The Art of *Joseph Andrews*

THE ART OF *JOSEPH ANDREWS*

BY

HOMER GOLDBERG

The University of Chicago Press

CHICAGO / LONDON

Library of Congress Catalog Card Number: 69-14826

The University of Chicago Press, Chicago 60637
The University of Chicago Press, Ltd., London W.C.1

Published 1969
Printed in the United States of America

For my father, who taught me the value of laughter

Contents

Preface

In this book I have tried to write the kind of literary history "founded on the principle of artistic synthesis" called for by the late R. S. Crane in his "Critical and Historical Principles of Literary History" (*The Idea of the Humanities and Other Essays, Critical and Historical* [Chicago, 1967], 2: 45–156), in which the "constructional aspects of literary works" are considered from the standpoint of the "problems faced by writers in the process of making poems, dramas, or narratives of different kinds." The kind of narrative Henry Fielding undertook in his first novel was one he had admired in other literatures. His conception of the problems entailed in the construction of a work of this kind and the means to their solution, as well as his definition of the essential characteristics of the species he called comic romance, was influenced by his reading of Cervantes, Scarron, Lesage, and Marivaux. But more than two centuries after the event we have still to determine the precise sense in which *Joseph Andrews* can be said to be "written in imitation of" *Don Quixote*. Study of the novel's relation to its continental antecedents has never gone beyond general similitudes and the casual attribution of particular material indebtedness, while in recent years interpretation of the novel's structure has ranged increasingly far afield—to neoclassical epic theory, the practice of historians and biographers, and latitudinarian homiletics—for the key to Fielding's thinking.

Taking Fielding at his word, I have chosen to begin again by trying to see what he saw in his avowed models and what he did with what he found there. Analyzing the continental comic romances in a fashion consistent with his own way of reasoning about this "species of writing," I have sought to establish the composite "idea of romance" they presented him. Focusing on what he did with these resources, I have attempted to move beyond technical and material indebtedness to an understanding of the form of the novel as a complex adaptation of structural components from several sources to produce a new kind of narrative synthesis. Obviously the works of Cervantes and his fellow "biographers" were not the only important influences at work in the process of Fielding's composition. One cannot ignore the ethical concerns he brought to the novel from his periodical journalism, nor its special relation to *Pamela.* But for this kind of literary history the significant questions are whether and how he managed to subsume these concerns to his controlling artistic aim of constructing a comic fiction of a certain kind. I have tried to demonstrate how he enlisted these preoccupations as integral elements of the novel's peculiar comic form. In the second and third parts of this study I have further elucidated the distinctive character of Fielding's achievement by examining the ways in which he adapted and reshaped particular materials and devices, and by comparing his practices with those of his predecessors. At the same time, this analysis tends to verify the definition of the novel's form and exhibit Fielding's awareness of its constructional problems by showing how its various elements are shaped and ordered to function toward this hypothesized end. Whatever the novel's relation to its continental antecedents, the validity of that definition, and of my analysis of Fielding's realization of the form, must ultimately depend on their adequacy as formulations of the reader's perception and experience of the work.

From what I have said, it should be evident that this is not a conventional source study. Nor is it an essay in comparative literature. Viewing the continental comic romances from Fielding's perspective, I have inevitably overlooked significant aspects of these works which might deserve consideration in other contexts, and done them less than full justice. But to claim for Fielding a remarkably inventive sense of comic form is not to diminish Cervantes' genius. Conversely, to acknowledge that *Joseph Andrews* is perhaps less profound than its "great original" is not to deny its historical significance in bringing to the novel a kind of constructive awareness that seems, in the light of its subsequent development, remarkably modern.

This inquiry was originally suggested to me, more years ago than I can comfortably acknowledge, by Ronald Crane, who supervised the doctoral dissertation from which it evolved. My analysis of the novel derives from principles developed in his exemplary essay on *Tom Jones*. His trenchant criticism of early drafts prevented many errors, and I regret that the final version could not benefit from his rigorous common sense. I remain his debtor for invaluable inspiration, guidance, and friendship. For generous financial assistance over an extended period, I thank the Research Foundation of the State Univeristy of New York and the Graduate School of the State University at Stony Brook. For encouragement to develop the dissertation into a book, I am grateful to Arthur Friedman, Gwin Kolb, Alan D. McKillop, and Hollis Rinehart, who read the original version. For helpful criticism of portions of the manuscript in various drafts, I thank my friends and sometime colleagues, Wayne Booth and Robert Marsh. To Leigh Gibby I owe special thanks for asking, a long time ago, "Why two protagonists?" Martin Battestin and William Coley very kindly provided an early copy of the Wesleyan edition of *Joseph Andrews.* To Mrs. Cecilia Grimm and Mrs. Rosemary Vanni, my gratitude for typing and sympathy on their respective sides of the Atlantic. Chapter 7 was originally published, in slightly different form, in *Modern Philology*, volume 63 (1966), and is reprinted here with the permission of the editor and the University of Chicago. Lastly I thank my wife, for her forbearance and confidence.

The Art of *Joseph Andrews*

"Showing What Kind of a History This Is; What It Is Like, and What It Is Not Like"

For Samuel Richardson, the genealogy of Henry Fielding's first novel was simple and plain: "The Pamela, which he abused in his Shamela, taught him how to write to please, tho' his manners are so different. Before his Joseph Andrews (hints and names taken from that story, with a lewd and ungenerous engraftment) the poor man wrote without being read."[1] Fielding may indeed have been indebted to Richardson's "little book" for disclosing the possibility of popular success in narrative fiction exceeding that he had enjoyed (Richardson's detraction notwithstanding) in the theater. But he obviously did not consider it the "hitherto much-wanted standard or pattern for this kind of writing" it proclaimed itself to be. In introducing his own novel to the public he took pains to make clear that it was

[1] From a letter to Lady Bradshaigh in *The Correspondence of Samuel Richardson*, ed. Mrs. Barbauld, (London, 1804), 4 : 286. Later in the same correspondence he renews the attack: "As to the list of Fielding's performances, I have seen at least twenty of them; for none of which, before Joseph Andrews (except for such as were of a party turn), he gained either credit or readers" (p. 312).

an essentially different kind of book, grounded in a conception of fiction deriving from an older and more remote tradition.

As the editor of Pamela's "authentic papers," Richardson sought to dissociate her story from those "pernicious novels and idle romances" he had denounced in the volume of exemplary *Letters* he published a few months earlier. As that work was designed to exemplify "not only the requisite Style and Forms . . . But How to Think and Act Justly and Prudently, in the Common Concerns of Human Life," *Pamela* was no tale "calculated for Amusement only," but a narrative published "in order to cultivate the Principles of Virtue and Religion in the Minds of the Youth of Both Sexes," for whom the "main applications of its most material incidents" were spelled out at its close. If a prepublication notice did acknowledge *Pamela* to be a novel, it was "an *English Novel*," infused "with a truly *English Spirit* of unaffected good Sense."[2] As such, according to one of its prefatory letters, it offered "an Example of Purity to the Writers of a neighbouring Nation; which now shall have an opportunity to receive *English* Bullion in exchange for its own Dross, which has so long passed current among us in Pieces abounding with all the Levities of its volatile Inhabitants."[3]

Like portions of the novel itself, Fielding's editorial preliminaries to *Joseph Andrews* seem to have been written with their Richardsonian counterparts in mind. In studied contrast to the self-righteous insularity of *Pamela's* editorial rhetoric, Fielding proclaimed his book on its title page an imitation of Cervantes, and in a Preface addressed to "the mere *English* Reader," pro-

[2] From the introduction to a letter "To my worthy Friend, the Author of Pamela," published in the *Weekly Miscellany* for October 11, 1740, quoted in Alan Dugald McKillop, *Samuel Richardson, Printer and Novelist* (Chapel Hill, N. C., 1936), p. 42.

[3] The letter was actually written by a Frenchman, J.B. de Ferval, but as McKillop remarks, it obviously had Richardson's approval and "may have been inspired by him," and Fielding might understandably have considered it the work of "the editor" himself. It is quoted here from McKillop, p. 39.

posed to acquaint him with a kind of writing "which I do not remember to have seen hitherto attempted in our Language."[4] In the following mock-introductory discussion "Of writing Lives" (1:1), he derided Richardson's notion of the novelist as schoolmaster or governess by classing *Virtue Rewarded* with *Jack the Giant Killer* and similar works "of excellent Use and Instruction, finely calculated to sow the Seeds of Virtue in Youth, and very easy to be comprehended by Persons of moderate Capacity." Having reversed the cross-channel flow of literary gold by citing in the Preface as his only example of modern serious prose fiction the Abbe Fénelon's rigorously pure *Télémaque*, he went on in the preface to the second of his "little Volumes" (3:1) to honor along with Cervantes as fellow "Biographers" (in whose works "Truth is only to be found") some of the "neighbouring nation's" most popular exporters of "levities": Lesage, Scarron, Marivaux, and the translator of the *Arabian Nights*.

In doing so, Fielding was not merely pursuing a less direct form of the byplay he indulged in the prefatory materials to *Shamela*, displaying his cosmopolitanism at Richardson's expense. He was also trying to establish what his offended rival chose to ignore: that his "lewd and ungenerous engraftment" was in fact conceived as an autonomous fiction of a kind which he had read and admired in other literatures. If, like Richardson, he sought to dissociate his work from the run of novels and romances, he did not hesitate to acknowledge at the outset of his Preface what his reader could infer from the title page: that his "true history" was a romance, that is, an extended narrative prose fiction. If he echoed Richardson, and most writers of his time, in claiming his work was grounded in "truth" and "nature," the truth he valued was not the pretence of literal authenticity with which Richardson, and Defoe before him, appeased the puritan

[4] *Joseph Andrews*, ed. Martin C. Battestin (Oxford, 1967), p. 3. All subsequent references to the novel are to this edition. Text references are to book and chapter.

distrust of fiction per se. Condemning "those Romance-Writers," the historians, for their unreliable interpretations, he espoused that poetic rendering of the probable and universal in the "Actions and Characters of Men" which made a pure invention like *Don Quixote* "the History of the World in general."

This fidelity to "nature" distinguished the fiction of Cervantes and the French writers Fielding associated with him from "a different Idea of Romance": the works of "those Persons of surprising Genius, the Authors of immense Romances, or the modern Novel and *Atalantis* Writers," who depicted "Persons who never were, or will be, and Facts which never did nor possibly can happen"—strictures which might also have applied, for all its pretended veracity, to the Cinderella story of the paragon of virtue and her suddenly transformed persecutor-prince. These are the works he has in mind at the close of the Preface when he speaks of having distinguished his work from "the Productions of Romance Writers." His earlier opposition of *Télémaque* to these same "immense Romances" suggests that he found that sober didactic work similarly faithful to nature. But Lesage, Scarron, and Marivaux had more in common with Cerantes than this generic realism. At the outset of his second volume Fielding was naming, under the facetious designation of "biography," his best-known precedents—*Don Quixote, Le Roman comique*, *Gil Blas*, *La Vie de Marianne*, and *Le Paysan parvenu*—in a "kind of Writing" he called, using conventional terminology of his day, comic romance.

In the Preface in which he defined this literary species, he accentuated the distance between this "Idea of Romance" and the run of popular novels and romances by taking Homer and Aristotle as initial reference points. If he did so partly to give neoclassical legitimacy to a literary tradition some of his readers might consider "low," it is also clear that the *Poetics* provided him analytic procedures through which he could formulate the differentiating characteristics of the distinctive kind of book he had undertaken.[5] Following the pattern of Aristotle's reasoning in the opening chapters of the *Poetics*, he proceeded through a systematic classification of literary kinds to arrive at his familiar definition of the comic romance as a "comic Epic-Poem in Prose."

Fielding might have been surprised by the implications critics and scholars have drawn from this formula.[6] He tried to make its meaning plain in amplifying his formal definition of the species through contrast with dramatic comedy and serious romance, the genres which in different ways it most nearly resembled. Even as his use of the term *romance* in naming the species carried no "romantic" or other qualitative implications, it is clear from the opening paragraphs of the Preface that he did not intend the term *epic* to designate a literary species with distinctive qualities of substance and effect; indeed the first part of the Preface endeavors to reorient the reader who comes to it with such a definition in mind. As it is used there, *epic* carries no more specific or qualitative meaning than "extended narrative." This limited signification is implicit in Fielding's initial division of the whole realm of plotted literature into the parallel modes of drama and epic, each in turn divisible into its comic and serious species. It is also plainly inferrable from the abstract technical contrast between the comic romance and its dramatic counterpart which completes the definition sentence: "differing

[5] Although the authors of the *romans de longue haleine* also rationalized their performances in terms of neoclassical epic theory, they seem to have regarded the *Poetics* as a body of doctrine rather than a source of analytical method. See Arthur L. Cooke, "Henry Fielding and the Writers of Heroic Romance," *PMLA* 52 (1947): 984–94.

[6] I have discussed some of these in my article, "Comic Prose Epic or Comic Romance: The Argument of the Preface to *Joseph Andrews*," *Philological Quarterly* 43 (1964): 193–215, where I have argued in more detail the interpretation of the Preface summarized here.

from Comedy, as the serious Epic from Tragedy: its Action being more extended and comprehensive; containing a much larger Circle of Incidents, and introducing a greater Variety of Characters." Of all the implications which he might have drawn from the idea of epic, Fielding alludes only to these aspects of magnitude deriving from the difference between narrative and dramatic manner. The limitation of the term's significance is even more evident when this passage is compared with the immediately following sentence, where the term *comic* specifies qualitative attributes through a hiearchy of compositional elements from the structure of the whole action to the language in which it is presented. "It differs from the serious Romance in its Fable and Action, in this; that as in the one these are grave and solemn, so in the other they are light and ridiculous: it differs in its Characters, by introducing Persons of inferiour Rank, and consequently, of inferiour Manners, whereas the grave Romance, sets the highest before us; lastly in its Sentiments and Diction, by preserving the Ludicrous instead of the Sublime."

In its implications for the distinctive qualities of the species, *comic* is clearly the most significant element of Fielding's formula. It was also a concept which he thought was not very well understood. Accordingly, he devoted most of his Preface to clarifying its meaning. To begin with, the comic romance or comic prose epic was not to be confused with mere anti-romance or mock-epic. This mistake could easily result from the antithesis of ludicrous and sublime, give the common view of his proclaimed model as a travesty of the chivalric romances, his own reputation as a writer of theatrical burlesque (acknowledged in the Preface), and the apparent parodic intention conveyed by the novel's opening chapter. To retrieve his own work and others (presumably *Don Quixote* and *Le Roman comique*) "truly of the Comic kind" from mistaken classification as burlesque, he anticipated the point he was to develop more fully in book 3, chapter 1.[7] Whereas the "surprizing Absurdity" of burlesque derives from its "Exhibition of what is monstrous and unnatural" (the writer deliberately distorting his objects for amusing effect), the comic writer "should of all others be the least excused for deviating from Nature," from "the just Imitation of which, will flow all the Pleasure we can this way convey to a sensible Reader." If *Joseph Andrews* was to take off *Pamela*, it was not to make its parodic points at the expense of the credibility of its own actions.

In effect, this distinction only extended the process of antithetical definition which runs through the opening paragraphs of the Preface. It remained to define the essence of the comic—or as Fielding called it, the ridiculous—directly and positively. In addressing himself to this question, Fielding offered what he evidently regarded as his most original and venturesome opinions. Finding the practice of some professed comic writers misguided and the theory of Aristotle and Bellegarde inadequate, he sought to cut through the traditional external distinctions of rank and manners employed in his initial classification, and isolate that aspect of "nature" which he considered the specific object of the comic writer's imitation and the source of its distinctive quality. Those authors who would "expose the Miseries of Poverty and Distress to Ridicule" mistook condition and fortune for the index of a category whose essential determinant was to be found in a distinctively motivated kind of behavior. Those who would "ridicule the blackest Villanies" failed to discern precisely the range of moral defect peculiar to comedy. For, he argued, "the only Source of the true Ridiculous (as it appears to me) is Affectation."

The parenthesis indicates that this formulation was not to be taken as a simple assertion of fact, like the initial division of

[7] If, as seems likely, the Preface was composed after the novel was substantially complete, then the order of composition would conform with the logic of the argument.

epic into tragic and comic forms, nor as the conclusion of a chain of deductive reasoning, like the definition of the comic romance, but as a theory or hypothesis. Restrictive as this derivation might seem, it is evident from the ensuing discussion that Fielding was not seeking to reduce the comic to dogmatic formula in the interest of literary taxonomy. Instead of attempting a theoretical or inductive proof of the legitimacy of his definition, he tried to show its relevance by analyzing the psychology of affected behavior and describing the mechanism by which he saw it producing the comic effect. Tracing the "only source" still further from external circumstances and into the domain of character, back to two of the most prevalent of human motives—the vain desire to "purchase Applause" by pretending to qualities we do not possess, and the hypocritical endeavor to "avoid Censure by concealing our Vices under an Appearance of their opposite Virtues"—might strengthen the claim that this apparently limited conception encompassed a "copious Field" of behavior. Fielding's central aim, however, in discriminating these two modes of affectation which, "as they proceed from very different Motives . . . are as clearly distinct in their Operations," seems to have been to elucidate their differing potential for producing the comic effect. Although both vanity and hypocrisy fall within the comic writer's proper purview, the latter offers more promising material for two reasons. Having a "violent Repugnancy of Nature to struggle with," hypocritical pretense sits more awkwardly on its affecter. In addition, it is more surprising to the reader "to discover any one to be the exact Reverse of what he affects . . . than to find him a little deficient in the Quality he desires the Reputation of." Hence the hypocritical affectation produces both the "Surprize and Pleasure" of the ridiculous "in a higher and stronger Degree," a theoretical conclusion Fielding saw confirmed by the practice of Ben Jonson, "who of all Men understood the *Ridicúlous* the best."

The "good-natur'd Reader" who accepted Fielding's invitation at the end of the Preface to "apply my Piece to my Observations" could thus expect to find an extended narrative prose fiction incorporating a great variety of characters in a wide-ranging scheme of action, reflecting at every level of composition—from its "light and ridiculous" plot and "inferiour Manners" to its "Ludicrous" thought and expression—a central comic intention. Though he could expect the verbal comedy to include a measure of burlesque, in the more substantive aspects of the work the author would not attempt to arouse laughter by radically distorting or transposing the natural order of things ("as in appropriating the Manners of the highest to the lowest, or *è converso*"), but would draw his materials from the "copious Field" of ridiculous behavior which "Life every where furnishes an accurate Observer." If the characters were "Persons of inferiour Rank," their "low" condition would not in itself be the object of laughter but only those pretences engendered by vanity and hypocrisy. And if the novelist were to act on the implication of his own argument, the reader could expect greater emphasis on hypocrisy than vanity.

To this rather sketchy characterization of his work and its kind, Fielding subsequently added two further specifications in the course of praising his sister's novel, *David Simple* (1744), which he considered another specimen of the comic epic in prose. The first of these, concerning the structure of the plot or "fable," derives from the "more extended and comprehensive" scope that distinguishes the epic action from that of drama.

The two great originals of a serious air, which we have derived from that mighty genius [Homer], differ principally in the action, which in the Iliad is entire and uniform; in the Odyssey, is rather a series of actions, all tending to produce one great end. Virgil and Milton are, I think, the only pure imitators of the former: most of the other Latin, as well as Italian, French, and English epic poets, choosing rather the history of some war, as Lucan and Sillius Italicus; or a series of adventures, as Ariosto,&c., for the subject of their poems.

In the same manner the comic writer may either fix on one action, as the authors of Le Lutrin, the Dunciad, &c.; or on a series, as Butler in verse, and Cervantes in prose have done.

Of this latter kind is the book now before us, where the fable consists of a series of separate adventures, detached from and independent on each other, yet all tending to one great end; so that those who should object want of unity of action here, may, if they please, or if they dare, fly back with their objection in the face even of the Odyssey itself.[8]

The kind of unity attributed to the *Iliad* is what is generally understood by "unity of action"—a sequence of causally linked events constituting a single process of change with a perceptible beginning, middle, and end. The nature of Fielding's second kind of unity is less apparent. If its actions are "detached" and "independent," they could hardly "tend to one great end" in the sense of producing some climactic event. Nor do Fielding's examples seem to bear out this conception: although the episodic action of the *Odyssey* culminates in the hero's rout of the suitors and restoration to his rule and family, neither *Hudibras* nor *Don Quixote* ends in a similar climactic resolution, and the marriages concluding *David Simple* are no more than a mechanical device of termination. Fielding's reasoning becomes clearer if the "one great end" that the several actions are "all tending to produce" is taken to mean not a climactic event but the intended overall effect or quality of the work as a whole. Interpreted in this way, the second kind of unity can be seen to reside in what the author aims at in the creation of his actions rather than in the causal mechanism by which he connects them. Thus the distinctive character of the *Odyssey* is present in some measure in each of its heroic and marvelous adventures; the separate episodes produce similar

[8] *The Complete Works of Henry Fielding, Esq.*, 16 vols. ed. W. E. Henley (New York, 1902), 16 : 10–11 (hereafter cited as *Works*). Text references are to volume and page.

effects, and they combine to produce a unified total effect. Again in *Hudibras* and in *Don Quixote* the comic power of the work derives from its accumulated generally similar episodes rather than from an extended intrigue culminating in a comic triumph or catastrophe.[9]

This reading seems to be confirmed by the immediately following paragraph, in which Fielding goes on to define in rather general terms the essential qualities or characteristics of the comic prose epic or comic romance plot:

> This fable hath in it these three difficult ingredients, which will be found on consideration to be always necessary to works of this kind, viz., that the main end or scope be at once amiable, ridiculous, and natural.

The "main end or scope" is evidently the central story line or overall system of actions. That it should be "ridiculous" and "natural" had already been made explicit in the Preface and book 3, chapter 1 of *Joseph Andrews*. Some idea of what he meant by the added stipulation may be gathered from the next paragraph, in which he digressses from his enumeration of the "beauties" of his sister's work to argue the essentiality of this quality to "every work of this kind."

> If it be said that some of the comic performances I have above mentioned differ in the first of these, and set before us the odious instead of the amiable; I answer, that is far from being one of their perfections; and of this the authors themselves seem so sensible, that they endeavour to deceive the reader by false glosses and colours, and by the help of irony at least to represent the aim and design of their heroes in a favourable and agreeable light.

Here Fielding moves beyond the earlier limitation on moral depravity in comedy to suggest a positive ethical specification, with particular reference to the work's protagonist. He articu-

[9] Fielding acknowledged this when he alluded to "the loose unconnected Adventures in Don Quixote; of which you may transverse the Order as you please, without any Injury to the whole" (*The Covent Garden Journal*, 2 vols., ed. G.E. Jensen [New Haven, 1915], 1 : 281 [hereafter cited as *CGJ*] Text references are to volume and page).

lated the idea implicit in these remarks more fully ten years after the publication of *Joseph Andrews* in an analysis of *Don Quixote*, the model from which it derived. Reviewing *The Female Quixote*, he praised Mrs. Lennox for equaling their mutual master in "that Care which both have taken to preserve the Affection of their Readers for their principal Characters, in the midst of all the Follies of which they are guilty" by endowing them with attractive intellectual and moral qualities.[10] This idea of a virtuous comic hero is already hinted at in the concluding paragraph of the Preface to *Joseph Andrews*, where Fielding speaks of Parson Adams' "worthy Inclinations," and hopes "the Goodness of his Heart will recommend him to the Good-natur'd"; and its theoretical groundwork is laid earlier in the careful differentiation of the two branches of affectation. Hypocrisy, "concealing . . . Vices under an Appearance of their opposite Virtues," is "nearly allied to Deceit." Vanity is comparatively innocent. It is "nearer to Truth," and "doth not imply an absolute Negation of those Qualities which are affected." Though the vain man "hath not the Virtue he affects, to the degree he would be thought to have it," he is, by definition, not vicious. This moral differentiation of two kinds or degrees of affectation provides the basis for the conception of an amiable comic protagonist in whom the ridiculous is mingled with the appealing. A character can be vain of qualities he lacks and still exhibit moral and intellectual virtues which "preserve the affection" and even excite the admiration of the reader.[11]

The stipulation of amiability as an essential attribute of the comic romance fable implies more than a definition of the comic hero. It distinguishes Fielding's sympathetic mode of comedy from that of Ben Jonson, in which the foibles of affectation are exposed through the machinations of rogues and schemers.

[10] *CGJ* 1 : 280

[11] Moreover, one can be vain without dissimulation (see the discussion of Adams' character below, p. 79), whereas it is the very essence of hypocrisy.

Actions involving such an amiable figure or figures with a "'great variety'" of affected persons will not only produce amusement; they will also entail other responses generated by the reader's approval and sympathy for the comic hero and antipathy toward his antagonists. (In the 1742 Preface, the acknowledgment that he has depicted vices is accompanied by the assurance that they are set forth as objects of detestation.) If the "main end or scope" is to be "amiable," it would appear that the eventual fortunes of the sympathetic and antipathetic persons must be commensurate with the reader's sense of their desert.

The concept of a unified "series of actions" and the idea of amiable comedy furnish important further clues to Fielding's conception of his work and of the "kind of writing" he thought it was; but beyond this the remarks in the Preface to *David Simple* confirm a fundamental characteristic of Fielding's thinking about his novel that is significant for an understanding of his art. The overall direction of the argument in the Preface to *Joseph Andrews* as well as its individual points shows him consistently reasoning about his work, and others, not in relation to some general or particular moral or instructional goal but in terms of their attainment of the emotive effects specific to their kind. His description of the analytical parts of the comic romance is not simply an enumeration of its constituent elements but a specification of their affective qualities as determined by the postulated comic intent of the whole. The distinction between comedy and burlesque is not a simple contrast of subjects and methods; it involves a judicious discrimination of apparently similar but significantly different emotional effects, through an analysis of their diverse causes.[12]

The question on which the whole argument of the Preface

[12] The "exquisite Mirth and Laughter" of burlesque is "Physic for the Mind," purging "Spleen, Melancholy and ill Affections" and promoting "Good-Humour"; though it "agitate(s) the Muscles" less, comedy produces "a more rational and useful Pleasure."

progressively converges—the definition of the Ridiculous—concerns not only the comic writer's materials but the means of producing the effect he seeks. Affectation is the *source* of the Ridiculous, which in turn is not simply a designation of the comic writer's subject, or object of imitation. It is also Fielding's name for the distinctive emotional effect specific to the kind of writing he is attempting to define. It is thus a term of the same order as "the sublime" or, more precisely, "the tragic," and the response it designates is as essential a part of the definition of this species as pity and fear are of Aristotle's definition of tragedy. This sense of the term is most evident in the discussion of how the Ridiculous "arises" from the discovery of affectation, striking the reader with "Surprize and Pleasure . . . in a higher and stronger Degree when the Affectation arises from Hypocrisy." The Preface to *David Simple* carries this reasoning in terms of qualities and effects a step further. As "natural" refers to the generic quality that the comic prose epic exhibits in common with *Télémaque* and all other "true" narrative and dramatic poetry, and "ridiculous" designates the specific effect aimed at in this kind of writing, "amiable" differentiates the distinctive character of Fielding's particular mixed or qualified mode of the comic.

Fielding's remarks on the writer's choices are in keeping with this general orientation. Ben Jonson is praised on the same general grounds on which the author of "*the Comedy of* Nero, *with the merry Incident of ripping up his Mother's Belly*" is earlier condemned. Although he displays great moral obtuseness, that fictional writer is not being held up as an object of shame or moral reprobation, but derided as a misguided practitioner who must fail of attaining the truly comic because he seeks for it in the wrong place. Similarly, Jonson is not lauded as the censurer of fraud and dissimulation but as a great comic artist who "understood" the *poesis* of the Ridiculous, and "used" hypocrisy as the material most conducive to this end.

Fielding's sense of his own work as a product of similarly judicious "use" of materials is reflected in the seemingly conventional disclaimer near the end of the Preface of having "against my own Rules introduced Vices, and of a very black Kind." The rules are those concerning the choice of literary subjects in relation to their emotional effects, enunciated in the immediately preceding paragraph: "Great Vices are the proper Objects of our Detestation, smaller Faults of our Pity: but Affectation appears to me the only true Source of the Ridiculous." To show that his practice is consistent with his theory, Fielding claims he has not made vice an object of amusement and indicates how he has managed to depict it without impairing the comic character of the novel. He has confined himself to "accidental Consequences of some human Frailty, or Foible" rather than vices "habitually existing in the Mind"; and he has conceived his incidents ("They never produce the intended Evil") and represented them ("They are never the principal Figure at that Time on the Scene") so as to insure that this already qualified evil may not arouse responses injurious to the intended comic effect.

Fielding's tendency to define compositional problems in terms of intended emotional effects is revealed more particularly, and dramatically, in a letter to Richardson in praise of *Clarissa*.[13] This remarkable document complements his formal literary pronouncements with a unique view of the novelist talking shop with a fellow practitioner, at the same time unexpectedly disclosing him in the role of "good-natur'd Reader," responding sensitively to the work of the man whose earlier novel he had publicly derided. Fielding's own way of formulating this dual capacity is to ascribe some of his remarks to "my head" and some to "my heart." After complimenting Richardson on preserving a "vein of Humour" in Lovelace's narrative

[13] E. L. McAdam Jr., "A New Letter from Fielding," *Yale Review*, 38 (1948): 300–310.

and introducing "natural and entertaining" new characters, including one with "much of the true Comic Force," he focuses upon the dramatic climax of the installment he has just read, the events surrounding the rape of Clarissa. The head begins by noting how Richardson, "with great Judgment," has affected the reader's attitude toward "Loveless" to insure the intended impact of the climactic episode: "His former Admirers must lose all Regard for him on his Perseverance, and as this Regard Ceases, Compassion for Clarissa rises in the same Proportion. Hence we are admirably prepared for what is to follow." At this point the analytic novelist gives way to the affected reader:

> When Clarissa returns to her Lodgings at St. Clairs the Alarm begins, and here my heart begins its Narrative. I am Shocked; my Terrors ar[e ra]ised, and I have the utmost Apprehensions for the poor betrayed Creature.—But when I see her enter with the Letter in her Hand, and after some natural Effects of Despair, clasping her Arms about the Knees of the Villain, call him her Dear Lovelace, desirous and yet unable to implore his Protection or rather his mercy; I then melt into Compassion, and find what is called an Effeminate Relief for my Terror. to continue to the End of the Scene. When I read the next Letter I am Thunderstruck; nor can many Lines explain what I feel from Two. . . . The Circumstances of the Fragments is Great and Terrible; but her Letter to Lovelace is beyond any thing I have ever read. God forbid that the Man who reads this with dry Eyes should be alone with my Daughter when she hath no Assistance within Call. Here my Terror ends and my Grief begins which the Cause of all my Tumultuous Passions soon changes into Raptures of Admiration and Astonishment by a Behaviour the most Elevated I can possibly conceive, and what is at the same time most Gentle and most natural.

One could not ask for a more circumstantial account of emotional effects produced by a work of literature. Like a patient recording every variation of his pulse and blood pressure, Fielding reports to Richardson on the success of his artistic strategy. His inference that Richardson has deliberately constructed the sequence to produce terror, then grief, then admiration and wonder, becomes explicit when the head inadvertently reasserts itself:

> During the Continuance of this Vol. my Compassion is often moved; but I think my Admiration more. If I had rec'd no Hint or Information of what is to succeed[14] I should perceive you paving the way to load our admiration of your Heroine to the Highest Pitch, as you have before with wonderfull Art prepared us for both Terror and Compassion on her Account. This last seems to come from the Head. Here then I will end: for I assure you nothing but my Heart can force me to say Half of what I think of *the* Book.

Flushed with the achievement of *Tom Jones*, Fielding may have been generously writing what he thought the vain Richardson wanted to hear; but the intensity of his enthusiasm seems utterly unfeigned and without irony. More significantly, "the Head's" evident predisposition to reason in terms of the conscious shaping of the reader's responses tells as much about Fielding's own art as it does about his opinion of his rival's. Although this letter was written in 1748, its conformity with the distinctive orientation of earlier formal remarks suggests that this was not a new habit of mind, and it is at least a tenable working hypothesis that he thought in analogous fashion about the construction of episodes and sequences to achieve corresponding comic effects in *Joseph Andrews*.

The "heart" that expressed such a feeling response to the horror of Clarissa's situation and the nobility of her conduct reveals a keen moral sensibility. A similar, if more dispassionate, moral awareness underlies Fielding's reasoning about the Ridiculous, his distinction of two degrees of affectation, and the conception of amiable comedy. Although he is primarily concerned in the Preface to *Joseph Andrews* and in the associated remarks on *David Simple* and *Clarissa* with moral discrimina-

[14] Apparently Fielding had learned of Richardson's plan from his sister, who was a member of Richardson's circle.

tions as they relate to poetic effects, it is also apparent that he was concerned with the ethical implications of literature. He would not have reacted so emphatically to *Pamela* if the work praised from the pulpit had not inculcated "Principles of Virtue and Religion" antipathetic to his own understanding of these basic values. In *Shamela* he derided Richardson's brand of piety as a blend of ostentatious ritual activity and complacent spiritual passivity ("Dost thou not teach us to pray, to sing psalms, and to honour the clergy? Are not these the whole duty of man?"), savoring more than a little of Methodism ("the useful and truly religious doctrine of *grace* is everywhere inculcated"; " 'tis not what we do, but what we believe, that must save us"). In *Joseph Andrews*, he opposed to it his own energetic and self-effacing ideal of Christianity, which he had expounded in "An Apology for the Clergy."[15] Centered in the "virtue of charity, which . . . comprehends almost the whole particular duty of a Christian,"[16] his religion stressed good works over faith and rite. Against the prudential and essentially negative copybook morality of *Pamela*, stressing purity, discretion, propriety, and conquest of the passions, he espoused an impulsive virtue, stemming from benevolent feelings rather than Richardson's overestimated precepts, not solipsistically absorbed in its own preservation but actively promoting the good of others.[17]

But if Fielding would thus "mingle Instruction with Entertainment," it was surely not, in the simple pedagogic relation conceived by Richardson, "so as to make the latter *seemingly*

[15] *The Champion*, March 29, April 5, April 12, and April 19, 1740.

[16] *Works* 15 : 272.

[17] There is a clear connection between this anti-egoistic ethic and the exposure of affectation, both branches of which are grounded in the essentially selfish desire to purchase the good opinion of others—Fielding describes his archetypal stagecoach lawyer as one "who made Self the Centre of the whole Creation." Recognition of this selfish motive would account for the presence of affectation tranforming what would otherwise be objects of compassion into figures of mirth.

the *View*, while the former is *really* the End."[18] In describing himself, in book 3, chapter 1, as a satirist whose aim it was "to hold the Glass to thousands in their Closets, that they may contemplate their Deformity, and endeavour to reduce it, and thus by suffering private Mortification . . . avoid public Shame," he was hardly disclosing the real compositional end concealed beneath the carefully elaborated comic intention of the Preface. Nor is it plausible that the writer who followed his serious analysis of his work with a mock-introductory derision of the literary *exemplum* would conceive of his story as the allegorical emblem of a moral idea or the working out of an Aesopian fable, either in the positive pattern of Pamela's perseverance and reward or in the negative example of Sally Godfrey's fate. Although he likened himself, in his role of satirist, to an admonitory parent, he did not address himself (except in facetious chapter titles) to youths and maidens in need of guidance. He envisioned mature readers, sophisticated enough to be amused by his jests upon conventional didacticism, yet not so jaded or cynical as to resist the appeal of innocence adrift in a sea of meanness and fraud. His heroes and heroine were not presented as models for the reader's imitation, but as sympathetic figures whose foibles and embarrassments might still be a source of amusement. Although he valued innocence and thought chastity a virtue which "all mankind are bound to the observance of,"[19] he would generate mirth out of the plight of an innocent lad attempting to preserve his virtue. Although he regarded charity as the quintessence of the ideal Christian minister, and specified among its laudable manifestations a disposition "void of suspicion" and "inclined to maintain good and kind thoughts of men,"[20] he made such a pattern priest the principal comic figure of his novel, and these very qualities

[18] In a manuscript letter, cited by McKillop, p. 62.

[19] It is listed among "those virtues which we have been taught by morality, such as patience, fortitude, temperance, chastity, &c." (*Works* 15 : 272).

[20] *Works* 15 : 271, 272.

the wellspring of his habitual comic error. Out of this good man's solemn exhortation of submission to divine providence and his friend's reciprocal effort to comfort him for the loss of a child with the hope of heavenly restoration—a hope Fielding described in the contemporaneous essay, "Of the Remedy of Affliction for the Loss of our Friends," as the "sweetest, most endearing and ravishing" consolation afforded by religion[21]—he created two of the funniest scenes in the novel.

It may be assumed that Joseph spoke for his creator when he defied "the wisest Man in the World to turn a true good Action into Ridicule" (3:6). But the man who saw the "amiable, ridiculous, and natural" as "difficult ingredients," and who recognized the need to prevent the reader's admiration for Lovelace and enjoyment of his "vein of Humour" from obscuring his essential villainy, must have realized that to place an innocent youth and a truly Christian parson at the center of a series of comic adventures without making "a Jest of Religion, and the Clergy, of Virtue, and Innocence" (as he sarcastically inferred "the Town" would have preferred him to do in *Amelia*)[22] posed a delicate problem. In theory he might assume a natural conformity of emotional response to the ethical character of the objects depicted, so that only a "very ill-framed Mind" or "very diabolical Natures" could view scenes of deprivation with amusement. In practice he recognized that to have the reader enjoy the comedy of the good parson's inapt preaching and even smile at the facetiously ironic introduction of his "Exhortations" as "calculated for the Instruction and Improvement of the Reader," without contemning the substance of these remarks or his earnest good intentions, he needed to shape and guide his responses—as he was later to praise Richardson for doing.

How Fielding managed to preserve the reader's respect and

21 *Works* 16 : 109.
22 *CGJ* 1 : 178.

affection for Adams while making his difficulties and mistakes the objects of laughter, and the broader question of the relation of his ethical concerns to his informing comic intention, can best be investigated through an analysis of the novel. His "few hints" concerning his "kind of writing" may also be extended by considering precisely how and to what extent the "series of actions" in *Joseph Andrews* might be seen to constitute a unity, and in what ways Fielding can be observed to have shaped the reader's estimates and responses in the service of that "one great end." But, since his definition of these and other problems inherent in the particular conception of his novel and his strategies for their solution were both influenced by his observation of the practice of his predecessors in comic romance, we are likely to gain a better understanding of Fielding's achievement in *Joseph Andrews*—what it is as well as how it came to be—if we consider the completed form of the novel in the context in which it was created.

From his student essay at dramatizing Cervantes to his disposition of Richardsonian matter within Virgilian structure in *Amelia*, Fielding was an inveterate literary imitator. In composing *Joseph Andrews* he had before him, not a single model, but a broad literary mode offering a range of possibilities. The kind of encyclopedic memory and attentive scrutiny reflected in that remarkable quodlibet, *The Tragedy of Tragedies*, was here at the service of a more sympathetic adaptation, and he evidently drew from Cervantes and the other continental writers many hints for characters, incidents, and devices. But to a writer of his analytic bent this body of fiction presented more than a repository of materials and conventions; nor was it only a general affinity of spirit that made these works the collective source of the "Idea of Romance" he expounded in the Preface and the opening chapter of book 3. They presented him with a variety of formal prototypes whose positive and negative examples influenced the conception and design of his own unique comic structure. By placing ourselves in Fielding's position as he surveyed the works of his fellow "biographers," we may undertake to answer some of the questions he left unresolved about *Joseph Andrews* and its relation to the continental comic romances.

I

The Main End or Scope: The Art of the Whole

Fielding's Prototypes: From Cervantes to Marivaux

It is not surprising that Fielding should have looked to *Don Quixote* for inspiration and guidance when he turned his hand to narrative fiction. Fourteen years earlier, while he was still in university, he had tried to make his first play by transplanting Cervantes' knight and squire to an English inn. Even in this rather feeble youthful sketch, which he abandoned for five years in despair of "going beyond" or even "keeping pace" with his master, Fielding transcended the then common view of the knight of La Mancha as a low comedy lunatic or simple burlesque figure, recognizing another dimension of character beneath the mock-chivalric armor. At the climax of *Don Quixote in England*, he has the mad Spaniard intercede in behalf of its young lovers against the "good" match with a grossly stupid country squire favored by the heroine's father.

DON QUIXOTE: Sir . . . I suppose you look upon yourself as a reasonable sort of person?

SIR THOMAS LOVELAND: What?

DON QUIXOTE: That you are capable of managing your affairs; that you don't stand in need of a governor?

SIR THOMAS LOVELAND: Hey!

DON QUIXOTE: And if this be true of you, is it possible you can prefer that wretch, who is a scandal to his very species, to this gentleman, whose person and parts would be an honour to the greatest of it?

SIR THOMAS LOVELAND: Has he made you his advocate? Tell him, I can prefer three thousand to one.

DON QUIXOTE: The usual madness of mankind! Do you marry your daughter for her sake, or your own? If for hers, 'tis sure something whimsical, to make her miserable in order to make her happy. Money is a thing well worth considering in these affairs; but parents always regard it too much, and lovers too little. No match can be happy which love and fortune do not conspire to make so. The greatest addition of either illy supplies the entire absence of the other; nor would millions a year make a beast, in your daughter's eye, preferable to this youth with a thousand.[1]

The suggestion that the worldly "prudent" man is the one truly "in need of a governor" is Fielding's own, part of the broader innovation of making Quixote the spokesman of the kind of satiric observations he was later to express through his discursive narrator.[2] The rest of the knight's conduct, however, is patterned as closely on his role in the episode of Camacho's wedding (pt. 2, chaps. 21–22)—where, after defending the humble lovers against the disappointed wealthy bridegroom, he expounds the identical recipe for marital happiness—as his thinking the Guzzle Inn a castle and a pack of hounds an army are upon their more obvious Cervantean counterparts. Adhering to the master's practice with the fidelity of the cautious apprentice, Fielding thus gave us his earliest recorded view of the Cervantean hero as a mixture of folly and wisdom, a view not surprisingly like that expressed in the refrain of Cervantes' own choric characters:

1 *Works* 11 : 65.

2 See p. 280, n. 10, below.

The Canon gaz'd on him, admiring his unparallell'd sort of Madness, the rather because in all his Words and Answers he display'd an excellent Judgment; and, as we have already observ'd, he only rav'd when the Discourse fell upon Knight-Errantry.[3]

The same paradox remains at the core of Fielding's formulation of the knight's character two decades later in his review of the *Female Quixote;* but "excellent Judgment" is only one of the complex of worthy traits evidencing Cervantes' and Mrs. Lennox' equal care in preserving the amiability of their protagonists. Quixote and Arabella are both "represented as Persons of good Sense, and of great natural Parts, and in all Cases, except one, of a very sound Judgement, and what is much more endearing, as Persons of great Innocence, Integrity and Honour, and of the highest Benevolence."[4] There is little evidence of this lovable ingenuous humanity in Fielding's student version of Quixote, a moral censor rather than an amiable humorist. Even at the end of the play, when Sir Thomas and his future son-in-law remark choricly on the madman's wisdom, they do so more in wonder than affection. But if Fielding's supplement to the theory of the comic prose epic in the Preface to *David Simple*—where he rated the amiability of the comic protagonist an essential characteristic of the species—is any gauge of his thinking two years earlier, he had already arrived at the more benevolent idea of Quixote's character articulated in the *Covent*

[3] *The Ingenious Gentleman Don Quixote de la Mancha,* trans. Peter Motteux rev. John Ozell (New York: The Modern Library, 1950), p. 416. Although he owned a Spanish dictionary, there is no evidence that Fielding read Cervantes in the original. The only copy of *Don Quixote* listed in the sale catalogue of his library is in Jarvis' translation, published after *Joseph Andrews.* Parallels in phrasing between *Don Quixote in England* and Motteux's translation indicate that this, rather than Shelton's translation, was the source of his notion of "the Manner of Cervantes," probably in Ozell's revised version published in 1725, two years before he alluded to the novel in *Love in Several Masques.* References are to the most readily available modern edition of this version. Part 1 is divided into four books; in part 2, chapters are numbered in a single consecutive series.

[4] *CGJ* 1 : 280.

Garden Journal when he undertook his most significant imitation of Cervantes. Parson Adams' specific "Character of perfect Simplicity" might not "be found in any Book now extant," but Fielding had certainly recognized his general prototype in another figure whose good heart, even more than his good head, appealed to the good-natured reader in spite of all his folly.

Conceivably a writer who would try to bring the hostile invective of the *Dunciad* within reach of amiability, as Fielding did in the Preface to *David Simple*, might have reasoned, for the sake of his theory, that this folly and absurdity could be traced to affectation. There is something like vanity in Quixote's view of himself at the outset of his adventures ("O happy Age! O fortunate Times! . . . decreed to usher into the World my famous Atchievements; Atchievements worthy to be engraven on Brass, carv'd in Marble, and delineated in some Masterpiece of Painting, as Monuments of my Glory, and Examples for Posterity!"); and the description of compassion turned to mirth "when Ugliness aims at the Applause of Beauty, or Lameness endeavours to display Agility" might apply to the actions of the decrepit romanticist. But it is most unlikely that the man who praised the knight for his lack of dissimulation could equate the desire to "purchase everlasting Honour and Renown" by "redressing all manner of Grievances, and exposing himself to Danger on all Occasions" with that selfish "Vanity [that] puts us on affecting false Characters, in order to purchase Applause." If Quixote's heroic role "sits . . . aukwardly on him" as do the virtues affected by the vain and hypocritical, this is only a secondary element of Cervantes' comedy. The fountainhead of that comedy is not the attempt to deceive others, but a radical self-delusion; its wellspring is not false profession or false behavior, but false perception.

Fielding developed a formula more pertinent to the knight's ridiculousness, and one which takes into account his nobler traits, in the *Covent Garden Journal*, where he defined humor as "a violent Bent or Disposition of the Mind to some particular Point" that enlists "the Affections, Spirits, and Powers of the Mind" under its "own absolute Command," coloring all a man's actions and setting him off from his fellows. Such a "Violent Impulse," Fielding argued, is not ludicrous per se, but its subject may become "ridiculously distinguished from all other Men" according to "the Manner or the Degree in which it is exerted":

> By either of these the very best and worthiest Disposition of the Human Mind may become ridiculous. Excess, says Horace, even in the Pursuit of Virtue, will lead a wise and good Man into Folly and Vice—So will it subject him to Ridicule; for into this, says the judicious Abbé Bellegarde, a Man may tumble headlong with an excellent Understanding, and with the most laudable Qualities. Piety, Patriotism, Loyalty, Parental Affection, &c. have all afforded Characters of Humour for the Stage.[5]

Don Quixote is not among the half-dozen works Fielding cites in this discussion, but he had already equated humor with "wild unruly passion" and associated both with Quixote in one of his earliest plays,[6] and his list of laudable qualities would easily accommodate the pursuit of justice and defense of the defenseless. Allowing that the "violent impulse" of Quixote's mind, which radically distorts his judgement in all matters impinging upon the "particular point" of his chivalric obsession and distinguishes him from other men, is not a natural "Bent or

[5] *CGJ* 2 : 62–63.

[6] At the end of Act II of *The Coffee-House Politician* (1730), the choric Worthy soliloquizes about the title character's eccentricity: "I recollect the dawnings of this political humour to have appeared when we were at the Bath. . . . What an enthusiasm must it have arrived to. . . . The greatest part of mankind labour under one delirium or other: and Don Quixote differed from the rest, not in madness, but the species of it. The covetous, the prodigal, the superstitious, the libertine, and the coffee-house politician, are all Quixotes in their several ways."

> That man alone from madness free, we find,
> Who, by no wild unruly passion blind,
> To reason gives the conduct of his mind. [*Works* 9 : 108]

Disposition" but a subversion of its normal state, this description and the subsequent characterization of humorous behavior as "throwing the reins on the neck" of one's "favourite passion, and giving it full scope and indulgence" fit Cervantes' hero very well. His basic inclinations—to defend the helpless and succor the innocent—reflect the honor, integrity, and benevolence Fielding ascribed to him; in this sense his madness manifests the "worthiest Disposition of the Human Mind." When it is not leading him into folly or causing him to rage, it may even foster his nobility, sagacity, and brilliance. When he discourses on the Golden Age or compares the merits of arms and letters, he seems not so much mad as deliberately dedicated to the way of life he considers the noblest a man can pursue. But by the "manner of exerting itself," in the preposterous conceit of riding about the countryside armed *cap-a-pie* in search of "adventures," and through the excesses to which he allows his devotion to the chivalric ideal (which he cannot distinguish from the conventions and extravagances of chivalric romance) to carry him—he becomes ridiculous.

Cervantes' lengthy two-part narrative provided Fielding with a record of his master's successive experiments and strategies in developing a "series of actions" from the nucleus of his hero's habitual distortion of the situations, events, and persons of ordinary life, a kind of incremental handbook on comic invention and the problems of episodic narrative form. In the early chapters of part 1, Cervantes could be seen making his way by a kind of trial and error. In Quixote's first knightly endeavor—the rescue of a lad whom he subsequently relinquishes to the mercy of his brutal master on the strength of that peasant's "oath as a knight" and his own illusory reputation as an avenger—he focused on the disparity between his imagination of heroic achievement and his actual ineffectuality, pointing up the adverse effect of his chivalric vision upon his noble intentions and their supposed beneficiary. This rather rueful ironic view of the knight's endeavors was not to be maintained, nor was he to confront other real wrongs to be righted. His next adventure, in which he roils a group of innocent travelers with demands of homage to his unseen mistress and receives a beating for his pains, sets the pattern for many subsequent episodes. But the abruptness with which this incident ends Quixote's scarcely begun sally suggests that Cervantes may have recognized the limitations of his subject as initially conceived and brought his adventurer home for a fresh start. In depicting Senor Quesada's domestic situation and his friends' extensive critical survey of the literature propelling him out of it, Cervantes would appear to be expanding his sketchy introductory context in keeping with an enlarged idea of the potential scope of his invention.

Equipping the heroic idealist with an appetitive, cowardly, proverb-grinding peasant squire before sending him abroad again added considerably more than a second amiable comic figure to vary the comedy. Sancho Panza's craving for spoils supplemented the knight's own manic compulsion for adventures. The presence of a disciple still in need of conversion inspires him to those wilder imaginings—giants out of windmills, armies of sheep, "Mambrino's helmet" from a barber's basin—for which he is most remembered. But more than this, the fellow traveller provided an antiphonal sounding board for Quixote's eloquence and wisdom, and an object for his often furious but sometimes gentle, almost fatherly reprobation, affection, and concern, enriching and humanizing the figure who as solitary adventurer was confined to extravagant actions and chivalric vaunt. For his part, though simple enough to follow his eccentric neighbor in hopes of acquiring an island kingdom, Sancho still insists that windmills are windmills, and discretion the better part of valor. Between the insanely courageous and ingenuously selfless master and the shrewdly covetous, prudently craven man, Cervantes was able to develop an interaction of character not to be found in Quixote's bizarre encounters with the neutral personages or inanimate objects that occasion his adventures. As the knight lectures on knight errantry and argues the validity of his wild visions, while the shrewd empiric looks for holes in his master's rhetorical armor, lobbies for a liberal interpretation of the stern chivalric regimen, and threatens to leave rather than follow a madman, their amiable contest becomes as much an object of comic anticipation as the adventures themselves.

In the meandering actions of the first part of the second sally (pt. 1, 1:7–3:9), where one discrete episode succeeds another without consequence, this interaction provides the only sustained center of relatively specified expectation. Fielding probably had this portion of the novel, containing the memorable battles with the windmills and sheep, uppermost in mind when he described *Don Quixote* as a series of "loose unconnected Adventures" that might be reordered "as you please, without any Injury to the whole."[7] But in the next portion of the narrative (pt. 1, 3:10–4:9) he could have seen Cervantes replacing this rudimentary open-ended organization with a more complex web of incident in which initiative passes from Quixote to his friends, who plot to bring him home by playing upon his delusion, and the paths of both are made to intersect with those of two injured lovers. Although he was later to describe the stories of Cardenio and Dorothea as "extravagant and incredible" actions in which Cervantes "approaches very near to the Romances which he ridicules,"[8] in *Joseph Andrews* (3:1) Fielding cited Cardenio's madness and the perfidy of his and Dorothea's betrayer, Ferdinand, as instances of his fidelity to nature (see below, p. 177). Whatever his opinion of these actions, he must have recognized this portion of the novel—in which the knight's penitential antics, Sancho's abortive mis-

[7] *CGJ* 1 : 281.
[8] *Ibid.*

sion to Dulcinea, and the curate and barber's hoax are interwoven with the unexpectedly connected histories of the two young people so as to heighten the melodramatic effects of the interpolation while enlivening the primary narrative by continually shifting the center of interest—as a more sophisticated structure than the "loose unconnected Adventures" he alluded to in the *Covent Garden Journal.* Cervantes intimated a principal reason for introducing the new material when he later observed, concerning Quixote's adventures, that "too much of one thing clogs the Appetite, but Scarcity makes every thing go down" (pref., pt. 2). But as the inn to which the aggregated characters descend for the contrived denouement of the crossed lovers' fortunes becomes the backdrop for the completely autonomous "novel," "The Curious Impertinent," the lengthy captive's history, and lesser romantic episodes, Fielding could hardly have failed to take critical note of the reverse effect remarked by Cervantes himself at the beginning of part 2: initially introduced for variety, the romantic material itself produced a surfeit, and Quixote's scarcity did not help the bolus to go down.

Cervantes answered the need to reestablish his primary subject with a sustained buildup of comic activity at the end of the long agglomerative section. Starting with a gross physical prank played on the old gentleman, he developed a continually renewing sequence of innyard commotion from the delayed and unexpected repercussions of his last exploits on the road, culminating in a pitched battle in which all the romantic characters side with Quixote against the authorities, even to maintaining that the liberated barber's basin is indeed Mambrino's helmet. The effectiveness of this accelerating action as the climax of *Don Quixote,* part 1—bringing chickens home to roost and accumulating characters and momentum in the manner of Jonsonian comedy, and ending in the mad knight's triumphant vindication—apparently impressed Fielding sufficiently to influence his thinking about the denouement of his own novel. In the chapters of the brief coda that followed, he could still see Cervantes' invention at work, improvising Quixote's "enchantment" in place of the "Princess Micomicona" hoax when Dorothea's reunion with her errant lover requires her abdication of that role; reviving memory of the early, more purely Quixotic, part of the novel with recapitulative incidents as the adventurers rewind the thread of their journey; and sustaining interest to the end by an ironic turn of the old contest between knight and squire. For Sancho is now as eager for his master to resume his quest as he formerly was to abandon it; and his efforts to disabuse the knight of the trick played upon him founder on the same invulnerable fantasy and rhetorical ascendancy that formerly sustained their errantry.

In the first part of *Don Quixote*, Fielding could observe Cervantes progressively enhancing the initial potentially crude idea of a comic madman with a subtler and more substantial interplay of the antithetical knight and squire; experiencing difficulty in sustaining the narrative on even this enlarged conception of his original subject and experimenting with more extended plotting and more complex narrative organization; lapsing into a succession of mechanically introduced independent stories; and finally bringing his original vein to a climax. The benefits of this process of incremental revision and exploration were to be found in part 2, where a generally similar narrative structure—wandering adventures followed by a sustained central sequence in a fixed milieu, and a recapitulative homeward journey—was planned with some care and realized with better effect. The lesson was not to be lost on Fielding, who would not require the prompting of the characters' introductory reflections on part 1 to alert him to the differences perceptible from the outset of part 2, where in place of the abortive first venture there is a deliberate buildup of anticipation for the volume's single sally. Quixote's goals are more specifically defined; the jousting at Saragossa is established as his destination, and the reader is encouraged to look forward to the mad knight's appearance in this latter-day chivalric setting as the climax of his adventures.[9] In contrast to the isolated opening exploit of the Don's first sally, the first incident on the road (Sancho's improvisation of an unknown peasant girl as Dulcinea) is the germ of a protracted comedy of deception whose sequence of ironic turns is not completed until the close of the book, and Dulcinea's mysterious enchantment is the knight's recurrent preoccupation.[10]

Instead of the wholly unprepared appearance of the curate and barber in the Sierra Morena, Fielding could observe Cervantes establishing the threat to the knight's adventuring at the beginning of part 2 and using it to affect the reader's responses. Hints of a young friend's scheme of defeating Quixote in single combat, like the extensive conversations between him, Quixote, and Sancho preceding the sally, whet the appetite for new adventures; the subsequent defeat of the "knight of the mirrors" (pt. 2, chap. 14) clears the way for a long sequence of adventures without an unexpected intervention like that in part 1. At the same time, the plain hints of young Carrasco's eventual return provide a specified long-range anticipation. Cervantes' apparent plan was to stage this return combat in the appropriate setting of the Saragossa tournament (the suggestion that the knight set out for this destination comes from Carrasco), and to make this convergence of expectations the climactic event

[9] This expectation is initiated at the end of part 1, where the narrator alludes to his hero's "third Expedition in quest of Adventures" after which "he was present at certain famous Tilts and Tournaments made in the City of *Saragosa,* where he met with Occasions worthy the Exercise of his Sense and Valour" (pp. 438–39). In the same passage, he refers to Quixote's death.

[10] The duchess persuades Sancho that in thinking he invented the transformation he has himself been deceived by Dulcinea's enchanters, and he is hoaxed into bringing about the disenchantment by self-flagellation. In the end, the joke is brought full circle as Sancho deceives the knight into thinking his back has borne the blows he has applied to trees.

of part 2. But in reaction to Avellaneda's spurious sequel to part 1 he changed his hero's itinerary, made "the knight of the white moon" (Carrasco) deliver his successful challenge on the strand outside Barcelona, and hurried the novel to a close. Despite the apparent haste of composition, the extent of the homeward journey even in its truncated rendition indicates that Cervantes planned to make it a much more comprehensive recapitulation of the knight's adventures than its counterpart in part 1.[11]

Within this more carefully planned and shaped structure, the Quixotic comedy could be seen to have mellowed. The knight's actions are more pacific, and he shows less manic compulsion for adventures. Though still capable of accepting a stranger as transmuted Dulcinea, of thinking "the knight of the mirrors" is enchanted to look like his young friend Carrasco, and of fabricating a supernatural fantasy out of an hour's nap, only once does he make that wildly "creative" misappraisal of simple objects that sparks the most characteristic incidents of part 1.[12] He rages a good deal less at Sancho, whose proverbs are increasingly a match for his master's learning. Their debate about the nature of reality gives way to more expansive dialogues on a variety of topics, occupying a greater part of the narrative, through which both protagonists appear more appealing and less fantastic. As Quixote's wisdom is more and more in

[11] In the coda of part 1, there is a terminal review of books of chivalry, a parody of the earlier romantic story of Chrysostom and Marcella (see below, chap. 7, pp. 181–82, especially n. 5), and a final bizarre battle like those in the beginning. The longer corresponding sequence of part 2 (chaps. 66–73) includes an analogue of Sancho's gubernatorial judgments and a final hoax by the duke, in addition to echoes and reminiscences of various adventures on the road. The pattern of part 2 is blurred somewhat by the resumption of random adventures between the climax of the central sequence and Quixote's final defeat, perhaps in reaction to the discovery of Avellaneda's piracy, and it is not clear whether bracketing his defeat with the happy resolution of a love story begun before the end of the central sequence was a hasty contrivance or part of the original plan. In any case, Fielding might have noted the strategy with interest (see below, p. 86).

[12] In the discovery of the "inchanted Bark" (chap. 29).

the forefront, and his madness manifests itself more in talk than action, the sometimes extravagant caricature of part 1 gives way to the picture of a "natural" human being with a bizarre eccentricity. This is in part the result of Cervantes' humorous play upon the prior existence of part 1. Thanks to Cid Hamet's history, the travelers are no longer regarded as freaks but recognized and welcomed wherever they go. His redoubtable valor acknowledged, the old gentleman is less driven to seek out new exploits; delighted with his own fame, and the hospitality of friendly "castles," Sancho is not inclined to question the chivalric way of life. By a kind of *tromp l'oeil*, their universal reception and their discussion of the first installment of their adventures make the protagonists seem to transcend the fiction of which they are part.

The most striking change in the sequel, and the one to which Cervantes most pointedly called attention, was in the central sequence of the narrative (pt. 2, chaps. 30–57). In response to criticism of part 1, he undertook to avoid "Novels, as *The Curious Impertinent*, and that of the *Captive*, which were in a manner distinct from the Design."[13] Instead he developed the central comedy in a direction first explored in the corresponding section of part 1, expanding the Micomicona ruse into an extended series of elaborate stunts and charades played upon the knight's fantasy and the squire's simplicity by a pair of highborn pranksters whose contrivances and the resources available for their execution produce adventures whose comic wonders not even Quixote's imagination could engender without a cooperative universe.

As in part 1, the sequence falls into two stages, but instead of interweaving actions in the first stage and falling off to a tedious addition Cervantes here built to a climactic second stage in which the narrative alternates between the separate adventures of Quixote and Sancho. For the greatest of the jests perpetrated

[13] *Don Quixote*, p. 728.

by the duke and duchess is the presentation of Sancho's island. To make the most of the realization of that absurd wish, the source of so many comic and wistful moments throughout the novel, Cervantes complemented his shrewd gubernatorial judgments and bedevilments with the reactions of Sancho's wife and neighbors back home. For sixteen chapters he kept the narrative moving among these comic centers and Quixote's endeavors to resist the pretended ardors of a pretty young member of the duke's retinue, until the whole sequence culminates in the island's "invasion," Sancho's abdication, and, most unexpectedly, Quixote's formal combat in behalf of an actually betrayed maiden.

The creation of this climactic sequence out of materials from which he had already spun more than five hundred pages of narrative was marked by Cervantes in characteristically droll fashion. On the eve of Sancho's government, precisely the point at which the reader would be least likely to yearn for "Equisodes and Digressions that might be of more Weight and Entertainment," he made his fictitious historian pause conspicuously to complain of being confined to "so dry and limited a Subject" as "the bare History of Don *Quixote* and *Sancho*."[14] Fond of such narrative jokes himself, Fielding would not have been likely to miss Cervantes' irony; even without it, he would have recognized and appreciated the difference between this sequence and its counterpart in part 1, as he doubtless did Cervantes' generally greater concern with manipulating the reader's expectations and responses throughout part 2. But his admiration for Cervantes' ingenuity must have been qualified by some reservations concerning his heavy reliance on the pranks of the duke and duchess.

In an essay in the *Champion* on "a certain diversion called roasting," he expressed strong disapproval of would-be wits

[14] *Ibid.*

who amuse themselves by drawing out and playing upon the infirmities and eccentricities of others.

> I have often observed in life, the person roasted to be infinitely superior to those who (to use a word of their own) have enjoyed him. To say the truth, the least oddity of behaviour, the most inoffensive peculiarity often exposes a man of sense and virtue, to the ridicule of those who are in every degree his inferiors.[15]

Later in the same essay, he associated the roaster with those who find madness amusing: "nor should I entertain a good opinion of him, who could go to Bedlam, and divert himself with the dreadful frenzies, and monstrous absurdities, of the wretches there." Obviously Fielding thought the purely fictional madness of Quixote a proper object of amusement. But there is a significant difference between escapades and discomfitures engendered by the knight's own folly, or his friends' playful contrivances to rescue him from it, and the noble pair's calculated manipulation of that weakness solely for their own amusement. At the beginning of the sequence, after the relatively tame adventures of the first stage of part 2, even a reader with Fielding's contempt for practical jokers might be delighted with the mischievous play-acting organized by the witty couple. As their guest, Quixote himself feels for the first time that he is truly a knight-errant, and a priest who objects early in their stay to the duke's humoring of knight and squire is clearly made out to be a mirthless prig (pt. 2, chaps. 31–32). There is comic justice in the duchess' turning of Sancho's trick of the enchanted Dulcinea back upon him, and, in another sense, in Sancho's attainment of his island. One must feel grateful to the duke for fulfilling this ancient fantasy. But as the stunts accumulate, the duke's initial humane restraint gives way to a general license to michief on the part of his retinue (including making sport of a foolish girl's misfortune). He is

[15] *Works* 15 : 241.

amused when his henchmen reward Sancho's remarkable gubernatorial sagacity with a thorough *guignol* beating, but for a reader of Fielding's moral sensibility the joke must long since have gone sour. Nor could he have readily assented to Cervantes' approving characterization of another "Gentleman of good Parts," who later parades Quixote through the streets with a sign pinned to his back, as a lover of "Diversions . . . innocently . . . obtain'd without Prejudice to his Neighbours."

Cervantes eventually allowed his narrator to express some misgiving about these pranksters in commenting upon a final elaborate charade performed by the duke's company near the end of the novel. In Cid Hamet's opinion, "those that play'd all these Tricks were as mad as those they were impos'd upon: And . . . the Duke and Dutchess were within a Hair's Breadth of being thought Fools themselves, for taking so much Pains to make Sport with the Weakness of two poor silly Wretches."[16] Even in this lone criticism, however, the objection is to the extremity of the duke's pursuit of a prank rather than his victimization of the protagonists. There is no trace of qualm or qualification in the zestful account of Quixote's drubbing near the end of part 1, when his friend and neighbor, Barber Nicholas, contrives to give his goatherd opponent the advantage so that he may produce a "shower of blood"—to the unrestrained delight of the canon and curate and other witnesses.

This kind of treatment was bound to generate an increasing dissatisfaction for the reader cumulatively impressed by Quixote's noble and endearing qualities. At the beginning of the novel, and again at the outset of part 2, such a reader might well agree with the gentleman who chides Carrasco for finally defeating Quixote because the good of having him cured cannot match the loss of pleasure from his vagaries. By the end of the novel, he would be more likely to agree with the angry Cas-

[16] *Don Quixote,* p. 909.

tilian who, on the occasion of the same gentleman's parading him through Barcelona, laments that the "Whim of Knight-Errantry" should spoil his good parts and advises him to "leave playing the Fool" and go home. Whether he thought Cervantes intended it or not, Fielding might well have considered this modification of attitude and its lesser analogue in the course of part 1 essential elements in the emotional form of the novel. The conclusion of part 1 is not merely arbitrary but satisfying, because the transformation of the knight into a passive manipulated victim is eventually a sad one; in the course of part 2, as the kindnesses of the travelers' various hosts give way to the bedevilments of the duke and duchess and the cruder jests of their subsequent "enjoyer," the reader's desire for an end to the comedy grows stronger. In the course of the whole novel, as the sum of the heroes' wisdom and goodness mounts beside their accumulated buffetings and victimizations—and particularly in the closing chapters after the knight fails to shake off his final defeat, and his old romantic enthusiasm turns to weariness and melancholy—the wish grows to see the old gentleman placed beyond the reach of further folly. Thus his restoration to sanity and the insurance of its permanence by his death constitute not merely Cervantes' safeguard against subsequent false sequels but the most emotionally satisfying conclusion to the novel. Or so it might have seemed to Henry Fielding, who reasoned in generally similar fashion about Richardson's strategy in *Clarissa*, and who saw Cervantes' lengthy series of actions "all tending to one great end." For he was to make similar progressive modifications of attitude an important constituent of the form of his own imitation of Cervantes.

Of the French works Fielding associated with *Don Quixote* in the ranks of "truthful" fiction, only the earliest, *Le Roman comique*, could be regarded as an adaptation of specific elements of Cervantes' formula. As Scarron's title suggests, his account of the intertwined fortunes of a troupe of players is a "low" humorous version of the *romans heroiques* of La Calprenède and Scudéry—latter-day successors to the vogue of chivalric romance. Acknowledging his affiliation with Cervantes in the same passage in which he derided those "voluminous Works" which Fielding disparaged in the Preface to *Joseph Andrews*, Scarron adapted Cervantes' mock-heroic narrative manner and facetious chapter titles, and revived Quixote's feats of arms in his own brand of comic violence. He also made his principal comic figure—"le plus grand petit fou qui ait couru les champs depuis Roland"—a debased Quixote. Like his Spanish ancestor, the dwarf Ragotin envisions for himself a romantic and heroic role for which he is radically unqualified, pugnaciously engaging in a succession of grotesque battles in which he is invariably the loser. But this little pettifogger has no trace of the knight's disinterested virtue or wisdom; he is motivated solely by contumacious vanity. His character is as far removed from that of the noble Manchegan as his physical deformity is from the radical mental transfiguration at the core of Cervantes' novel, and Scarron's comedy is correspondingly lacking in depth and subtlety.

Insofar as his irrepressible "mauvaise gloire" provokes him to play the lover and affect talents he does not possess, this rash little coxcomb seems to correspond more closely than Quixote to Fielding's idea that "the Imperfections of Nature, may become the Objects of Ridicule . . . when Ugliness aims at the Applause of Beauty, or Lameness endeavours to display Agility." Insisting on gallantly escorting the actresses, he brings them tumbling downstairs with him; infatuated with the success of a *nouvelle* he has recited as if it were his own, he makes advances toward one of them and is rebuffed by a rap of a buskin. But the humor derives less from Fielding's "only source of the true ridiculous" than from the "imperfection of nature" itself. In the continuation of the latter incident, after the whole company tease him by keeping "son histoire" out of his reach, the enraged dwarf flails impotently at the lower parts of his chief antagonist, "ne pouvant pas aller plus haut," while "les mains de l'autre, qui avaient l'avantage du lieu, tombèrent à plomb cinq ou six fois sur le haut de sa tête et si pesamment qu'elle entra dans son chapeau jusques au menton."[17]

The comedy of Ragotin's *disgraces* is predominantly physical. When his vanity is not producing pratfalls or his friends are not tricking or tormenting him, he is beset by gross accidents. In one chapter near the end of Scarron's composition, the drunken dwarf is thrown from a horse, stripped, bound and dragged in a cart, pitched into a muddy ditch, attacked by flies, whipped by a coachman, chased by a dog, and stung by a swarm of bees. These gross misadventures are matched by such grotesqueries as a naked madman wandering the countryside, an elaborate practical joke with a corpse, and an antediluvian procession of animals through the corridors and bedrooms of the novel. Like Ragotin, a corrupt and cowardly constable who attaches himself to the strolling players and the troupe's would-be poet both vainly pretend to capacities they do not possess, but these potential sources of character comedy, and the more prominent mischief of the rascally old actor Rancune, are overshadowed by simple mistakes and a general fractiousness which frequently erupts into comic violence.

The inhabitants of Fielding's fictional world live in a comparable state of explosive irascibility, and the example of Scarron's extended and lively inn-brawls probably contributed more directly than Cervantes' more bizarre encounters to the exuberant dynamics of his comic battles. But though he probably enjoyed the Scarronian fracas, the man who thought only an "ill-framed mind" could find infirmity ridiculous must

[17] *Le Roman comique*, ed. Emile Magne (Paris, 1955), p. 43 (hereafter cited as *Roman comique*). All subsequent references are to this edition. Text references are to book and chapter.

have considered the persistent bedevilment of the little man as distasteful in its own way as the pranks played upon Don Quixote eventually become. More generally, in view of the centrality of character and motivation to his own notions of the ridiculous, he must have found Scarron's comedy, deriving more from external causes than from peculiarities of disposition or thought, generally inferior to that of Cervantes.

Evidently more to Fielding's taste, and more significant for his conception of *Joseph Andrews*, was Scarron's modification of another aspect of the Cervantean formula, its allusive relation to a popular mode of serious romance. Scarron made uncomplimentary references to the heroic romances, and parodied some of their epic mannerisms; but in transplanting the conventional plot motifs and narrative structure of this exalted genre to the *milieu declassé* of the provincial theater, he was not attempting to reduce it to absurdity. Instead, like Cervantes in his interpolations, he sought to create his own more realistic version ("plus à notre usage et plus selon la portée de l'humanité") of those "aventures de princes" substituting for the "héros imaginaires de l'antiquité qui son quelquefois incommodes à force d'être trop honnêtes gens" a personable and unassuming young leading man. But neither Destin, nor Étoile, as the actress who passes for his sister is called, is an ordinary stroller, and, as Parson Adams says of Joseph and Fanny, "there is something singular enough in their history."

The hero, though lowborn, has been the protegé of a nobleman and the companion of his sons. His beloved is a lady of higher lineage whom he rescued from the assault of a villain who has since dogged their steps from Rome to Mans. When the novel opens, these lovers, whose identity and relationship are unknown to their fellow comedians as well as the reader, have been members of the company for some time. Destin recounts most of his involved history to the other actresses, and it advances very little beyond the conclusion of his retrospective narrative. As it stands, it follows a clear, if incomplete, tragicomic pattern. Destin's initial heroics put him on a good footing with Léonore until the rival son of his patron discloses his low station and the girl's mother closes her doors to him; later, his protector banishes him for defending himself in a duel provoked by the same villainous son. From this low point, his fortunes turn upward as he reencounters Léonore and is able to assist her distressed mother, who charges him on her deathbed to protect her daughter and restore her to her long-absent father. At the point the story is brought up to date, the only apparent obstacles to the lovers' happiness are that long-sought reunion and the continued persecution of Saldagne, their original assailant, which reaches a climax in the kidnapping of the heroine in part 2.

The failure of this attempt (the object of dramatic preparation from the beginning of the novel) and Saldagne's wounding in the process may have been the preliminaries to a projected conclusion in which the villain's death would be followed by achievement of the other long-range goal. Scarron's preparations for the girl's reunion with her father, whom the pair have pursued across Europe, are begun in the opening chapters of the novel, where curiosity is focused on the theft of a jeweled picture of the parent she has never seen. They are renewed with its recovery near the end of part 2, an event which is apparently delayed until this point in anticipation of its use in a recognition scene in the projected final installment.[18] The happy ending might have been planned to follow directly, with the grateful father's blessing on the lovers' union, but Scarron seems to have been preparing from the beginning of Des-

[18] Destin learns near the beginning of the novel that the thief is the rascally constable la Rappinière, but he does not confront him with this knowledge until the end of part 2 (see n. 22 below).

tin's story for a denouement of another kind. That "bassesse de ma naissance," acknowledged by the hero in commencing his narrative, which leads him to the "pensée . . . criminelle" that Léonore might not be a "fille légitime d'un homme de condition" so that "le défaut de sa naissance" might match his own—and which subsequently causes the girl's mother to deny him her company—would once more bar the way to his happiness. For the girl's aristocratic father, who has not been able to acknowledge his private marriage to her mother, could hardly accept a baseborn stroller as his son-in-law. But Scarron did not name his hero Destin for nothing. He would snatch him from the brink of misery by the discovery that his birth is as exactly *en rapport* with Étoile's as he had wished: he is in fact the quasilegitimate offspring of a similar secret union between a Scotch lord and a lady of good family, changed in his cradle by the grasping schemers supposed to be his parents.

Such a denouement would be consistent with the adaptation of comparably melodramatic conventions of heroic romance in the lovers' first encounter and at subsequent turns in their history, and its early foreshadowings are evident. Shortly after Destin's birth, his miserly and dishonest supposed parents are given the care of a highborn babe. From infancy they favor the supposed lord over their own offspring, though young Garigues, as Destin is called, displays natural superiority to the cloddish young count. Most significantly, when the grown lad returns from his travels, his putative father, entrenched as the manager of the young count's affairs, hastily sweeps him away from any possible encounter with the noble family and orders him never to return. These indications of an exchange of infants (the virtually undepicted young "Comte de Glaris" has no other discernible function) are borne out by Scarron's early narrative hints. He plays with the reader, much as Fielding does in the opening sentence of his narrative, having Destin begin his story by saying "Je vous ferais bien croire, si je voulais, que je suis d'une maison très illustre";[19] and he supplements this a few pages later with a broader stroke:

Pour moi, je paraissais être ce que je n'étais pas, et bien moins le fils de Garigues que celui d'un comte. Et si je ne me trouve enfin qu'un malheureux comédien, c'est sans doute que la fortune s'est voulu venger de la nature, qui avait voulu faire quelque chose de moi sans son consentement, ou, si vous voulez, que la nature prend quelquefois plaisir à favoriser ceux que la fortune a pris en aversion.[20]

One may discern in this complaint the prospect of a denouement in which fortune will relent in her persecution of the "malheureux comédien" and nature will be vindicated.

The sequels to Scarron's narrative extant in Fielding's time show no recognition of these signs of the intended resolution of Destin's story, but they were less likely to be lost on Fielding, whose interest in denouements of this kind, first evinced in *The Author's Farce* (1729), was carried over into his novels.[21] Although the idea of using such a venerable device as exchanged infants to resolve his own comically qualified version of the

[19] *Roman comique*, p. 57.

[20] *Roman comique*, p. 61.

[21] Scarron was completing part 3 at his death, but it did not survive him. In the "troisième et derniere partie" attributed to Jean Girault (1662?), reprinted in subsequent editions of the novel and included in the English version by Tom Brown that went through six editions between 1700 and 1741, Saldagne is killed by the players in another attempt to abduct Étoile, and Destin and Étoile are united without further mention of the girl's father. A "suite" by de Preschac (1679) was appended to this conclusion in a number of eighteenth-century French editions (including the 1730 Paris edition that might have been read by Fielding), although it preserves Saldagne and does not advance the lovers' fortunes beyond their state at the end of part 2. The two volume "suite et conclusion" of 1771 is the first to pick up the hints of the hero's birth. After learning he is the true Earl of Glaris, Destin rescues a gentleman who is discovered by the jeweled picture to be Étoile's father, and the marriage receives both fathers' blessings. It was not until 1849 that the brief sequel of Louis Barré got the two discoveries in the order that Scarron seems to have contemplated, with the threat of parental disapproval breathlessly averted by Destin's transformation; but in addition to making Destin and Étoile first cousins, and confusing the false Glaris with Saldagne, Barré's tangled plotting requires old Garigues to confess the exchange of infants almost before it could have taken place.

conventional romantic story might have occurred to Fielding independently, the more idiosyncratic resemblance between the pattern of Destin's story and Joseph's, each reaching its preliminary melodramatic climax near the close of the penultimate part of the novel in the abduction and immediate recovery of the heroine, and the fact that the handsome young player is involved in a comic seduction scene with an older woman of higher position (see below, pp. 155–57) give weight to the hypothesis that he had *Le Roman comique* before him in devising it.

More important, perhaps, than any such material suggestions was Scarron's interweaving of Destin's story with the other threads of the narrative to develop suspense and surprise. Adapting the *commencement par le milieu* favored by writers of heroic romance and held by contemporary theory to be the proper epic order, Scarron conceived his whole narrative in the pattern Cervantes attempted when he departed from his linear sequence of episodes to interpolate the stories of Cardenio and Dorothea, unfolding the past histories of Destin and Étoile and other members of the company within the framework of their ongoing adventures; but he interwove his several strands with noticeably greater delight in playing upon the reader's expectations. Among the initial comic broils, he rouses curiosity concerning the mysterious young player and the apparently unrelated depredations of a band of horsemen, then explodes a comic fracas just as Destin is to begin the narrative that will resolve it and unexpectly connect the two. After bringing the story of the lovers' vicissitudes up to date and foreshadowing new trouble with the disclosure that their old enemy is close on their trail, he diverts attention to the misadventures of Ragotin and the other low comedy figures and to a completely autonomous *nouvelle*, the better to startle the reader with the dramatic eruption of a whole new line of romantic interest. His original readers were made to wait six years for the appearance of part 2, and a few chapters beyond, to resolve the mystery of the abduction of Angélique, one of the actresses, and to learn that her apparent abductor, Léandre, was in fact her unsuccessful rescuer. A few chapters later the corpulent Mme Bouvillon's assault on Destin's virtue is disrupted by Ragotin's hysterical announcement of the girl's safety, but now it is discovered that Étoile has been taken in her place! The ease with which Destin effects her rescue indicates that Scarron was less interested in sustaining romantic suspense than in dazzling the reader with successive turns of his story; and, although the narrative is again given over to episodic comedy and inserted tales after the lovers' reunion, the pattern of parts 1 and 2 points toward a final burst of dramatic developments such as I have sketched for Scarron's projected conclusion.

Although he facetiously cast himself in the role of an author who needed to pause at the end of his first chaper to think what to write in the next, Scarron obviously planned this sequence of developments with some skill, concealing parts of the plot, giving true and false hints, and interrupting and intertwining actions so as to make anticipated or prepared events surprising. In retrospect, it is obvious that Saldagne has kidnapped Angélique, thinking she is Étoile: he has been seen mistakenly molesting a number of other travellers in his quest for her early in the novel. But the abduction is made to appear mysterious as well as unexpected because attention has been diverted from the principal center of suspense before it occurs, and the reader is encouraged by plausible signs to think it is part of a wholly new line of action in which Angélique's ardent admirer is the culprit. When Étoile is abducted in turn this long-anticipated event is unexpected because attention has been focused on the story of this secondary pair of lovers. Even after the heroine is rescued, there remains the mystery of how she came to be on the road, enabling the villain to correct his mistake, and the surprising discovery that the players' supposed friend, the provost La Rappinière, also tried to steal the lady. Yet this too has been prepared, as has the subsequent disclosure that he had earlier stolen the jeweled picture of her father, unexpectedly resolving the novel's earliest mystery.[22]

Whereas Cervantes roused curiosity by such peripheral wondrous circumstances as the love-crazed Cardenio's living like a wildman, Dorothea's transvestite disguise, and Ferdinand and Lucinda's masked arrival at the inn, Scarron developed it out of integral elements of his story. Whereas Cervantes arbitrarily brought Cardenio and Dorothea together in the wilderness and even more palpably contrived their meeting with their common betrayer and his subsequent reformation, Scarron, by alternately directing and deflecting the reader's attention, produced surprising turns out of the "natural" consequences of earlier events. Although he was not to attempt so involved a complex of intrigues in *Joseph Andrews*, Fielding might well have appreciated these differences in Scarron's method, for he was to employ similar means toward similar effects. He might also have noted with approval another difference between Scarron's romantic story and Cervantes'. Although Dorothea, and to a lesser extent Cardenio, take part in the hoaxing of Don Quixote, this seems to have no effect upon their roles as serious romantic figures. Under Scarron's hand, the story of Destin and Étoile takes on some of the comic coloration of its surroundings. It is not only that the hero and heroine are involved in grotesque encounters, or that he is drawn into the "low" free-for-all, countering bites and scratches with hoisting of skirts and laying on of hands. The wounded Destin's deathbed letter, begging Léonore not to begrudge him the undeserved honor of dying for her, reads like a burlesque of the sentiments of romantic

[22] La Rappinière asks Rancune to help him win Étoile near the end of part 1. Earlier, when the provost's servant is mortally wounded, he calls Destin to his bedside for a mysterious conference, and la Rappinière pales at Rancune's mention of the robbery.

heroes; his dry observation on the change wrought in her mother's attitude by her need to use him is an amusing departure from their conventional *bienséance*. There is something correspondingly ludicrous in the bungling dastardy of Saldagne, who repeatedly assaults the wrong persons and, when he finally gets Étoile by accident, immediately seeks the help of his brother-in-law, who he knows is Destin's best friend. The rapidity with which surprising turns develop in the central chapters of part 2 is almost comic in itself, or so it might appear to Fielding, who could have seen Scarron's facetious narrative intrusions in the otherwise serious interpolated *nouvelles* as another gesture toward the kind of overall comic synthesis he sought in his own work.

Neither *Don Quixote* nor *Le Roman comique* suggests any substantial connection between Fielding's reading of continental fiction and his idea of affectation as the source of the ridiculous. It is in *Gil Blas* that one finds the first clear anticipation of Fielding's comic exposure of pretense. Whereas Cervantes' comedy, and in a more diffused way that of Scarron, turns inward, directing laughter toward a few isolated butts who depart from the established norms of their respective fictional worlds, Lesage used his hero's journey through life as a means of exhibiting the prevalent vanities, delusions, deceptions, and vagaries of human nature. Gil Blas is not predisposed to a specific kind of humorous behavior by any peculiar bent; as he is carried from one situation to another by accidents or the whims of his betters, comic expectation is centered not on what he will *do* next, nor even what he will *become*, but what he will encounter. As the great Sangrado's apprentice, he is acquainted with the pretensions and stupidities of the medical fraternity, recurrent objects of satire throughout the novel; in the service of a beau he makes the frivolous rounds of "high life"; in the household of the Marquise de Chaves, he observes the affectations of a fashionable salon; through his friend Fabricio, he is introduced into the capricious self-centered realm of authors, and through his sometime sweetheart Laura to the coquetries, deceits, and jealousies of the green room. Throughout this quasisystematic survey of the various walks and stations of life, from his first post as the lackey of a valetudinarian priest to his ultimate eminence as confidential secretary to two prime ministers, he witnesses the chicanery of underlings, the ingratitude of superiors, and the parasitology of courts, from kitchen to royal closet.

The comedy made of these materials plays upon the ironic discrepancies between men's reputations or fortunes and their abilities, between their professions and their practice, between their "quality" and their humanity—between things as they ought to be or are thought to be and things as they are. Sangrado's practice and fame flourish, though he concedes "je n'ai souvent la satisfaction de guérir les personnes qui tombent entre mes mains." Fabricio's meaningless Gongorisms gain applause, but thanks to a patron's vanity his fortune is really made by the hissing of his play. While a set of *petit maitres* indulge their "wit" at the expense of an aspiring bourgeois, they are themselves easily gulled by their larcenous stewards, and even fleeced by their footmen, who at the same time foolishly affect the very affectations of their masters. In contrast to Cervantes and Scarron, who spin out particular consequences and ramifications of a set of ridiculous propensities established early in their respective narratives, Lesage presented Fielding with a mode of comedy in which the point or climax of many incidents is the disclosure of a character's eccentricity or pretense. A priest whom Gil Blas has restored to favor is effusive in his gratitude and hospitality, until he learns that his benefactor has himself fallen from grace; a reputedly profound sage proves to be a fool who knows how to keep silent and look wise; a bishop presses favors upon acquaintances he has no intention of helping, out of vain self-importance. This tendency is carried to its logical extreme on those occasions in which an insider presents the neophyte Gil Blas with a series of such vignettes by way of acquainting him with the foibles of the drawing room or tavern.

Although he is often only a spectator of these follies and chicaneries, Gil Blas is also frequently their victim. If there is any prevailing pattern in his comic misadventures and those of the barber Diego and the servant lad Scipio, who assume his role in their interpolated histories, it involves some kind of comic disappointment of the young man's expectations. In the early stages of his acquaintance with the world, Gil Blas is the classic dupe, swelling with conceit or congratulating himself on his amorous prowess, only to discover that he has been taken. As he progresses, he fancies himself a sharper, but as often as not his schemes end in some unexpected deflation. After getting on by cheating his masters as best he can, the nimble-fingered opportunist gradually finds he can serve himself best by serving his masters more or less faithfully. It is at this stage that the process of his worldly education through disillusionment is brought to a climax in a loosely articulated but clearly shaped ironic sequence.

In the first phase of this sequence (bk. 7), Gil Blas is twice on the way to making his fortune honorably, only to be disappointed by the vagaries of his masters. As the faithful literary secretary of the Archbishop of Granada, he carries out his solemn charge, informing him of the decline in his homiletic powers, and is dismissed for lack of literary judgment. Subsequently, he delivers Count Galiano from his bilking servants and exhausts himself nursing his master's ape, and is immediately abandoned when he himself falls ill. In the first instance he stubs his toe on his master's vanity; in the second he is the victim of simple ingratitude; in both cases there is an emphatic contradiction between the master's protestations at the outset and his conduct in the climax. In addition to the wry contrast between the nobleman's absurd concern for his pet and his fearful indifference toward his valuable assistant, the irony of the second episode is heightened by the fact that it is the story of his treatment by the archbishop which first commends Gil Blas to the Count, who presents himself as one who perceives the folly of the prelate's self-love and knows how to value the young man's service better. In the context of preceding adventures, the underlying irony of both episodes is that Gil Blas, who has not been averse to playing the world's game, here resists the temptations of easy flattery or belowstairs connivance, only to be dismissed for his pains. The ironic vision of the rewards of virtue is emphasized by Gil's observation at the close of the latter episode:

Quand il vous arrivera quelque grand malheur, dit un Pape, éxaminez-vous bien, et vous verrez qu'il y aura toujours de votre faute. N'en déplaise à ce saint Pere, je ne vois pas comment dans cette occasion je contribuai à mon infortune.[23]

In the second phase of the sequence (bk. 8) Gil Blas does succeed in attaining affluence and power as the prime minister's favorite, and the story takes another ironic turn. The erstwhile victim of the vanity and selfishness of his "betters" is no sooner elevated himself than he develops the same ill-natured affectation he formerly smiled at in others. The good nature which could not be corrupted by a series of criminal acquaintances, and resisted the temptations of the archbishop's palace and the count's menage, is now blown up with avarice and conceit. In the words of his old friend Fabricio, "Gil Blas n'est plus ce même Gil Blas que j'ai connu."

This ironic success story reaches its melodramatic catastrophe in the final phase of the sequence (bk. 9), as Gil Blas, on the eve of his marriage to a fortune, is tumbled from his high place into

[23] *Histoire de Gil Blas de Santillane*, ed. Auguste Dupouy (Paris, 1935), 2 : 102 (hereafter cited as *Gil Blas*). Subsequent references are to this edition. Text references are to book and chapter.

prison. This event, which Gil Blas takes more seriously than any of fortune's previous blows, initiates his purgation from vanity and ambition; but viewed from a more detached perspective it is also the delayed climax of the sequence of bitter comic letdowns. For while imprisoned, the erstwhile factotum slowly and reluctantly makes the discovery that a prime minister is no more humane nor less human than his other masters: he has once more been sacrificed to the convenience of the mighty.

Whereas Lesage thus managed to shape the second installment of his novel effectively, he did not always keep the vein of episodic comedy described above before him as his "main end or scope." Although Gil Blas is bilked by a flattering parasite in his first adventure, his peregrination through the world of affectations and eccentricity does not really get under way until book 2, and in the second half of the first installment this strain disappears in a welter of interpolations culminating in a lengthy rogue's tale. Again, when he had brought the novel to an appropriate conclusion by having his hero retire from the world at the completion of his moral education, he added an anticlimactic sequel in which Gil Blas is carried through a second round of ministerial intrigue, and his servant Scipio reenacts his earlier adventures. Fielding might well have relished the irony of a "cured" Gil Blas proclaiming no interest in reentering the corridors of power while waiting three weeks for an interview with the new prime minister, and then ingratiating himself by zealously denouncing the policies of his former patron; but he must have regarded Lesage's open-ended and overextended narrative, with its many interpolations, its extremely casual probabilities, and its almost total lack of concern with shaping expectations and responses, as a cautionary example in his own pursuit of a "series of actions, all tending to one great end."

On the other hand, the idea of a comparatively "normal" and

ingenuous protagonist traversing a world of venality, eccentricity, and pretense was an appealing divergence from the paths of Cervantes and Scarron. It provided scope for a much greater variety of comic characters and situations. Reflecting upon the foibles of specific professions and classes, and upon the frailties of human nature in general, rather than the oddities of a few idiosyncratic figures, it also conformed with Fielding's avowed satiric intention of describing "not Men, but Manners; not an Individual, but a Species." What Gil Blas must recurrently discover to his sorrow is closer to what Parson Adams experiences in his westward journey than anything else in the tradition of comic romance. In the world envisaged by Lesage, selfishness and cheating are the rule, and good nature a rarity. In keeping with this vision his comedy, from the invention of its materials to the form of its episodes and the manner of its narration, is laden with irony. In these respects Fielding's particular version of the "History of the World in general" has more affinity with *Gil Blas* than with *Don Quixote*. The passengers in his stage coach come from Lesage's Spain, rather than Cervantes', and the fate of its good-hearted postilion "transported for robbing a Hen-roost" reflects a corresponding ironic vision of the world's justice.

Of all the works cited by Fielding in his discussion of "Biography," the one most immediately before the reading public at the time of his writing would also appear to be the least likely source for his "idea of romance." *La Vie de Marianne*, the second volume of which had appeared in translation in the midst of *Pamela's* vogue, would seem to have more in common with Richardson's novel than with Fielding's "lewd and ungenerous engraftment," or his definition of the comic romance. Recounting "tout le pathétique" of an orphan girl threatened with seduction, following her through a succession of emotional crises toward the apparently intended denouement of a socially elevating marriage founded on romantic love, Marivaux's uncompleted novel resembled *Virtue Rewarded* in other ways as well. Each misfortune or complication in the heroine's relations with her Tartuffe guardian, the lady who befriends her when she flees his "protection" (who proves to be his sister), and the young man with whom she falls in love (who turns out to be her benefactress' son) presents her with a problem of conduct, and a challenge to her nobility. As Pamela's virtuous behavior in adversity converts her persecutor's lust to love, Marianne's selfless determination to reject her lover rather than disoblige his mother wins the mother's blessing on the unequal match. If Pamela, after her initial round of vindicated suffering, must go on to convert the implacable Lady Davers from violent abuse to approval and admiration of the shining beauty of her character, Marianne, having escaped her tempter and received her benefactress' blessing on her love, must melt the opposition of powerful relatives by nobly renouncing claim on her lover while refusing an advantageous match arranged by the prime minister himself. One cannot tell whether Marivaux contemplated bringing back Marianne's errant lover through the force of her goodness in his unwritten denouement, as Richardson in his sequel had Pamela win the straying Mr. B. back to her tearful bosom by her unexampled selflessness; but he approached this in the last installment published before *Joseph Andrews*, when Marianne's scrupulously considerate behavior toward her lover's correspondence with her rival moves that young lady to renounce him.

Both heroines are preoccupied with the analysis of their feelings and conduct. In keeping with Richardson's didactic intention, Pamela is conspicuously concerned to remain respectful toward the master bent on her undoing and the lady who abuses her; she even wonders if her efforts to avoid ruin are in keeping with a dutiful submission to providence. In similar fashion, Marivaux seems to invite admiration not only for his heroine's choices but for the acuteness and delicacy of sensibility she reveals in her very discernment of the problems of her situation. If anything, Marivaux is more preoccupied with the nuances of conflicting sentiments and obligations, and as psychologically or dramatically interesting objects in themselves, rather than for any illustrative or exemplary purpose. Thus the cause of Marianne's sighs and tears when subjected to M. de Climal's addresses is not anything so obvious as fear for her virtue, which she feels perfectly capable of protecting, but the conflict between her desire to put a favorable construction on the actions of her patron and her misgivings about his motives—and the embarrasments this ambiguous relationship creates for her simultaneous courtship by the gentleman's nephew. In subsequent episodes, she ponders comparable problems. Can she continue to accept her lover's addresses after learning he is the son of her benefactress without betraying that lady's kindness? Should she follow her own inclination against the counsel of so august a personage as the prime minister? What right has a feckless orphan to decline his generous offer of a secure marriage with a government official? Should she continue her engagement although it may prejudice her fiancé's career? How should she behave toward him, and his mother, and her rival, when she discovers that his affections have strayed?

Fielding could hardly have failed to remark resemblances noted by contemporaries with a less immediate and special interest in the two books. But there are also significant differences which would account for his divergent estimates of them, and it is even likely that Fielding's prior knowledge of Marianne's story, which Marivaux had carried as far as he ever did by 1737,[24] influenced his negative view of *Pamela*. The refine-

[24] The ninth, tenth, and eleventh parts, published in 1741, are completely given over to the story of a nun who befriends the heroine, a diversion which suggests that Marivaux had lost interest in his subject some years before he abandoned the novel. For a discussion of the relation of *Pamela* to *Marianne*, see McKillop, pp. 35–38.

ments of sentiment and internal debates over punctilios of *bienséance*, marks of subtlety and sophistication in Marivaux's low-key drama of sensibility, might well have appeared excessively nice and even perverse in the starker melodramatic context of Pamela's more desperate situation. To Fielding, Pamela's occasional flashes of witty spirit and sauciness in response to her master's indecencies must have seemed much more natural than her apologies for them or her pious concern for his welfare virtually *in medium raptum.* The unfailing propriety of the exemplary maiden's sentiments would appear all the more incredible—and to a writer of Fielding's satiric outlook, suggestive of hypocrisy—when placed next to the more "truthful" portrait of her older French cousin, drawn to serve no didactic function. For Marianne's heroism is mingled with a measure of selfishness, calculation, and acknowledged vanity. Although she suspects her patron's carnal motive almost at their first meeting, she avoids recognizing this suspicion as long as she can, partly out of timidity, respect, or generosity, but at least as much to keep the presents resulting from his "kindness." She is disgusted by the suggestion, made by the earthy linen-draper to whom she is apprenticed, that she accept the gifts and only repulse the old man when he tries to claim his reward, but her own more proper plan is to tell him his love is hopeless, then to accept the presents if he persists in making them. The limits of her nobility are clearly defined. After Mme de Miran approves her son's courtship of the orphan shopgirl, Marianne does not remind her of her own previously stated intention of taking the veil; to do so would be an "excès de désintéressement de ma part n'aurait été ni naturel ni raisonnable."[25] As this admixture of *amour propre* makes the young Marianne more natural than the little girl who seems to protest too much that

[25] *La Vie de Marianne, ou les aventures de Madame la comtesse de* ***, ed. Frédéric Deloffre (Paris, 1963), p. 200 (hereafter cited as *Marianne*). Subsequent references are to this edition.

the summit of her desires is a return to honest indigence, the older Marianne's disarming acknowledgment of the foibles of her younger self is more engaging than the epistolary Pamela's self-conscious aspiration to perfection.

This characterization is related to a more general difference that would obviously make Marivaux's novel more congenial to Fielding and bring it, at least from one aspect, within the definition of his "kind of writing." In keeping with its exemplary intention, *Pamela*, especially part 1, is a largely humorless work. The heroine's occasional sallies of wit and sprightliness are never allowed to impinge upon the fabric of her melodrama; if her solemn obsession with her precious "papers" and the related absurdities deriving from Richardson's epistolary method provoked Fielding's laughter, that effect was not intended. For Marivaux, on the other hand, Marianne's "pathétique" also has its comic perspective. She is upset when de Climal shatters the sweet confusion of her first interview with Valville and she learns the two men are related; painful in itself, the uncle's proposal to keep her is turned into a calamity when the nephew discovers them and departs in a rage. Yet from the reader's perspective the two men's successive discoveries of each other in identical suppliant postures also plainly constitute a little ironic comedy, in which amusement at the old hypocrite's uneasiness in the first instance is capped by delight at his complete discomposure when the roles are reversed. Similarly, the melodramatic collapse of her patroness' attempt to pass her off as a provincial lady and her consequent abduction are triggered by the primarily comic embarrassment of her unexpected encounter with the gossipy linendraper in the halls of the great. At other times the laughter is more directly at Marianne's expense, since even her agonizing is seen in a humorous light. The dilemma created by Valville's wish to see her home after their first accidental meeting—is it worse to have him discover that she lives in unfashionable surroundings or to let him think she is the kind of girl who travels through Paris without a companion?—may be a delicate problem for a sensitive maiden in the throes of first love, but the extent of its development makes it ludicrous. The internal monologue in which Marianne fashions out her distresses a pretext to wear her tainted presents one last time is a trenchant depiction of the power of vanity: grieving over the necessity of returning her fine clothes, she puts aside this petty concern to face the more serious aspect of her situation; she will expose M. de Climal to the monk who placed her in his care and seek his assistance; but how should she make the most favorable impression and show the proper respect?—and so the elegant dress is unpacked.

On this, as on other occasions, Marianne's own narrative invites a smiling view of her emotions: "ce coeur si fier s'amollit, mes yeux se mouillèrent, je ne sais comment, et je fis un grand soupir, ou pour moi, ou pour Valville, ou pour la belle robe."[26] The continuation of this passage exemplifies the kind of self-analysis that distinguishes Marianne from Pamela:

> Ce qui est de certain, c'est que je décrochai l'ancienne, et qu'en soupirant encore, je me laissai tristement aller sur un siège, pour y dire: Que je suis malheureuse! Eh! mon Dieu! pourquoi m'avez-vous ôté mon père et ma mère?
>
> Peut-être n'était-ce pas là ce que je voulais dire, et ne parlais-je de mes parents que pour rendre le sujet de mon affliction plus honnête; car quelquefois on est glorieux avec soi-même, on fait des lâchetés qu'on ne veut pas savoir, et qu'on se déguise sous d'autres noms; ainsi peut-être ne pleurais-je qu'à cause de mes hardes.

Whereas Pamela's up-to-the-minute narration strained credulity by requiring the persecuted innocent to act as simultaneous moral commentator, the distance of the Marianne recounting her history from the young girl undergoing it permitted Marivaux to indulge the worldly and derisive outlook of the one without nullifying the tender sufferings of the other. As an

[26] *Marianne*, p. 132.

event in the melodrama of sentiment, Valville's defection is a pathetic irony: having persevered so nobly for her love, and overcome all external obstacles to its fulfillment, the heroine now finds its object unworthy of her efforts. But a reader of Fielding's temper might have seen it as a refreshingly satiric turn of the conventional romantic story, and he would have been encouraged in this view by Marianne's own subsequent mocking comment on her imaginary correspondent-reader's chagrin. That lady's mistake is in regarding Valville as "un héros de roman" instead of "un Français qui a réellement existé de nos jours." "Homme, Français, et contemporain des amants de notre temps . . . Il n'avait pour être constant que ces trois petites difficultés à vaincre."[27]

Three years before he brought Marianne's fortunes to this ironic turn, Marivaux interrupted the serial publication of her story to develop a more straightforwardly comic "low" version of analogous materials in *Le Paysan parvenu.* Replacing the Virtuous Orphan (as she was called by a contemporary translator) with an innocent-seeming youth, he carried his more blatant social climb through several crises paralleling hers. Again the initial episode involves the attempted seduction of a servant girl by a gentleman, and again the title character resists corruption; but Jacob's girl friend is happy to cooperate with their master, and the hero's refusal to be bought or intimidated into donning prenuptial horns does not prevent his taking money from the girl whom he has no intention of marrying. The "romantic" phase of Jacob's story begins with a chance encounter similar to Marianne's accidental meeting with Valville, but here the damsel in distress, and the eventual object of the enterprising peasant's desires, is a fat and fiftyish old maid of comfortable means. As Mme de Miran's effort to introduce Marianne into society as a provincial lady is foiled by the unexpected presence of the garrulous Mme du Tour, so "M. de la

[27] *Marianne,* pp. 375–76.

Vallée's" wedding with his erstwhile employer "cousin" collapses when the officiating priest turns out to be the bride's former spiritual guide and the groom's old enemy. This comic catastrophe leads to another dramatic confrontation even more closely anticipatory of the pending portion of Marianne's story, again with a sardonic twist. Arraigned before a high official by his fiancée's sister (as Marianne is by Mme de Miran's family), the hero charms the assembled company into approving his suit; but among the most impressed is another less ingenuous *dévote*, and, with his declamation of the innocent sincerity of his love still echoing, Jacob is drawn into a flirtation with this supposedly austere friend of his bride-to-be. After this, the story departs from Marianne's and its direction becomes increasingly uncertain, as the married Jacob pursues opportunities offered by this lady and another more frankly predatory matron, the one culminating in a comically frustrated rendezvous, the other leading to Versailles, where he gallantly declines a sinecure rather than impoverish another, more conventionally romantic lady.

Although Jacob's initial servant role and a brief scene between him and his mistress in the beginning of the novel have led some critics to see him as the prototype of Fielding's footman, this is hardly the story of "how an obscure country boy made his way in Paris against poverty and the temptations of women."[28] The fortunate peasant would seem to be less nearly related to Joseph Andrews than to Felix Krull: "On dira de lui: parvenu par les femmes."[29] If he lets the lady take the initiative in each of his entanglements, this is not the reticence of a bashful youth but the calculated prudence of a lowly young man dealing with older women of higher station and pretended severity. His shrewd opportunism appears in the speed with which

[28] Wilbur Cross, *The History of Henry Fielding* (New Haven, 1918), 1 : 315.

[29] Marcel Arland, Preface to Marivaux, *Romans* (Paris, 1949), p. xlv.

he transforms himself from a meek servant to the pressing lover once he has his aging mistress away from her sister and priest, in his obvious delight in the contemplation of her wealth, in the alacrity with which he subsequently redirects his affection when confronted with the prospect of a more elevated conquest. Yet he will not accept his first master's offer to make his fortune at the cost of his masculine honor, nor can he accept a lucrative post at the expense of a suffering lady and her ailing husband; and his very roguery is ambiguous. The substantive attraction of his fiancée may be her *petit bourgeois* status and handsome income, but the good-natured peasant is so delighted with his prospect and so grateful for her kindness that he convinces himself of his affection for her. When he intimates to Mme Ferval that he does not love his wife-to-be, he does so because this is what the lady wants to hear. Is this opportunism—or a desire to please, an excess of good nature where women are concerned, a compulsion to play the lover on cue? Of course Jacob's own explanations of his conduct are not to be trusted, and, as in Marianne's vain rationalizations, much amusement arises from the discrepancy between what he says and what the reader sees. Although he begins his story by frankly acknowledging his low birth, contrasting his candor ("je ne l'ai jamais dissimulée à qui me l'a demandée"[30]) with the affectation of his nephews, he euphemizes his origins to Mme Habert and passes himself off as a *petit monsieur* with a nobleman he meets later. Yet, however disingenuous or lacking in self-knowledge he may be, he is never malicious, and his conquests or seducers feel amply repaid by his tender attentions, so that neither wife nor mistress seems cheated. Though his actions are questionable and his explanations unpersuasive, Jacob is an engaging figure, and it seems likely that the impulsive benevolence he displays at Versailles would be enough to make Fielding regard him as truly "amiable."

[30] *Le Paysan Parvenu*, ed. Frédéric Deloffre (Paris, 1959), p. 5. Subsequent references are to this edition.

He would appear all the more sympathetic because he usually encounters hypocrisy or ill nature in his superiors, in relation to which his spirited disposition and flexible sentiments may be the necessary weapons of a poor lad making his way. His low origin, the subject of his opening lengthy ruminations and seldom out of his consciousness as he moves upward, is crucial in each of his disasters and triumphs. The wedding collapses because of the revelation of his status, as does his rendezvous with Mme Ferval. Conversely, Jacob's vivacious denunciation of the artificiality of social degrees carries the day at his arraignment. Here, as in the climax of the first episode, where the corrupt master is astonished by the idea of honor in a servant, and again in Jacob's denunciation of the false-faced director of conscience, Marivaux aligns the reader's sympathies with the peasant of qualities against the snobbish, hypocritical, and ill-natured quality. The clearest expression of this intention occurs at the audience at Versailles, where an arrogant politician and his supercilious parasites are flabbergasted by Jacob's refusal to profit from another's misfortune, and his conduct is applauded by the rough but unaffectedly good-natured M. Bono (a name as well as a character Fielding might have relished).

The general pattern of Marivaux's comedy in both *Le Paysan parvenu* and *La Vie de Marianne* is closer to that of Lesage than to Cervantes or Scarron, but it also differs from the mode of *Gil Blas* in ways which prefigure more particularly the direction of Fielding's comedy in *Joseph Andrews.* The world in which Marianne and Jacob move is not such a maze of fraud and eccentricity as that of *Gil Blas,* but the subtler and more prevailingly ill-natured kind of pretense they encounter is more nearly akin to Fielding's antipathetic concept of affectation than the dogmatic folly of Dr. Sangrado or the self-deceiving vanity of the archbishop, which for all their harm to others lack the hard edge of malice. Like Fielding, Marivaux focuses on hypocrisy more than vanity and, in contrast to Lesage's wider satiric range, concentrates on religious and sexual hypocrisy, central targets of Fielding's comic attack virtually untouched in the other continental comic romances. In an episode that might be transposed to Fielding's novel without much modification, the true benevolence of Mme de Miran's warm-hearted response to the tears of the unknown girl is set off against the fulsome compassion of a prioress which evaporates when she learns her suppliant has neither means nor family. The pious posture of the lecherous de Climal, who would persuade Marianne that her submission to his advances is the will of divine providence, has its counterparts in the corrupt master who pretends a solicitous concern for his young servants' welfare as cover for his own adultery, and in the succession of *dévotes* whose holy facades conceal amorous appetites. In the household of Jacob's bride-to-be, where even the cook mixes pious expostulations with an inclination toward her fellow servant, the affected austerity of the gourmandizing and scandalmongering sisters is matched by the hypocrisy of their priest, whose ostensible concern for their souls masks a perverse pleasure in ruling them, and perhaps something more regarding the younger.

Like Gil Blas, Marivaux's protagonists are not themselves free from vanity and pretense, but the nobility of the one, the good nature of the other, and the moral sensibility (admittedly sometimes clouded) of each distinguish them from most of the persons they encounter. Despite their foibles, Marianne and Jacob are both more positively endearing figures than the simply extroverted Gil Blas, whose psychology remains largely a blank. Through their digressive narrations, Marivaux depicts the complexity of his hero's and heroine's unexpressed thoughts and feelings, and even their acknowledgment of their foibles is engaging. Another source of more active sympathy is the greater emphasis Marivaux gives to the seriocomic suffering of his protagonists. The effects of Gil Blas's victimizations or disappointments are sharply attenuated by his clownlike resilience. Although his adventures, particularly in the middle of the novel, imply that "high" people are the moral inferiors of the "low" people they rule, Lesage does not rouse much concern for his hero as the innocent underdog in a world of injustice.[31] This central premise of Fielding's conception is a more explicit and significant element of the internal rhetoric of Marivaux's novels.

The heightened awareness of the dimension of moral sympathy and antipathy is reflected in Marivaux's development of a gratifying counterweight to the pains and embarrassments of his young quasi-innocents. From Valville's discovery of his uncle on his knees before the little shopgirl to his own confusion when Marianne discovers his inconstancy, from the frustration of Jacob's master to the embarrassment of Mme Ferval at the interrupted tryst, numerous incidents in the two novels conclude with the discomfiture of the hypocrite. In pointed contrast to Gil Blas's disappointing discoveries, Jacob not only sees through the pretense of his beguiling betters but has the satisfaction of telling them off. The climax of the first phase of his story is the astonished master's frustration by the peasant's blunt refusal to play his game; and as he departs under the ample wing of Mlle Habert he leaves her spiritual director in confusion by denouncing his hypocritical civility and exposing his real motives. In this punitive comedy of hypocrisy's exposure, embarrassment, and frustration—a kind of effect not to be found in Lesage, Cervantes, or Scarron—as in the generally greater emphasis on moral deserts of which it is part, Marivaux's novels are a clearer prototype of the peculiar synthesis of sym-

[31] In the Preface to *Roderick Random*, Smollett objected that Gil Blas's insouciance "prevents that generous indignation which ought to animate the reader against the sordid and vicious disposition of the world."

pathetic and antipathetic comedy which Fielding achieved in *Joseph Andrews.*

Among the variety of materials and methods presented by the five continental comic romances Fielding knew best and esteemed most, he could observe two broad similarities. They all mingled their comic actions with somewhat more serious, usually tragicomic, stories of lovers' intrigues and trials in loosely structured narratives that were either redundant or uncompleted. From the analytic perspective of a seasoned professional writer approaching a new mode of composition, the four novelists could be seen to confront (with varying degrees of awareness, concern, and success) common artistic problems deriving from these common characteristics, problems initially adumbrated by Cervantes' procedures in the two generally similar but contrasting parts of *Don Quixote.* In introducing extensive romantic material in part 1, he acknowledged the difficulty of sustaining a lengthy narrative out of a single comic subject, however rich; if in part 2 he went on to demonstrate that he could do just that while showing the advantages of long-range planning over improvisation, the narrative still conspicuously lacked the kind of specified expectation resolved in a climactic terminal effect which seems to have been contemplated by Scarron in his incorporation of episodic comedy within an overall envelope derived from the pattern of heroic romance. *Le Roman comique* in turn showed only the evidences of such a plan and not its realization, and if Lesage was aware of Cervantes and Scarron, he heeded none of their lessons, relapsing into mechanical interpolation and, apart from the well-conceived ironic sequence in the middle of the novel, exhibiting general indifference to the problems of forming and shaping the narrative.

In this context, Marivaux's novels presented a strikingly different combination of the comic and romantic ingredients, not as distinct narrative elements, but two aspects of the same system of actions. The touchingly perplexed orphan and the candidly ingratiating peasant were not merely made to interact with comic figures, as were Cardenio and Dorothea, nor given occasional humorous strokes, like Destin and Étoile, but were at once the objects of compassion and amusement, the major turns of their fortunes comic as well as poignant or gratifying. If the actions producing these mixed responses were at times ambiguous, as if in his pursuit of ethical refinements the author himself were not sure what attitude he would have his reader take, they also reflected the "realistic" definition of his subject expressed in Marianne's comment on her wayward lover: "un spectacle de ce coeur naturel, que je vous rends tel qu'il a été, c'est-à-dire avec ce qu'il a eu de bon et de mauvais."[32] In this imperfect humanity, Fielding might have seen the image of his own young footman and foundling, and in Marivaux's novels seriocomic systems of action closer than any other precedent fiction to his characteristic mixed or intermediate mode. But while Marivaux also showed him some effective short-run comic and dramatic structures, neither of his uncompleted narratives betrayed any signs of an overall plan comparable to Scarron's.[33]

Contemplating this composite picture, Fielding might understandably have concluded that a conspicuous lack of form or structure was an essential characteristic of the "kind of writing" he was undertaking. Unlike any of his predecessors, however, he was to publish his comic romance complete in a single installment. And even as he was to combine their several modes of comedy into one distinctively his own, so, in retaining the conventional tandem of comic and romantic ingredients (ac-

[32] *Marianne*, p. 376.

[33] After Jacob's rendezvous with Mme de Ferval, the direction of Marivaux's last installment of *Le Paysan parvenu* (part 5, 1736) is increasingly uncertain, terminating in the promise of a survey of the contemporary theater. See also n. 24 above.

knowledged in the coupling of the adventures of Joseph Andrews with those of "his Friend Mr. Abraham Adams" on the title page), he was to weave these strands into a new kind of narrative unity.

The Reasoning Behind the Form of *Joseph Andrews*

Most readers of *Joseph Andrews* have found the novel's distinctive substance in the adventures of Parson Adams. Although he yielded primacy of place on the title page to Joseph's story as the object of long-range expectation and the focus of the novel's resolution, from Fielding's Preface, which contains no reference to the young footman or his fortunes, one might infer that the running encounter between his "Character of perfect Simplicity" and a "copious Field" of the vain and hypocritical lay closer to his central preoccupations in conceiving the book. Obviously it was through this strain that it derived most significantly from the work of which it proclaimed itself an imitation. Whatever the actual process by which Fielding arrived at his eventual conception of the novel's distinctive form, the hypothesis that the work as it stands represents his solution to problems posed by his adaptation of Cervantes' general formula is at least as plausible as the hard-dying notion that he set out to write a second *Shamela* and wandered astray. As good a place as any, then, to begin reconstructing the thinking behind the finished structure is with the definition of the nature of that imitation and the problems it entailed, commencing with "the most glaring [character] in the whole."

The essential formula Fielding perceived at the heart of Cervantes' novel was a character set off from the other inhabitants of his fictional world by a persistent tendency to misconstrue that world in a certain way, yet exhibiting, for all his error and oddity, moral and intellectual qualities that earn the reader's affection and admiration. The most obvious modification he made in devising his own particular version of this formula was to narrow the scope of his comic hero's misapprehension. Whereas Quixote's obsession works its transformations upon all aspects of reality, Parson Adams' mistakes are confined to the characters of men.[1] Fielding may have seen the path of his deviation marked out by Cervantes himself in the "most fortunate and noble Beginning" of Quixote's "Feats of Arms." The adventure of the whipped serving lad's rescue involves no wild metamorphosis of the situation. The joke turns upon Quixote's error in assuming that the peasant will honor his pledge to pay the lad and refrain from punishing him; while the knight rides off exultant at having "redressed the greatest Wrong and Grievance that ever Injustice could design or Cruelty commit," the reader remains to see the farmer take out his resentment on the boy's hide. Cervantes' primary point, underlined in the episode's long-delayed sequel, is that by intervening on the boy's behalf, the great avenger has only made him suffer more. For Fielding, the greater interest of the episode may have been in the knight's idealistic expectations concerning the master's adherence to his oath, an error acknowledged by Quixote himself in the sequel: "I might, by Experience, have remembered, that the Word of a Peasant is regulated, not by Honour, but Profit."[2] Coming at the very outset of Quixote's

[1] Exceptions to this general assertion are discussed below, pp. 105 and 147–49.

[2] *Don Quixote,* p. 262.

adventures, this atypical mistake might well have impressed Fielding. He also had before him the model of Gil Blas's repeated disillusionments to suggest the general direction of the adventures of his parson-errant. But though Adams was to undergo even more disappointing discoveries than Lesage's mistreated hero, his habitual assumption that the men he meets are as good as they profess was to be incorrigible by experience.

Obviously influenced by Fielding's specific ethical preoccupations, this concentration of Adams' Quixotism in the realm of character may also have been affected by his concern to make his adventures more "natural" than those of his master. He later praised Mrs. Lennox for similarly confining her heroine's folly to "mistakes [of] one Man for another," avoiding "the Absurdity of imagining Windmills and Wine-Bags to be human Creatures, or Flocks of Sheep to be Armies."[3] The *donnée* of these "much less extravagant and incredible" adventures also seemed to him more probable than that of the original: that "the Head of a very sensible Person is entirely subverted by reading Romances" was a "Concession . . . more easy to be granted in the Case of a young Lady than of an old Gentleman."[4] In his own revision of the Cervantean formula, he did away altogether with the artificial subversion of mind; the premise that a country parson immersed in ancient learning and Christian teaching might be "as entirely ignorant of the ways of this World as an Infant" required no comparable special "concession." In keeping with his praise of the "perfect Judgment and Art" with which the "Subversion of the Brain in Arabella is accounted for by her peculiar Circumstances, and Education," he provided his own comic hero a background against which his failure to "apprehend any such Passions as Malice and Envy to exist in Mankind" was, as he sardonically

[3] *CGJ* 1 : 282. Arabella's mistakes are still somewhat closer to Quixote's than Adams', for they concern the external "Rank and Conditions" of men, rather than their moral character.

[4] *CGJ* 1 : 281.

understated it, "less remarkable" than from the worldly perspective of a Colley Cibber.

By giving his hero's mistakes a more "natural" genesis, Fielding deprived himself of the abnormal fixation which, once conceded, "accounted for" Quixote's persistence in fantasy in the face of a hundred potentially disabusing adventures, and for his retention of amiable and noble qualities in the midst of his folly. He thus faced, in peculiarly aggravated form, the problem of combining the "difficult ingredients" of the "amiable, ridiculous, and natural" to which he referred, in full awareness of his own recent experience of their difficulty, in the Preface to *David Simple*. He had to persuade his reader that a mature, genuinely learned, and sane man of "good Sense" and "good Parts" could credibly persist in mistaking the characters of his fellow men after repeated exposure to their meanness and fraud; and to preserve affection for him in the face of his persistence in error.

He was able to do this without violating his own canons of fictional "Truth" by conceiving his "Character of perfect Simplicity" in accordance with notions about the constitution of character which he stated in his essays and gave dramatic embodiment in his novels. Adams' exclamations on the wickedness of the times and his suspicion that "he was sojourning in a Country inhabited only by Jews and Turks" do not really affect his perception of his fellow creatures, because this peculiar defect of vision stems from a more fundamental element of his character than "good Sense" or "good Parts." This is made apparent in the "very curious Adventure" of the false promising gentleman (2:16) "in which Mr. *Adams* gave a much greater Instance of the honest Simplicity of his Heart than of his Experience in the Ways of this World." Inexperience might account for the parson's original delusion; but his sustained failure to suspect the fraud in the face of mounting evidence must be traced to another source, the same characteristic which prompts him, even after he is convinced that his deceiver "is indeed a wicked Man," to detect "in his Countenance sufficient Symptoms of that *bona Indoles*, that Sweetness of Disposition which furnishes out a good Christian."[5] The irony is not simply that Adams mistakenly projects onto the psuedobenevolent his own disposition: it is this very constitution which is the source of his habitual error. Like the pattern priest Fielding describes in the "Apology for the Clergy," he is "void of suspicion" and "not apt to censure the actions of men" because he exercises to an extraordinary degree the virtue which "comprehends almost the whole particular duty of a Christian":

> . . . "charity believeth all things, hopeth all things." It is inclined to maintain good and kind thoughts of men. It . . . always turns the perspective, with a friendly care to magnify all good actions, and lessen evil. It weighs all mankind in the scales of friendship, and sees them with the eyes of love.[6]

Though this "brotherly love and friendly disposition of mind" is "everywhere taught in Scripture," in Adams it is not the product of instruction. It is the manifestation of the most important of the "goods" with which he is endowed—"good Nature." In an essay "On the Knowledge of the Characters of Men," probably written about the same time as *Joseph Andrews* and closely related to the preoccupations of the novel, Fielding offered a definition of this quality which, if it was not drawn with Adams specifically in mind, certainly describes accurately the central principle of his character.

> Good-nature is that benevolent and amiable temper of mind, which disposes us to feel the misfortunes, and enjoy the happiness of others; and, consequently, pushes us on to promote the latter, and prevent the former; and that without any abstract contemplation on the beauty of virtue, and without the allurements or terrors of religion.[7]

[5] *Joseph Andrews*, p. 180.
[6] *Works* 15 : 272.
[7] *Works* 14 : 285.

The incorruptible, and therefore incorrigible, "honest Simplicity" of Adams' heart is clearly of this order: this is the force behind his impulsive intercession at the sound of a woman's cries, his groans at the misfortunes of Leonora and the follies of the young Wilson, and his dance of joy at the reunion of Joseph and Fanny. In all these responses, as in his benevolent misappraisals of his fellowmen, his behavior is the unmediated product of the deepest impulse of his *nature*, a term through which Fielding expressed his concept of the primordial and essentially unchangeable individuating principle of character —that "unacquired, original distinction, in the nature or soul of one man, from that of another" which he infers from the "very early and strong inclination to good or evil, which distinguishes different dispositions in children, in their first infancy."[8]

Although the essential determinant of Adams' comic behavior is thus radical to his character, Fielding adapted another element of Cervantes' conception by relating the peculiarity of his protagonist's vision to his reading, which, if it is not the ultimate source of his characteristic error, serves to reinforce it. Adams' amazement at "the Wickedness of this World" stems not only from his own open nature ("As he had never any Intention to deceive, so he never suspected such a Design in others") but from his related tendency to assume that the noble sentiments of the ancient poets and philosophers and the virtuous conduct enjoined by the scriptures delineate human nature as it is, rather than as it might be or ought to be. Hence, even as he persists in misreading men's characters, he remains convinced of his superior knowledge of humanity, for "Knowledge of Men is only to be learnt from Books, *Plato* and *Seneca* for that."

This erroneous equation of learning with practical wisdom is paralleled by a corresponding overestimation of all that is to be drawn from books—precept, doctrine, rational argument—as

[8] *Works* 14 : 281–82.

influences upon the direction of behavior and the formation of character. (In this respect Adams is the unlikely vehicle for Fielding's derision of the views expounded and dramatized in *Pamela.*) Emblematically, the anecdote the parson cites in his argument with the innkeeper (2 : 17) as an example of the invaluable knowledge to be gained from books defines the character of Socrates as one in which a "Disposition . . . naturally . . . inclined to Vice" was "corrected . . . by Philosophy." At the heated close of this debate, unaware how his very contention contradicts what he contends, he declares the learning of the clergy "more necessary than Life it self," for it "clothes you with Piety, Meekness, Humility, Charity, Patience, and all the other Christian Virtues."[9] Thus Adams' "Blind side" extends from his ignorance of the failings of others, through his overestimation of the pedagogue as "the greatest Character in the World," to an incomprehension of the nature of his own spontaneous goodness, an irony Fielding is at pains to bring out in the immediately succeeding portion of the novel and again, most tellingly, near its close.

The particular doctrines of rational stoicism, submission to providence, and reliance on grace that Adams has drawn from his reading of classical philosophy and Christian scripture are contravened by his own impulsive humanity. But when Fielding, in the memorable episode of his son's supposed drowning, dramatically contrasts the parson's practice with his preaching, he is not exposing him as one "who *is* the very Reverse of what he would *seem* to be." His lack of self-knowledge is the antithesis of conscious dissimulation. If he is vain enough to envisage the publication of his sermons and to aspire to the role of Socrates; if, believing the schoolmaster "the greatest Character in the World," he regards himself as "the greatest of all School-Masters"; if he prides himself on his learned insight into the

[9] *Joseph Andrews,* p. 183.

characters of men, the area of his most essential blindness—he cannot be said to affect a false character in order to purchase applause. Because of his essential innocence and lack of selfish egoism, even these secondary and less appealing aspects of his character cannot be traced to Fielding's "only Source of the true Ridiculous."

Fielding might justly claim that this "Character of perfect Simplicity" was "not to be found in any Book now extant." By taking as his starting point the fundamental paradox he remarked in the Quixote character—the wondrous mingling of sagacity and madness repeatedly emphasized in Cervantes' narrative—he set his comic hero above the dreary run of one-trait imitation Quixotes, from Sorel's extravagant shepherd to Smollett's Launcelot Greaves. By compounding and intensifying his own version of this central irony, he created a figure whose internal complexity and life rival the richness of their great original. In place of Cervantes' single, endlessly fruitful source of comic error and mischance, he conceived a set of naturally related but amusingly inconsistent attributes out of which he was able to multiply comic ironies within a work of much briefer scope.[10] At the same time, he supplanted the often rather arbitrary concatenation of the ludicrous and noble in Quixote with a fusion of the amiable and ridiculous at the very heart of his protagonist. Fielding's remarks in the *Covent Garden Journal* and his own theatrical adaptation suggest that he saw Quixote, like Mrs. Lennox's Arabella, as a mixture of distinct elements deriving from independent sources—the good qualities of the sane Senor Quesada persisting amidst the follies

[10] The character of Adams is rounded out by a set of secondary and less idiosyncratic foibles. Of these, the belief in the science of physiognomy which he articulates in his argument with the ex-sailor host (2 : 17) and the pedantic impulse to correct minor errors are most directly related to his central peculiarities, but his absentmindedness and perpetual hurry, the motley costume which deteriorates as the journey progresses, and even his belief in ghosts are consonant with the primary conception of his character.

generated by his delusion. There are numerous incidents in Cervantes' novel that convey this impression: in the episode of the puppet show (pt. 2, chap. 26), for example, the quiet gentleman who comments critically on the narrator's management of his tale seems to have no necessary connection with the furious madman who suddenly begins hacking up the puppets whom he takes for real Saracens. If at other times Fielding saw the knight's obsession engendering flights of brilliance and nobility beyond the potential of the uncrazed hidalgo, there is no evidence that he ever found the knight's delusion itself amiable or appealing. In his own conception he heightened the paradox by making the very root of Adams' comic error the principal source of his amiability. Though his "good Parts," like Quixote's, merit respect and admiration, his good nature makes the strongest appeal to the reader's affections. Even as Fielding found innocence and "the greatest benevolence" among Quixote's "much more endearing" traits, so he would have his readers cherish Adams' good heart, and that simplicity which provokes their laughter.

This convergence of "difficult ingredients" was facilitated by an accompanying alteration of the context in which he placed his comic hero. Although Don Quixote describes his as a "degenerate Age, Fraud and a Legion of Ills infecting the World," except for such isolated vignettes as the galley-bound criminals this image is not reflected in the persons and situations he encounters. Were it not for his obsession, his life would be quiet and uneventful. If Adams traversed a prevailingly innocuous world like that which Quixote's imagination transforms into the stuff of "adventures," his perfect simplicity would not lead him into surprises and embarrassments. Demonstrating that "Life every where furnishes an accurate Observer with the Ridiculous," Fielding created a fictional universe answerable to his description of contemporary society as "a vast masquerade, where the greatest part appear disguised under false vizors and habits; a very few only showing their own faces, who become, by so doing, the astonishment and ridicule of all the rest."[11] Adapting Lesage's conception of a protagonist whose adventures serve to expose a range of foibles, he went beyond Lesage and Marivaux in peopling his actions with a parade of lascivious prudes, savage Christians, cowardly heroes, and learned illiterates. Even Joseph and Fanny have their innocent vanities and pretenses;[12] but none of the good-natured characters is driven, as are most persons they encounter, by an overriding self-love that seeks to satisfy itself at the expense of others.

Indeed, ill nature or a lack of feeling for one's fellows seems as important a component in defining the antipathetic side of Fielding's comedy as affectation. The callous indifference of Gil Blas's lordly masters and Jacob's "betters" is extended to the world in general. When Joseph is found wounded by the roadside, he is given aid only after debate on the propriety of such action, and then only for reasons of prudence. Adams, asking directions, is bid "*follow his Nose and be d——n'd.*" When Joseph strikes Didapper for pawing Fanny, Squire Booby reprimands him for impropriety; when Adams rescues her from a ravisher, the jealous Slipslop tells him such actions do not become a clergyman. Whenever a company gathers—at the sign of the Dragon, at the justice's, or at the squire's—there is someone ready to pounce upon and ridicule those in distress, or to show up the simple and the innocent. Among the knowledgeable citizens of this world, the fashion is to deny or sneer at

11 "On the Knowledge of the Characters of Men," *Works* 14 : 283.

12 In the aftermath of his second interview with Lady Booby, Joseph retires to his garret to lament "the numberless Calamities which attended Beauty, and the Misfortune it was to be handsomer than one's Neighbours" (p. 46). Barely out of the hands of her first would-be ravisher, Fanny responds to Adams' disclosure that Joseph is homeward bound thus: "La! Mr. *Adams* . . . what is Mr. *Joseph* to me? I am sure I never had any thing to say to him, but as one Fellow-Servant might to another" (p. 144). See also p. 124 below.

tender feelings, and the highest virtue is a calculating prudence which inclines to suspicion. In *Don Quixote*, the judge, recognizing the captive as his long-lost brother, "flew into his Arms with such Affection, and such abundance of Tears, that all the Spectators sympathiz'd in his Passions."[13] In *Joseph Andrews*, the long separated friends, Paul and Leonard, embrace "with a Passion which made many of the Spectators laugh, and gave to some few a much higher and more agreeable Sensation."[14]

Consequently, Adams' frequent involvement in battles or near-battles is another likeness with a difference. Though quick to clench a fist or brandish a crabstick, he never converts a peaceful situation into an arena out of manic belligerency. He is drawn into fights to protect himself and other bedeviled innocents. Only in the whipping of the servant lad does Quixote encounter a real wrong to be righted by the might of his arm (an exception underscored by the knight's pursuit of the chimerical rescue of the "Princess Micomicona" instead of avenging Andrew or even being acquainted with the real grievance of the betrayed maiden who plays the princess). Fielding's world abounds in particular wrongs and general injustice. In contrast to the isolated betrayal of Dorothea, Fanny Goodwill must constantly fear for her virtue; the object of four attempted rapes, she arouses even the money-obsessed Peter Pounce and the effeminate Didapper. Whereas all the company at the inn join in persuading Ferdinand to do right by the injured girl, the ladies and gentleman of Booby Hall try to persuade Joseph to abandon his beloved for a more "suitable" match. In this milieu, law serves the whims of the powerful, and justice obtains by accident; modesty is usually its own and only reward; the postilion who gives the victimized Joseph his coat is reproved for swearing and transported for stealing chickens;

[13] *Don Quixote*, p. 368.
[14] *Joseph Andrews*, p. 316.

and the "worthiest, best-natured creature" wears a ragged cassock, while the self-serving Barnabas and the hypocritical Trulliber thrive.

Thus it was not only the Quixote character that underwent a "sea change," as Cross put it, in Fielding's conception. Retaining the comic hero's essential goodness while altering the nature and source of his mistakes, combining them with the exposure of affectation found in Lesage and Marivaux, and making the persecution of innocent "low people" by inhumane "high people" (a theme diversely developed by Lesage, Marivaux, and Richardson) a central circumstance of his fictional universe—Fielding converted Cervantes' benign and relatively self-contained comedy into a more abrasively ironic mode, redirecting its satiric impact from the isolated target of the accursed romances to the more immediate foibles of his own society and mankind at large. If Adams, like Quixote, is a freak in the world he traverses, he is so not because of any bizarre aberration but because of his abnormal goodness, his unselfish, impulsive feeling for others. If, like Quixote, he mistakenly takes his books as reliable guides to the reality he encounters, his reading is not extravagant fantasy but the wisdom of antiquity and the teachings of Christianity. However nobly transfigured he may appear to some modern readers, Quixote acts on premises which the normative figures of the novel recognize as plainly absurd.[15] But many of Adams' difficulties result from his living or expecting others to live according to precepts which his fellow creatures (and Fielding's contemporary readers) profess to believe. Adams has not had his mind subverted by books; the denizens of his world have been subverted from the noble humanity whose image he retains.

As a consequence of the more clearly drawn moral disparity between the hero and most of the persons he encounters, the

[15] See Oscar Mandel, "The Function of the Norm in *Don Quixote*," *Modern Philology* 55 (1958): 154–63.

amusement of Fielding's comedy is qualified by other feelings even more than Marivaux's. Each time Adams is duped or guyed there is an increment of comic indignation, and there is a complementary satisfaction when the antipathetic figures are exposed and discomfited. In the long run, Fielding could count on the reader's accumulated sense of the world's injustice to generate a desire to see affectation and vice put down and virtue and innocence rewarded. Yet he would have the reader realize that, given the state of the world, Adams' innocent good nature, unqualified by a measure of prudence, is a weakness. He wrote his essay on "Knowledge of the Characters of Men" about the same time as the novel explicitly to "arm . . . against imposition" the "innocent and undesigning" whose "open disposition, which is the surest indication of an honest and upright heart . . . principally disqualifies" them to detect falsehood in others.[16] In the *Champion* he had remarked that "men often become ridiculous or odious by overacting even a laudable part: for Virtue itself, by growing too exuberant . . . changes its very nature, and becomes a most pernicious weed of a most beautiful flower"; and in another essay roughly contemporaneous with the novel he saw "good-nature itself, the very habit of mind most essential to furnish us with true good-breeding," as a potential source of error and opprobrium.[17] By manipulating the reader's sympathies and reservations concerning the comic hero in the service of his "one great end," Fielding made the sequential articulation of this complex view a crucial mechanism of the novel's structure.

The obvious structural weakness of the kind of episodic comedy Fielding envisaged in the adventures of Abraham Adams was its lack of a narrative goal. The reader would be carried

16 *Works* 14 : 281, 283.

17 "An Essay on Conversation," published in the 1743 *Miscellanies*, *Works* 14 : 250. The *Champion* passage is quoted from *Works* 15 : 244.

from one encounter between the character of perfect simplicity and the world of affectation to the next with no more specified expectation than further adventures of the same general kind. In Fielding's conception, as in Cervantes', the radical peculiarity of the protagonist's vision precluded a "learning" plot; the reader must soon sense that it is vain to wonder when the hero will discover his error or what it will take to open his eyes. Even in part 2, Cervantes had not made the uncoiling of his comic mainspring an object of long-range suspense, erecting instead the framework of expectation concerning Saragossa and the return of Samson Carrasco. Given the particular etiology of Adams' error, Fielding could not even resolve his narrative with a dramatic change of outlook comparable to Quixote's terminal cure without arbitrarily destroying the "natural" character he had so carefully constructed. Nor would Adams' loss of innocence be as satisfying as Quixote's return to pious sanity.

The most common way of dealing with this generic problem of episodic fixed-character comedy was to import an external source of specified suspense and dramatic resolution from the conventional staple of serious romance, the trials and triumphs of one or more pairs of lovers. Cervantes pursued this strategy for a time in part 1, when he intertwined the adventures of the knight and his friends with the stories of Cardenio and Dorothea. In generally similar fashion, Lesage made the happy ending of the interpolated history of Don Alphonse and the fair Seraphine, with the attendant elevation of Gil Blas into a secure stewardship, serve as conclusion to the original (1715) version of his novel. But it was Scarron, whose comedy was dispersed among a "demi-douzaine de héros," who offered Fielding the most cogent demonstration of this narrative strategy, carrying it to its logical commencement and incorporating the whole novel within the framework of mystery and suspense centering on Destin and Étoile.

The advantages of embedding the adventures of his parson-errant within a similar structure of expectation focused on an innocent and amiable youth and maiden were not likely to have escaped Fielding, who had regularly employed the fortunes of lovers in a similar fashion in his theatrical comedies—particularly since it avoided another difficulty peculiar to his revision of the Quixote formula. Whereas there could be no more fitting opening for *Don Quixote* than the old gentleman's sallying forth in obsessive quest of adventures, for Fielding to show his selfless priest setting out for London to sell his sermons, or on any comparable mission outside the parish to whose service he is devoted, would be to launch his story on a slightly false note. Beginning with Joseph's story permitted him to account for Adams' presence on the road "naturally"—as the result of a characteristic naïvely vain expectation—without focusing attention on the atypically worldly enterprise itself.

Some such reasoning might have produced a narrative resembling *Joseph Andrews*, except for the peculiarities of construction that support the tradition of its improvisatory development: the love between Joseph and Fanny is not disclosed until the eleventh chapter, and in the interim the eventual object of romantic expectation is cast in a mock-Pamelian role. If Fielding did not simply start to write a parody and then change his mind, it would seem that he was willing to sacrifice the consistency of the whole for the sake of the parodic introduction, which would be radically weakened if the figure of male chastity were presented as a faithful lover. But if we concede to Fielding the same awareness of what he was about in constructing his own narrative that he later attributed to Richardson's composition of *Clarissa*, the abortive seduction of Pamela's brother can be seen as an ingenious improvement upon either plunging Adams directly into adventures in the manner of Cervantes or establishing Joseph as a conventional romantic hero in the fashion of Scarron. Placing his titular hero in a broadly humorous situation would establish unmistakably that his was to be a comically qualified version of the standard romance plot. At the same time this preliminary bout between innocence and hypocrisy would prefigure the central comic interaction between the amiable parson and his antipathetic antagonists. By defaulting, after only two interviews between mistress and servant, on his initially promised story of how "the excellent Pattern of his Sister's Virtues" enabled Joseph to "preserve his Purity," Fielding could foster the desire to see this conflict resume, thereby establishing a stronger arc of *comic* expectation over the whole narrative than Cervantes had developed in part 2 from the scheme of Samson Carrasco. Such a beginning would also function, like the anticipatory opening chapters of part 2, to make the very commencement of the central line of comic adventures a satisfying event. Having named Adams as coprotagonist on the title page, and given teasing glimpses of his character in the Preface and third chapter, he would make the reader wait a dozen chapters to see him in action, whetting his appetite the while by beginning and suspending another comedy of innocence and affectation and displaying the "Ways of this World" of which his innocent is so "entirely ignorant." Adding to these reasons the obvious dividends in taking off on the still-current talk of the town, Fielding might well have considered the appearance of makeshift construction a small enough price to pay—especially since the sudden redefinition of Joseph's situation would serve to establish emphatically that his was no "simple Book," "*easily to be seen through.*"[18]

For this opening strategy was part of an overall narrative scheme which, while it may have been influenced by Marivaux's fusion of comic and romantic and Scarron's manipulation of the reader's knowledge for effect, was essentially different from any structure he had seen in earlier comic romances. Starting with two lines of action more closely and "naturally" related

[18] *Joseph Andrews*, p. 48, from the passage introducing the disclosure of Fanny's existence.

than the converging histories of a troupe of comedians or a parcel of chance-met travelers, he combined them in a dynamic synthesis in which the reader's expectations concerning each would be significantly modified in the course of the narrative. Going beyond Scarron's interweaving of strands to generate suspense and produce surprising turns, he conceived a system of actions in which what happened in one line would affect the reader's opinions and desires concerning the other, and expectations aroused in one would be satisfied in the other. As the comic anticipations aroused by the promised parody of *Pamela* were to be transferred from Joseph's story to Adams' adventures, in the second half of the novel desires for moral satisfaction generated by the good parson's misadventures in a world of vanity and hypocrisy would be redirected to the renewal of Joseph's conflict with Lady Booby. The result would be an integrated "series of actions" in which the peculiarity of the beginning would heighten the effect of the central sequence of misadventures, and developments in that sequence would make the eventual resumption of the transformed original conflict a satisfying completion of an emotional process controlled by the comic intent Fielding defined as the determinant principle of his composition.

To achieve the benefits of his peculiar beginning, Fielding had only to suppress the knowledge of Joseph's love until the parodic episode was over; the reader would need no persuasion this early in the narrative to transfer his vague anticipation of certain kinds of comic incidents from a rather meagerly defined character whose adventures had scarcely begun to one whose description promised a broader range of actions. To reestablish Joseph's story as the central preoccupation of the narrative two hundred pages later, and have it accepted as a satisfying alternative to further adventures of one of the most extraordinary comic figures in literature, constituted the major problem of Fielding's dynamic system of actions. His strategy for solving it involved modifying the reader's view of both Adams and Joseph and gradually altering their relationship in the context of an increasingly hostile environment. Without blurring the fundamental distinction between the amiable protagonists and the many antipathetic ridiculous persons they meet, he would guide the reader to a progressively more sympathetic view of Joseph and a somewhat less appealing impression of his old teacher. In the middle of the novel he would shift the emphasis of Adams' comedy from his endearing natural simplicity to his vanity, from his misestimates of individual character to his mistaken beliefs and misapplied doctrines, at the same time altering the perspective in which his perfect simplicity was to be viewed. Instead of the affected and ill-natured, he would now be contrasted with Mr. Wilson and his undiscovered son, good-natured men of generous inclination and pure motive who have nonetheless learned through experience the world's true moral state and the circumspection required to cope with it. In the light of their practical wisdom, his innocence would seem more of a flaw, especially as the inimical world's threats to the "innocent and undesigning" were intensified.

The complementary process of Joseph's emergence from a parodic role into a modest (and admittedly unparticularized) heroism, prepared early in the novel, would reach its most important development in a sporadic series of exchanges with his old master. In this structurally functional adaptation of the running dialogue between Don Quixote and Sancho Panza, the contrast between Joseph's worldly prudence and Adams' impulsive ineptitude would be reinforced by the pupil's display of the sounder understanding of moral character and its formation and the teacher's pedantically doctrinaire responses to his young friend's sufferings as a lover.[19] In a coordinated development,

[19] Dick Taylor, Jr. "Joseph as Hero of *Joseph Andrews*," *Tulane Studies in English* 7 (1957) : 91–109, claims a "noticeable and sympathetic change and development of character into maturity" for Joseph, citing as "signs of his

the cumulative sense of the world's injustice would be sharpened by the depredations of the vicious "hunter of men," the impact of which would be heightened by juxtaposition with the immediately preceding idyll at Wilson's cottage—a more sharply drawn version of Cervantes' implicit contrast between Quixote's entertainment in turn by the soberly wise and modest "knight of the green coat" and the pranking duke and duchess.[20] As a result of these converging developments, the reader's desire for moral satisfaction would be wound to its highest pitch as Adams was being disqualified to serve as its principal agent or object, thereby facilitating the reemergence of Joseph's story as the vehicle through which virtue would be rewarded and villainy routed. At the same time, in an inverted adaptation of the emotional process which culminates in Quixote's death, the progressive emphasis on the less appealing aspects of Adams' complex character, together with his subjection, in the final stage of the journey, to treatment whose nastiness comes uncomfortably close to the boundaries of comedy, would make the reader relinquish more willingly the prospect of his further adventures. Thus when the curtain rose on the reassembled principals at Booby Hall, the renewal of the now redefined conflict between Lady Booby and Joseph would serve as a satisfactory dramatic and comic climax to the novel.

---

growth" some of the same evidence I have used in the subsequent analysis of the protagonists' realignment. In my view, neither Joseph nor Adams undergoes any substantive character change, nor does the young man pass through any process of learning or reformation like that of Tom Jones. Their roles and relationship are modified by manipulating the reader's knowledge of the two characters and their situations, through ordering and emphasizing the representation of their various traits, and by changing the circumstances in which they interact and the context in which they are viewed. Despite Taylor's ingenuity in educing Joseph's "personality," and his "stature and force" as "the Master of the Event," he remains almost a lay figure in comparison to Adams or Tom, and the reader is not intended to respond to his fortunes with the same degree of seriousness as to Tom's.

[20] Like Fielding's "roasters," Cervantes' pranksters are first encountered as a hunting party. For the relation of the "knight of the green coat" to Wilson, see below, pp. 196–99.

Such reasoning about the form of the novel, capitalizing on hints from Cervantes' improvement of his own first version, would not be out of character for the analytic admirer of *Clarissa* and the creator of *Tom Jones*. The best available evidence that he thought in this way six years earlier is to be found in the "judgment and art" with which he disposed the elements of *Joseph Andrews* in the service of this hypothesized conception. To observe this, and to define more precisely how he engaged his ethical concerns in the service of the novel's distinctive form, it will be advisable to examine more closely its unfolding structure.

Fielding's Realization of the Form

When Fielding paused at the beginning of the second book of *Joseph Andrews* to discuss the authorial mystery of "dividing our Works into Books and Chapters," he joked about an aspect of his craft which in practice he took quite seriously. In placing this discussion at the first "joint" of his narrative he was not only cautioning the "common Reader" to "consider of what he hath seen in the Parts he hath already past through" lest he miss "some curious Productions of Nature," but also in effect inviting the "slower and more accurate Reader" to observe the art with which his formal division of the novel articulates its unfolding internal structure. Shaping each book into a clearly formed narrative unit, Fielding used the major breaks in the narrative to define and accentuate the stages of its evolution. Book 1 begins by promising the mock-exemplary history of Pamela's brother and ends with the completion of a carefully constructed transition away from this parodic subject to the principal comic business of the novel; book 2 builds the comedy of the character of perfect simplicity in a world of affectation to a climax; when the narrative resumes in the second volume (bk. 3), it is already moving away from this center of interest, realigning the two protagonists and generating somewhat more serious responses in preparation for the resumption of the modified initial conflict which occupies the final book.

Book 1—Milady's boudoir and the Dragon Inn. Fielding's control and planning of the novel are manifest from the opening pages. His composition of the first ten chapters, constituting his supposed false start, clearly reflects his awareness of the need to subordinate the parody to his overall comic intention and to reconcile Joseph's mock-Pamelian part with his long-range plan. Between the ironic claim for the edifying value of Pamela's story as exemplified in the conduct of her brother (1:1) and the bedside interview which actually begins the promised comedy (1:5), he is careful to create favorable first impressions of both protagonists of his double-track narrative,[1] and to devote the first little quasidramatic scene of the novel (1:3) to establishing the mentor-pupil relationship whose transformation is to constitute a principal structural span of the narrative. The unequivocal tributes to Joseph's honesty and intrepidity embedded in the playful account of his early history (1:2), the "singular Devotion" and "Industry and Application" which bring him to Adams' attention, and the unaffectedly cheerful acceptance of his lot which wins the parson's warm praise (1:3)—all these signs encourage a more sympathetic view than his anticipated parodic role would warrant.[2] Simplicity,

[1] Joseph and Adams are introduced in successive parallel expository chapters: "Mr. *Joseph Andrews*, the Hero of our ensuing History, was esteemed to be the only Son . . ."; "Mr. *Abraham Adams* was an excellent Scholar." For a discussion of the narrative context of Adams' introduction, see below, pp. 254–55.

[2] After the comic hyperbole of "his Voice being so extremely musical, that it rather allured the Birds than terrified them . . . the Dogs preferring the Melody of his chiding to all the alluring Notes of the Huntsman," Adams' surprise at "such Instances of Industry and Application in a young Man" who

we are told, is Adams' "Characteristic"; but in successive scenes with Joseph and Slipslop Fielding emphasizes his goodness and sagacity, with no trace of comic qualification. Joseph's credulous response to the extravagances of Baker's *Chronicle* only serves to heighten our sense of the superiority of the apparently more knowledgeable parson over the naïve protege whom he catechizes.

Defining the country parish as the story's home base and bearing out the prefatory hints that Adams is to be as important a figure as Joseph, these preliminary scenes place the seduction episode in a context which implies that the parody is not to be the central preoccupation of the narrative. Nor is parody the formal principle of the episode itself. Ridicule of *Pamela* is incorporated within an autonomous comic episode bearing, like the thematically linked episodes for which he praised *David Simple*, "a manifest impression of the principal design"—an encounter between innocence and hypocrisy culminating in the frustration of the hypocrite. Though Joseph's priggishly self-conscious virtue and his epistolary protests of secrecy while blabbing arouse our laughter, he is never allowed to become the object of derision one would expect a parodic figure to be. Any such potential response is checked by the contrast with his clearly antipathetic female assailants; in the face of their hypocritical assaults, his Pamelian posture must seem a lesser foible, and our sympathies, however attenuated, are with him. Contrary to the impression created by traditional accounts of the novel, the prime target of the ridicule is not the footman but his mistress, a figure with no derisive implication for Richardson's novel.

When viewed in its entirety, the episode appears clearly designed with the comic sufferings of Lady Booby as its principal

---

"employed all his Hours of Leisure in reading good Books" can be read as parodic, but the account of his horse-racing prowess and integrity (an activity well chosen to dissociate him from the hothouse world of *Pamela*) is perfectly straight.

object: her effort to intimate her desires without compromising her hypocritical "Honour" is complicated by the internal conflict between her pride and her passion and embellished by her difficulties with the suddenly insubordinate Slipslop. The climactic scene between Joseph and his mistress (1:8) is the culmination of her mounting discomfiture. Here, amusement at the footman's mock-heroic posture is clearly subordinate to the comedy of the flabbergasted lady's frustration and anger. We are to laugh at Joseph when he caps the defense of his virtue by solemnly declaiming, "Madam . . . that Boy is the Brother of *Pamela* . . . ," but a moment earlier, when he fails to see why a great lady's "having no Virtue should be a Reason against my having any," he delights us not as a comic simpleton so much as a kind of deadpan wit, a plain speaker of disconcerting home truths. For Lady Booby the pangs of admitting her feelings to herself and disclosing them to her servants are rewarded by the ultimate humiliation: having exposed herself to the refusal of her footman, she must endure his moralizing as well.

By drawing the curtain on this little comedy with "the Heroine of our Tale" in an agony of unconquered passion, Fielding encourages the reader to anticipate its eventual resumption. Meanwhile he employs the second half of book 1 to transfer our comic expectations from Joseph's troubles with his mistress to Adams' encounters with the world. This is accomplished in a three-step process: Joseph is forcibly removed from his parodic role, the pair of female hypocrites is replaced by a representative aggregation of affected ill natures, and Adams is moved into Joseph's place as the innocent encountering this world.

The first of these steps is initiated by the most overt manipulation in the novel, the sudden disclosure of Joseph's love life. Though it serves to jar the obtuse reader out of any lingering expectation of parody, this radical surprise is, on examination, not so entirely unhinted as it first appears.[3] But before one has much time to reconsider Joseph's earlier behavior in the light of this new knowledge, Fielding executes a brilliant rhetorical stroke, casting the former foolish virgin as the victim in a modern reenactment of the parable of the Good Samaritan. The parallel is clearly drawn. Like his scriptural counterpart, "honest Joseph," as he is now called, is robbed, stripped, beaten, and left for dead; and as the biblical account contrasts the charity of the Samaritan with the indifference of the other travellers who pass the poor man by, so in Fielding's episode the impulsive kindnesses of a postilion and a chambermaid are set off against the ill-natured conduct of their "betters." But Fielding wryly altered the conclusion of the parable to emphasize his satiric characterization of the world and to heighten the reader's sympathy for Joseph. For he is at last taken up by the coach passengers, not out of compassion, as is his biblical counterpart, but out of purely selfish motives—to be delivered (after furnishing the travelers amusement) not to the comfort and safety

[3] The narrator's blithe allusion to Joseph's "other Inducements" for hastening to the country "which the Reader, without being a Conjurer, cannot possibly guess; 'till we have given him those hints, which it may be now proper to open" (p. 47) indicates the revision of the *donnée* is no mere clumsiness. Joseph, like his sister, is not above that "innocent" deception which is the common resource of servants dealing with their masters. His assurance to Lady Booby "that all the Women he had ever seen were equally indifferent to him" is of a piece with his pretense of understanding less of her intention in their first interview than he reveals in the immediately subsequent letter to Pamela (1 : 6), the counterpart of Fanny's later response to Adams' reference to Joseph (see chap. 3, n. 12). Attributable on first reading to youthful embarrassment, his answer "with some Confusion" to his mistress' query about having been in love, "it was time enough for one so young as himself to think on such things," can be seen in retrospect as a flustered evasion. In the light of the disclosure of a person "whom *Joseph* (tho' the best of Sons and Brothers) longed more impatiently to see than his Parents or his Sister," the letter conveying his intention of returning "to my old Master's Country Seat, if it be only to see Parson *Adams*," reveals a similar practice upon the best of sisters. Fielding also plays with the reader by calling attention to Lady Booby as "the Heroine of our Tale" two chapters before declaring "He is a sagacious Reader who can see two Chapters before him" and disclosing Fanny.

of the biblical inn but to the hostile mercies of Mrs. Tow-wouse and the indifferent ministrations of a quack surgeon and a self-serving priest.[4] Following hard upon the recasting of the male Pamela as a healthy young lover, this sharp change in the character of his victimization, underscored by the implied contrast with the scriptural analogy, completes the transformation of his suffering innocence from an object of amusement to one of sympathetic concern. Cognizant of his long-range plan, Fielding thus prepares for Joseph's eventual emergence in a straightforward heroic role by thoroughly modifying our original attitudes and expectations concerning him before he is allowed to recede into the background.

At the same time these actions serve to expose dramatically the moral ambience of the central comedy. As the use of a gospel analogy might suggest, the scope of the subject is enlarged from the isolated foibles of Lady Booby, Slipslop, and Joseph to the failings of mankind in general. The stagecoach and the Dragon Inn are the world in little: the passengers, whose several pretenses are exposed in their confrontation with the robbers; the hypocritical Mrs. Tow-wouse, whose charity is proportional to the recipient's ability to pay; the surgeon, whose "science" is humbug; and Barnabas, whose Christianity is verbal—all are drawn to fit Fielding's affectation theory. While the center of comic expectation is being shifted from Joseph to Adams, these are the principal comic objects before us. It is only after he has thus dramatically impressed upon the reader (and aroused his antipathy toward) the predominantly affected and ill-natured state of the world that Fielding brings his unsuspecting protagonist on the scene.

The appearance of the presumably parish-anchored parson in

[4] Martin C. Battestin, *The Moral Basis of Fielding's Art* (Middletown, Conn., 1959), pp. 94–95, focusing on the positive side of the analogy, sees the "Samaritan offices of two social outcasts" sounding "the theme of Christian charity" that "principally informs" the novel from this point to the end of book 3.

this arena is the novel's second major surprise. With a more vivid sense of the dramatic than he usually displayed as a playwright, Fielding heightens this effect, focusing attention on Adams as he is about to assume the central role, through a modest version of the anonymous entrance conventional to romance. In this procedure he also found an effective means of enlisting our sympathies for Adams in his introductory encounter with the world, represented by the surgeon. Although this "dry Fellow" exposes the unidentified grave gentleman's pretense of medical knowledge to the laughter of the assembled company, the reader recognizes that the man of science is the real fool, and that the butt of his wit, "having sufficiently sounded his Depth" and "contentedly suffered the Doctor to enjoy his Victory," is clearly the wiser man. By presenting this scene before revealing Adams' identity, Fielding produces a more telling impression of his probity and goodness and a more sympathetic response to his conduct than might have ensued if the reader witnessed it knowing that the surgeon's victim is the "Character of perfect Simplicity" whose comic adventures we have anticipated since the opening of the novel. This is only one of the means by which Fielding emphasizes Adams' amiable qualities at this stage of the novel in order to differentiate him from the ridiculous figures he will confront, and to stress the dimension of his character likely to be lost sight of in his impending journey of comic discovery. His immediate and spontaneous solicitude for the injured lad whose identity is unknown to him (1:14) is contrasted with the prevailing attitude in the inn; and his eloquently stated creed of good works, brotherhood, and simple piety (1:17) is set off against Barnabas' empty and vested religiosity.

The direction of Adams' adventures is forecast by the interview with the surgeon and by his naïve expectations in negotiating with Tow-wouse and the bookseller, but just as the first full-blown scene of the central comedy is developing out of the carefully set up interaction of the true and false parsons (1:17)

Fielding interrupts it with the explosion of the Tow-wouses' domestic row. In so doing he apparently was adapting Scarron's procedure in delaying the start of Destin's story with a similar outbreak of violence (*Roman comique* 1:12), sharpening the reader's anticipation of Adam's interaction with the world by forestalling its full commencement. By the same means he brought the transitional sequence to an effective climax fittingly centered on the keepers of the Dragon, even managing to make this incidental action unexpectedly provide a comically appropriate conclusion to the whole of book 1. For the explanation of Mrs. Tow-wouse' mock-tragic fury leads to a brief resuscitation of the now remote parodic comedy, with Joseph in a last fleeting appearance as vigilant virgin and Betty the chambermaid amusingly reenacting Lady Booby's part, even to the conflict of passions within her when her advances are rebuffed. Unlike the highborn hypocrite entrapped in that conflict, the down-to-earth chambermaid is quick to find an outlet for her thwarted desire.[5] And so after Joseph's several escapes and the frustrations of Lady Booby and Slipslop, the illicit sexual act contemplated since the beginning of the action is at last unexpectedly consummated.

Book 2—The first phase of the journey: Adams' adventures on the road. The central comedy of Adams' innocence in the world of affectation is adumbrated in preparatory incidents in the latter part of book 1 and revived intermittently in the second half of the novel, but it is in book 2 that Fielding develops it most extensively and concentrates its most memorable incidents. Although the two heroes are now journeying to-

[5] One of Fielding's nicest strokes of "nature" is his amusingly straight-faced description of the girl's unconscious mind at work: "*Betty* was in the most violent Agitation at this Disappointment. Rage and Lust pulled her Heart . . . but the latter Passion was far more prevalent. . . . In this Perturbation of Spirit, it accidentally occurred to her Memory, that her Master's Bed was not made" (p. 88).

gether, Joseph is quickly lost sight of, while the narrative follows Adams, who, with one brief exception (2:6), is continuously on the scene. Having arrived at his central subject, Fielding does not, in the manner of Cervantes at the comparable stage of his narrative, present a random succession of adventures stemming from Adams' misappraisals. Within the sequence there is an apparently planned progression in the kinds of comic actions in which Adams is shown, and these adventures are interwoven with developments in the other line of action and the independent "History of Leonora" to heighten their effect, activate long-range expectation of the final crisis of the novel, and shape book 2 itself into an effective narrative unit.

Beginning with Joseph's discovery that the parson has left the occasion of his London trip at home, the comedy moves quickly from Adams' absent-minded mistakes about road and reckoning —actions apparently designed to proclaim him Fielding's latter-day Quixote—to his centrally characteristic unawareness of the world's moral state. The first incident in this vein (2:3) is carefully drawn to demonstrate the extremity of the parson's benevolent unworldlines. Compared to some earlier actions in the novel, the two lawyers' oppositely distorted accounts of the same gentleman are a relatively innocuous extension of the normal procedure of their profession. But Adams, shocked at the suggestion that their divergent views might reflect their divergent interests, refuses to believe that men might be so evil as to let self-love affect their allegiance to truth. As he proceeds on his journey, the selfishness of the worldlings becomes more reprehensible and their folly more extreme, and the naïve observer of their ways becomes their victim. Yet he remains unenlightened, and the progression from gross mistakes to the display of his essential simplicity culminates in his vain defense of classical learning as the essential source of the knowledge of men. Thus Fielding concludes the second book and first volume of his history with the explicit formulation of the erroneous doctrine which serves to confirm his comic hero in his habitual mistake, reserving his expounding of it until the moment at which its absurdity can be fully appreciated and enjoyed in the light of Adams' preceding actions.

The effect of this developing comedy is heightened by its disposition in the narrative. Extending the procedure employed at the end of book 1, Fielding continues to whet the reader's appetite for Adams' adventures by periodically balking expectation. The parson's shock at the behavior of the lawyers and the easygoing philosophy of their host, whose belief in a future life does not deter him from being "for something present," makes us wonder what will happen when he encounters the real beasts of this jungle. But at the point where the central comedy might be expected to resume, after Slipslop's gossip about her mistress has served to keep alive the suspended first line of action, Fielding introduces "the Unfortunate Jilt," and the reader must content himself with Adams' childlike responses to the tale and his embroilment in the brief kitchen battle which punctuates it.[6]

The twice-frustrated anticipation of seeing the comic hero take center stage begins to be fulfilled in his more extensive second sally (2:6–13), which opens (as if to indicate that his adventures are now only properly commencing) with a fuller account of his history than is given at the start of the novel. Typically, Adams' chronicle of his adventures in borough politics is a record of exploitation by callously corrupt candidates in a succession of meaningless contests, yet the naïvely vain innocent interprets it as the record of his "Opportunities of suffering for the sake of my Conscience," of laying out "Talents" (control of a nephew's vote) "in the Service of my Country." From the successive ironic turns in this wry tale, comic injustices accumulate in a rapid series of unexpected develop-

[6] For discussion of this interpolated story, see chap. 7 below.

ments. The fire-eating patriot who elicits Adams' "notable Dissertation" flies at the sound of a woman's cries; Adams prevents a rape, only to find himself and the victim made the criminals in the case; that victim, in the novel's third major surprise, is discovered to be the lodestone of Joseph's journey; in the ensuing juridical farce, the innocent virgin as baited by lewd jests, Adams' learning is disproved by his inability to match a wager, and both are only accidentally saved from commitment on the damning evidence of the parson's possession of a Greek text. The mounting dissatisfactions of this restless sequence serve to heighten the gratification as well as the dramatic impact of the event in which it culminates—the unexpected reunion of Joseph and Fanny, with its attendant frustration of the predatory Slipslop. But in the dramatic confrontation which prefigures the novel's conclusion (with Slipslop standing in for her mistress) attention is once more deflected from Adams' adventures. Only after the romantic story has been brought to a point of temporary equilibrium with Joseph's acceptance of Adams' stipulation that the marriage await their return to the parish does Fielding fully pay off the promise of his neo-Cervantean comedy, appropriately concluding the first half of the novel with Adams' quintessential encounters with the world.

The scenes with Trulliber and the false promiser are clearly conceived with this climactic effect in mind. Each of these figures is an extreme exemplar of the world's hypocrisy, and each is peculiarly apposite to the central preoccupations of the novel: the porcine Trulliber, a brutalization of the complacently self-serving parson to whom Adams is contrasted at the outset of his adventures, is the complete antithesis of Fielding's model Christian clergyman; and the gentleman's cruel foible is the affectation of that cherished benevolence at the heart of Adams' character and so conspicuously lacking in the citizens of the world. Each incident is more extensively developed than any of Adams' preceding encounters, and in each the central process is the innocent's slow and reluctant discovery of the true character of his adversary. The two situations are arranged in a dialectical progression from Trulliber's more "naturally" motivated negative *response*—which is, after all, only an extreme extension of the lawyers' self-love—to the gentleman's gratuitous *initiative*, an apparently motiveless mischief which necessitates a more extended and involved discovery. Even after the record of his past crimes persuades Adams that "he is indeed a wicked Man," he still finds traces of Christian charity in his countenance. And so, fittingly, through his symptomatic belief in the "science" of appearances, Adams is drawn into the argument over the merits of learning versus experience with which Fielding wittily caps the comedy of the whole preceding sequence of his adventures. Having wandered cross-country blindfolded, and having just obtusely presumed on one "brother's" humanity and been presumed upon by another's, Abraham Adams, innocent of any comic irony, declares: "If a Man would sail round the World, and anchor in every Harbour of it, without Learning, he would return home as ignorant as he went out."

Book 3—The second phase of the journey: Wilson and the hunter of men. The division between volume 1 and volume 2 marks two distinct stages of the journey, and a corresponding modification in the preoccupations and tone of the narrative. Throughout book 2, as he follows Adams' eccentric course, the reader is outward bound in pursuit of new and unexpected comic adventures, as in the sallies of Don Quixote. But from Slipslop's parting threat of invoking her mistress' wrath (2:13) we are aware that a renewal of the conflict between Joseph and Lady Booby only awaits their arrival at the parish, and we are informed at the outset of book 3 that "we are now drawing near the Seat of the *Boobies*." In keeping with this refocus of expectation on the destination of the journey, Adams is permitted no independent sallies and has only one or two more passing encounters with the world's hypocrisy. The comic emphasis shifts in the direction forecast by the argument with the host at the close of book 2—from the opposition of Adams and the affected to a contrast between him and less eccentric good men, from his benign simplicity to his mistaken ideas and doctrines, from his innocence to his vanity. Rambling adventures are replaced by two sustained and pointedly contrasting sequences, the sojourn with the Wilsons and the serial encounter with the perverse country squire and his retinue. Each of these is in its own way more serious than the preceding actions, and together they are designed to prepare the final conflict by modifying our views of Adams and Joseph and amplifying that faint strain of comic apprehension which begins when Slipslop's threats are immediately followed by Adams' insistence on delaying the marriage.

The narrative reopens with a little night sequence obviously intended to dramatize the realignment of the two protagonists. In a rare misapprehension truly of the Quixote kind, Adams, believing the sheep stealers to be ghosts, advances to confront them, but Joseph prudently catches hold of him and persuades him to withdraw. Then the parson tumbles headlong down a hill (a sight which, "if the Light had permitted," the lovers "would scarce have refrained laughing to see") after which Joseph, carrying Fanny, "walked firmly down . . . without making a false step." Finally, coming to a river, Adams is for plunging in until Joseph reasons that there must be a bridge nearby.

This preliminary differentiation of the level-headed Joseph from his abstracted and impulsive mentor is followed by the more penetrating contrast between Adams and the man who is in the end discovered to be Joseph's father. The mature Wilson functions as the novel's central norm of sensible humanity. Though he has retired from the world after concluding its

"Pleasures . . . chiefly Folly, and the Business of it mostly Knavery," his is not the misanthropic withdrawal of the Man of the Hill. But the charitable disposition which prompts him to assist his neighbors and to take in the ragtag trio of midnight strangers is monitored by a prudence in his dealings with his fellowmen comparable to Joseph's in the mechanics of travel. In contrast to Adams' naïvely affectionate trust, Wilson knows "too much of the World to give a hasty Belief to Professions," and his reception of the travelers does not go beyond a decent but reserved hospitality until the suspicions aroused by their appearance are supplanted by confirmations of their true character. Not until Adams has astounded him with his eloquent discourse on Homer does "the Goodness of his Heart" begin "to dilate to all the Strangers"; then Joseph's modest behavior begins "to work on the Gentleman's Affections"; and only after Adams' plain account of the lovers' history has removed his last doubt is he "enamour'd of his Guests." This prudential behavior is the result of Wilson's youthful education in the ways of the town. His more drastic experience of the world's vices and follies has brought him to an understanding of the characters of men of which Adams' potentially eye-opening journey has given the parson no inkling. Wilson's history, a representative survey of "the World's" behavior which universalizes the inferences to be drawn from Adams' idiosyncratic experiences, is designed to inculcate in the reader the same moral vision. Its satiric exposure of the moral state of the world *as it is* forcibly points up the error of Adams' persistent naïve vision of it *as it ought to be*, and this contrast between the two men's diversely derived perceptions confirms the folly of Adams' belief in the superiority of books to experience as the source of ethical knowledge. Of the general remarks made in the course of his history which Wilson modestly considers "too obvious to be worth relating," one formulates the aspect of human nature to which Adams is persistently blind in others ("Selfishness is much more general than we please to allow it, so it is natural to hate and envy those who stand between us and the Good we desire"), and another ("Vanity is the worst of Passions, and more apt to contaminate the Mind than any other") is immediately confirmed by the parson's own unconsciously self-contradictory agitation at not being able to read "a Sermon, which he thought his Master-piece, against Vanity."[7]

The implications of Wilson's history for the reader's view of Adams and for the underlying thought of the novel continue beyond the travelers' departure from his house. Ignoring Wilson's own attribution of the folly of his youthful course to his premature departure from school and consequent "early Introduction into Life, without a Guide," Adams traces the "Cause of all the Calamities which he . . . suffered" to a public school education, and, obliterating the most obvious point of the tale, declares such schools "the Nurseries of all Vice and Immorality." In the consequent "Disputation on Schools" between the parson and his pupil (3 : 5), Fielding obliquely questions Richardson's excessive estimate of the power of moral tutelage and laughingly rebuts Pamela's lengthy critique of Locke's educational theory[8] while showing Adams' error to penetrate

[7] For a different view of the Wilson episode as the "philosophic, as well as structural, center of *Joseph Andrews,* comprising a kind of synecdochic epitome of the meaning and movement of the novel," see Battestin, pp. 119–29. For the relation of Wilson's story to *Gil Blas,* see below, pp. 130–32, especially n. 2.

[8] About a third of Pamela's fifty pages of commentary, undertaken at Mr. B's behest, is devoted to her perplexity in "knowing how to judge which is best, a *home* or a *school* education" (Everyman edition, 2 : 383). Persuaded by Locke's argument against the corrupting influence of servants and the bad example of parents, she first favors a "middle way" in which "a *few* young gentlemen" would be taught by a single master—that is, the kind of school Adams himself runs—but in the end prefers a home education for her own children, since Locke's objections would not apply "where the behaviour of servants can be so well answered for" as that of Mr. B's and "where the example of parents will be, as I hope, rather edifying than otherwise" (p. 387). While conceding the excellence of Locke's "noble *theory*" of a tutor knowledgeable in "the ways, the humours, the follies, the cheats, the faults of the

beneath his imperception of the world's moral state and his misconception of how knowledge of that state is gained to his very assumptions about the etiology of virtue and vice. As a corollary of his vain appraisal of the schoolmaster as "the greatest Character in the World, and himself the greatest of Schoolmasters," the parson believes environmental conditioning to be the crucial determinant of character. Projecting his own nature onto mankind in general, he regards moral education as a process by which "Boys may be kept in Innocence and Ignorance." Hence a private school is to be preferred to a public one, where, in Joseph's words, "a Boy of any Observation may see in Epitome what he will afterwards find in the World at large." The evident comic contradiction between Adams' view of the world in the abstract as corrupting and his previously demonstrated persistent assumption that each of its citizens is predisposed to goodness indicates what judgment we are to make of his position.[9] In the ideology of the novel, experience is neither so corrupting as Adams assumes nor is it so critically determinant of

age," who can "pull off the mask which their several callings and pretences cover" men with, and teach his pupil "to guess at, and beware of" their designs "neither with too much suspicion, nor too much confidence," Pamela, with characteristic piety, fears he may be "governed by partial considerations" and "take advantage of the confidence placed in him, to the injury of some worthy person" (pp. 382–83). However congenial Fielding might have found her other views (which are mostly in agreement with Locke), he must have been amused at the heroine's detection, in her first look at the treatise, of "some few things, which I think want clearing up"; one can imagine his hearty assent to her coy question: "Won't it look like intolerable vanity in me, to find fault with such a genius as Mr. Locke?" (p. 277).

[9] In *Tom Jones* (3 : 5), Allworthy takes Adams' stand: "Having observed the imperfect institution of our public schools, and the many vices which boys were there liable to learn, [he] had resolved to educate his nephew, as well as the other lad, whom he had in a manner adopted, in his own house, where he thought their morals would escape all that danger of being corrupted to which they would be unavoidably exposed in any public school or university." Fielding's judgment on the wisdom of this course is implicit in his characterization of the tutors to whom the lads' morals are entrusted, and more immediately in the fact that this account of "that singular plan of education" is given in the course of describing young Blifil's hypocritical manipulation of the favorite notions of Thwackum, Square, and Allworthy in turn.

character as a careless reading of Wilson's history might suggest —because human natures are not so originally uniform as the parson assumes. Wilson's life indicates that experience of the world is valuable in developing ethical judgment and prudence, but no education or environmental influence can account for those good impulses which impose limits on his involvement in the world's vice and folly and eventually enable him to transcend its values. As Joseph observes, "When I was in the Stable, if a young Horse was vicious in his Nature, no Correction would make him otherwise; I take it to be equally the same among Men: if a Boy be of a mischievous wicked inclination, no School, tho' ever so private, will ever make him good; on the contrary, if he be of a righteous Temper, you may trust him to *London*, or wherever else you please, he will be in no danger of being corrupted." The validity of this equine analogy is confirmed by Joseph's own London history, and by the behavior of Adams himself, whose ingenuously benevolent inclination is unaffected by his experience, and at odds with some of his own doctrine. More immediately and pointedly, the correctness of Joseph's view is brought out by the contrasting lives of Wilson and the next gentleman the travelers are to encounter. Slightly misquoting Addison, Adams declaims: "If Knowledge of the World must make Men Villains,/May *Juba* ever live in Ignorance." But Wilson's intimate knowledge of the world has not made him a villain: though in his youth he is led by passion and vanity to detestable acts, he is prevented by his natural goodness from being lastingly or fundamentally corrupted by the town. On the other hand, the squire, who has had the benefits of an extended private education "at his own Home, under the Care of his Mother and a Tutor" (the very method espoused by Pamela!), is thoroughly and irredeemably vicious.

The dispute on schools is the most significant step in the process by which Fielding realigns his two protagonists. Up to this point, Joseph has been shown to be superior to his mentor only in the pragmatic common sense displayed in the opening scene of book 3 and in that particular knowledge of the world's ways reflected in his recognition of the false promiser's stratagem of declaring himself not at home. But in this scene Joseph enunciates general ideas of considerable significance in the thought of the novel, challenging and clearly getting the better of his teacher on his own special ground. If he concludes by diffidently deferring to Adams' superior learning, as he did earlier in the promiser episode, he does so this time only after he has been sagacious and persistent enough to cause the good-natured Adams to lose his temper. To solidify this impression of Joseph's superior wisdom, Fielding concludes the dramatic exposition of ethical premises concentrated in the first half of book 3 by putting in Joseph's mouth "Moral Reflections" which summarize the world's hypocrisy and lack of charity as Wilson's remarks had its vanity: "Nobody scarce doth any Good, yet they all agree in praising those who do. Indeed it is strange that all Men should consent in commending Goodness, and no Man endeavour to deserve that Commendation; whilst, on the contrary, all rail at Wickedness, and all are as eager to be what they abuse. This I know not the Reason of, but it is as plain as Day-light to those who converse in the World, as I have done these three Years." It is thus left to Joseph to formulate that aspect of the world which occasions Adams' most characteristic and memorable errors.[10]

It is in the same speech that Fielding allows Joseph to remind the reader of the ethical limits of the comedy. And no sooner has he defied "the wisest Man in the World to turn a true good Action into Ridicule" than the travelers are beset by a "great Lover of Humour" whose "strange Delight . . . in everything

[10] Of course, the speech is given comic coloration, not only by Joseph's burlesque rendition of painters' names, but by the very image of him delivering it fixed "in one Attitude, with his Head reclining on one side, and his Eyes cast on the Ground" in the midst of a meadow with Adams snoring at his feet.

ridiculous, odious, and absurd in his own Species" requires his minions to "turn even Virtue and Wisdom themselves to Ridicule." From the moment the idyllic interlude extending from the meeting with Wilson is shattered by the hunting pack's emblematic dismemberment of a "poor innocent defenseless" hare, and their master incites them to the "sport" of attacking the sleeping parson, as dogs are valued more than humans and humans degraded to curs, moral dissatisfaction mounts until it reaches a climax in the "Scene of Roasting very nicely adapted to the present Taste and Times" (3:7). Here the world's baiting of Adams, which began with his entrance into the Dragon Inn (1: 14), is carried to its savage extreme.

The "cruelty is extended too far for good humor" in this episode is not, as Irvin Ehrenpreis would have it, a "miscalculation."[11] Through these practical jokes and the depredations preceding them, Fielding steers the reader away from a derisive view of Adams, awakening our recently dormant sympathies and arousing an active desire to see an end to his buffetings by the world. Far from having "failed to appreciate the degree of distress . . . he was eliciting" in this final sequence of the journey, he seems to have designed it as the protagonists' most "fearful" adventure. The "hunter of men" is not only the most powerful and perverse adversary encountered on the journey but also the most persistent, pursuing them, as no other assailant does, after they have left the scene and subjecting them to three separate attacks. Whereas the worst deeds of his less savage precursor in perversity, the false promiser, are only recounted retrospectively after he has quit the scene, Fielding here acquaints the reader early with the squire's viciousness and unrestrained power; in contrast to the earlier sexual assault on Fanny (2 : 9), in which the evil is disclosed only as it is being averted,

[11] "Fielding's Use of Fiction: The Autonomy of *Joseph Andrews*," in *Twelve Original Essays on Great English Novels*, ed. Charles Shapiro (Detroit, 1960), pp. 38–39.

and the victim's identity is not known until some time later, here the villain's designs on the girl are revealed before the roasting scene begins. Only in this instance and in the subsequent report of the pursuit following the trio's escape from the squire's house is the reader invited to contemplate a danger to the protagonists before they are aware of it themselves. But counterbalancing these means of heightening apprehension is Fielding's careful attenuation of the reader's "distress," confining it within limits consistent with his overall comic aim. The dogs' attack, which might have been a truly unpleasant incident, is made the subject of the most extended burlesque description in the novel. What Ehrenpreis calls the "painful suspense" of the abduction is undercut by the narrator's disclosure, at the close of the roasting scene, of the long-range consequences of the villain's dunking ("He caught a Cold by the Accident, which threw him into a Fever, that had like to have cost him his Life"), intimating that he is not to be seen again and implying that the subsequent kidnapping is not to succeed. Between the first escape and the battle with the pursuing human pack, when apprehension might be mounting, our attention is directed to a brief resumption of the comedy of book 2 in Adams' conversation with a hypocritical papist priest. And while Fanny is being borne to the arms of a ravisher the narrator turns with playful arbitrariness from "this Tragedy" to devote two chapters to the vanities of poets and players and the comically inept "Exhortations of Parson Adams to his Friend in Affliction."

In this agony at the bedpost, reminiscent of Parson Barnabas' ministry to the castoff footman at the outset of the journey (see below, pp. 119–20), Fielding continues to readjust the reader's attitudes toward the two protagonists. Like his earlier Pamelian "deathbed" speech (1:13), Joseph's "Despair . . . more easy to be conceived than related" ("'O that I could but command my Hands to tear my Eyes out and my Flesh off!'") cannot be taken very seriously. But though the reader, assured that no real harm will befall Fanny, is amused by these mock heroics, and much more by the misapplied rhetoric of Adams' "grave and truly solemn Discourse," his sympathies, as in the scenes with Barnabas, are with the young lover. The formal sermonizer who "comforts" his young friend by invoking images of "the prettiest, kindest, loveliest, sweetest young Woman" subjected to "the utmost Violence which Lust and Power can inflict" is seen in a less amiable light. The stern preacher who admonishes Joseph in the manner of the comforters of Job—interpreting his loss as a punishment for his sins, reprimanding his "stubbornness" in persisting in "the Folly of Grief," and rebuking him for swearing when he mildly protests ("upon my Soul") the involuntary nature of his feelings—is closer to the unfeeling Barnabas than to the Adams who responds to the same lovers' earlier reunion by "dancing about the Room in a Rapture of Joy."[12]

Coming after the disagreeable attacks of the four-legged and two-legged dogs, Adams' doctrinaire response to Joseph's plight

[12] Henry K. Miller, *Essays on Fielding's "Miscellanies"* (Princeton, 1961), pp. 242–43, points out that Fielding's essay "Of the Remedy of Affliction for the Loss of our Friends" directly contravenes the classic and patristic *consolatio* tradition only in its opposition to the commonplace that the mourner console himself with recollection of his friend: "What is all this less than being self-tormentors, and playing with affliction?" Whereas Fielding cautions against "all circumstances which may revive the memory of the deceased" in happier times, Adams pictures Fanny in the worst imaginable plight. Miller also remarks (p. 251) that the arguments which Adams stresses are among the fundamental points of the conventional treatises of the time that Fielding's conspicuously avoids. Significantly, Fielding revised one of Adams' speeches in the second edition to reinforce his injunction of submission to providence with the singularly inapropos stock assurance that "all the Misfortunes . . . which happen to the Righteous, happen to them for their own Good."

Fielding also specifies that the philosophic and religious arguments of consolation he propounds are not appropriate and cannot be expected to function until some time after the traumatic event, "the first emotions of our grief" being "so far irresistible, that they are not to be instantly and absolutely overcome" (*Works* 16 : 102). For the applicability of this limiting assumption to Adams' conduct in the subsequent incident of his son's supposed drowning (4 : 8), see below, pp. 120–21 and 280.

makes the reader more willing to see him relinquish the center of the stage. At the same time the abduction, the first threat to the lovers since their reunion, focuses attention on Joseph's story, now fully redefined as comic romantic melodrama. For all its attenuation and psuedosuspense, the "fearful" quality of the sequence makes the self-contained drama of the final book appear the continuation of a pattern of threats and dangers begun before the travelers reach home. (To enhance this effect Fielding omits his customary prefatory chapter at the opening of book 4.) But the arrival home is also a victory for the travelers. Adams' first condition for performing the marriage has been fulfilled, and whatever difficulties await the protagonists they are free from the monetary troubles of the journey and the unpredictable depredations which have assailed them on the road. After the malignity of the perverse squire, there is a kind of comfort in the known and domesticated villainy of Peter Pounce, who rescues Fanny as Slipslop did Joseph earlier. The fortunate accident which brings this rescue about and the narrator's humorous treatment of the "tragedy" of the abduction encourage the reader to view the final action with comic confidence. Before that action begins, Fielding concludes book 3 and the journey with an exploding discussion of charity between Adams and Pounce. In this colloquy at cross-purposes between good-natured Adams and his avaricious opposite on the crucial virtue which Adams so abundantly possesses and the world so radically lacks, an exchange which echoes Adams' comparable confrontations with Barnabas and Trulliber at the close of books 1 and 2, Fielding epitomizes the long encounter between innocence and hypocrisy as it is drawing to an end.

Book 4—The parish: Lady Booby versus the lovers. With the convergence of all the principal characters on the starting point of the narrative, Fielding initiates a sustained dramatic conflict within a limited scene and a clearly defined time, progressively filling the stage, as in the climax of a theatrical comedy, with secondary figures, including not only the peddler and Wilson but Pamela, her husband, and the aged recipients of her celebrated letters. The action has the classic form of a tragicomic complex plot: the lovers' adversary engages the law on her side, turns Mr. Booby's good nature, Pamela's snobbery, and Didapper's epicene lust to her use, and even finds allies in Adams' family; then fortune itself seems to desert the lovers, as their former rescuer, the peddler, reveals their apparent kinship, and even Adams rejoices at the prevention of their marriage; but while their situation is steadily worsening, the lovers are in fact progressing steadily toward the attainment of their wishes, and the fateful discovery which seems to place happiness beyond their grasp actually initiates the process by which Joseph is not only freed from the power of Lady Booby and the influence of Pamela but brought to a greater good fortune than he could have anticipated.

Fielding turns this whole melodramatic structure to comedy. Though the lovers are supposedly threatened, from the opening of the sequence the sufferings depicted are those of the "powerful" villainess, who, like Didapper and Pamela, is hardly a fearful antagonist, especially when compared to the tormentor from whom the innocents have just escaped. The stock external obstacles to lovers' felicity—opposition of the mighty, family interference, social distinctions, threats to the maiden's virtue, and finally the classical impediment of incest—are raised and resolved in such rapid succession as to constitute almost a burlesque. The appearance of Pamela in the flesh and her opposition to the marriage as a social mismatch (mocking her comparable sentiments and actions in the sequel of Richardson's novel)[13] contribute to the air of joking make-believe. Didap-

[13] In a letter advising her father against employing relatives in the exercise of the stewardship bestowed by her husband, she writes condescendingly: "You may lend them a little money. . . . You can fit out my she-cousins to

per's inability to overpower Fanny, his delegation of her seduction to a servant (not at all the same thing as the squire's dispatch of his henchmen to kidnap her), and his fumbling of his subsequent assault by mistaking the girl's room are all ludicrous; and, as in Mrs. Heartfree's adventures in *Jonathan Wild*, the cumulative frequency of the attempts upon the girl's virtue begins to be comic.

In this context, the final drama of identities—introduced with a deadpan joke on the uncertain pronunciation of the literary name of Richardson's "real life" heroine, involving two independent but interlocking thefts of infants by gypsies and a recognition by strawberry mark, and likening the protagonists' situation to that of Oedipus—is clearly a spoof. This might be inferred from the very complexity of the final "classical" peripeties, in which the lovers are first plunged by the discovery of Fanny's birth from the verge of happiness to the depth of despair and then quickly brought by the more surprising discovery of Joseph's parentage through a second, more extreme reversal. These final turns of the wheel, like the threatening movement of the sequence as a whole, heighten the impact and satisfaction of the lovers' terminal good fortune by making their

good reputable places. The younger you can put to school, or, when fit, to trades, according to their talents; and so they will be of course in a way to get an honest and creditable livelihood. But, above all things, one would discourage such a proud and ambitious spirit in any of them, as should want to raise itself by favour instead of merit," adding the traditional sigh of the poor little rich girl, "for undoubtedly, there are many more happy persons in low than in high life, take number for number all the world over" (Everyman ed., 2 : 13). To her husband she writes: "O that your lordly sex were all like my dear Mr. B.—I don't mean that they should all take raw, uncouth, unbred, lowly girls, as I was, from the cottage, and, destroying all distinction, make such their wives; for there is a far greater likelihood, that such a one, when she comes to be lifted up into so dazzling a sphere, would have her head made giddy with her exaltation, than that she would balance herself well in it" (p. 414). Describing the bad marriage of Lady Davers' foolish nephew, she concludes: "In short, she is quite a common woman; has no fortune at all, as one may say, only a small jointure incumbered; and is much in debt" (p. 432).

attainment of the goal toward which they have been progressing more or less uninterruptedly since their reunion in book 2 seem dramatic and surprising. But the relation of these terminal events to the rest of the novel is not truly analogous to the apparently similar resolution of *Tom Jones*, where the discovery of the hero's parentage, resulting from a complex chain of events running through the whole plot, reverses the sustained downward trend of his fortunes and resolves long-standing curiosity and suspense. In *Joseph Andrews*, where the title character's identity is part of the parodic *donnée* of the novel, the sudden raising of the question of birth in the closing pages of an extended narrative is a final comic embellishment, capping the literary comedy, like the mock-romantic joke with which he concluded *The Author's Farce*. Of course this denouement is prepared for, as the discovery of the King of Bantam and the romantic resolution of Mr. Wilson's tale are not.[14] But in hinting at this development, in the ambiguous opening sentence of the narrative ("Mr. Joseph Andrews . . . was esteemed to be the only son of Gaffer and Gammer Andrews") and in subsequent passages, Fielding appears less intent on providing clues

[14] The itinerant peddler has been told to come to the parish to reclaim his loan, and Wilson has proposed to visit Adams "within a Week" on his journey into Somersetshire. The narrator's oversight of this "Circumstance which we thought too immaterial to mention" (until after the education dispute) is apparently designed to emphasize it. To the reader at all familiar with the staples of romance, Wilson's account of a kidnapped infant bearing a strawberry mark is a virtual announcement that a second romantic happy ending to his story is in the offing, and to make sure the broad hint is not lost, Fielding has Adams return to the subject in the following chapter. Given the novel's parodic *donnée,* the idea that even the recently more resourceful Joseph might be the lost son is at this point about as likely as Adams' hypothesis that he might be the King of Corsica. But in retrospect, Adams' early query whether Joseph "did not extremely regret . . . not having been born of Parents, who might have indulged his Talents" (1 : 3), Betty's belief, on the conventional romantic evidence of the whiteness of his skin, that "the Man in Bed was a greater Man than they took him for" (1 : 15), and Lady Booby's admission that he is "so genteel that a Prince might without a Blush acknowledge him for his Son" (4 : 6) all take on a new significance. For the denouement of Wilson's story, see below, p. 131.

or establishing probabilities than on enjoying these playful ironies which the reader might find amusing in retrospect. Similar compositional jests may be discerned in his beginning volume 2 with what proves to be the history of Joseph's parentage after opening the first volume with an unsuccessful search into his ancestry, and his having Joseph sleep through that part of Wilson's story which pertains to him, even as Adams a few pages later sleeps through Joseph's disquisition on the aspect of the world which he critically mistakes. But in view of the novel's beginning the climactic joke is the resolution of the birth tangle itself. Through the unexpected use of one of the most ancient of romantic plot devices, Fielding completes the demonstration, begun with the first disclosure of Fanny's existence, that this is no "simple Book," as the transformed Joseph proves to be no more kin to Pamela than the novel is to her exemplary history—and Fanny, the young virgin constantly threatened by assault, is revealed as her true sister.

Between the complication and denouement of this last-minute drama-within-a-drama, Fielding sets off a final explosion of physical humor, paralleling the Tow-wouses' row at the end of book 1 and the lesser comic disturbances which function analogously at the close of books 2 and 3. Involving all the principal characters in a wild sequence of mistakes in the night conspicuously reminiscent of his continental antecedents in "this kind of Writing," he combines the function of Cervantes' innyard melee and retrospective coda, recapitulating the whole novel while bringing its ubiquitous sexual comedy to a richly ironic climax. The man-hungry Slipslop, teased with the illusory consummation of her pursuit of Joseph (in the person of the feigning Didapper), entertains two men in her bed without satisfaction. And the transcendentally innocent comic hero, successively discovered in two different women's beds (having effortlessly attained in the second the situation most of the male characters have unsuccessfully sought by force or guile), is denounced by the libidinous hypocrite as "the wickedest of all Men" and even suspected by the girl whose chastity he has defended and the boy whose innocence he has nurtured.[15]

Joseph's skeptical confrontation of the bewildered Adams over Fanny's bed defines dramatically the completed change in the relationship of the parson and the disciple whom he catechizes with indulgent superiority at the beginning of the novel. The climax of the running opposition between the two friends is reached midway in the final book (4 : 8), where Fielding resumes their argument exactly where it left off in the dialogue at the bedpost. Again the lover's emotional response to his sweetheart's danger is rebuked by a formal sermon from the parson, which Fielding makes even more pointedly reminiscent of Barnabas than his previous "solemn Discourse." As Barnabas responds to the "dying" Joseph's complaints at leaving Fanny (1:13) by cautioning against "any Repining at the Divine Will" and bidding him "divest himself of all human Passion" and "forget all carnal Affections," so Adams, enjoining submission to "the Will of Providence," condemns setting "our Affections so much on anything here, as not to be able to quit it without Reluctance" and (misapplying to marriage a text against adultery) censures "the Indulgence of carnal Appetites." In warning that the lover's fear for his beloved "argues a Diffidence highly criminal," Adams echoes the very phrasing employed by Barnabas in a similar application.[16] To be sure, these are conventional Christian sentiments, and Adams' expression of them is doubtless more heartfelt than the complacent Barna-

[15] For an allegorical reading of this scene as the climax of the novel, entailing a progressive modification of the reader's view of Adams substantially opposite to that I have argued, see Mark Spilka, "Comic Resolution in Fielding's 'Joseph Andrews'," *College English* 15 (1953–54) : 11–19. For a discussion of the incident in relation to its particular antecedents, see below, pp. 146–49.

[16] "*Barnabas* said, 'that such Fears argued a Diffidence and Despondence very criminal; that he must divest himself of all human Passion, and fix his Heart above' " (p. 59).

bas' perfunctory formulas. But transcendence of human affections is more fittingly urged upon a young man departing this life than upon one entering matrimony, and the reliance upon Providence is more appropriately recommended when the object of his fear (Fanny's bereavement) is beyond his control.

Moreover, the particular passive version of Christianity implicit in these sentiments is far from that active eleemosynary love for one's neighbor embodied in Adams' conduct. The "slower and more accurate Reader" may recall with a smile that when Fanny was similarly threatened earlier (2 : 9) the preacher who here advocates responding to danger by "resort to Prayer only" did not confine himself to prayer "that she might be strengthened," as the jealous Slipslop subsequently defined his Christian duty. In the midst of the mounting threats of the final sequence, his advocacy of this recourse rather than the "unjustifiable or desperate means" of a wedding preceded by only two announcements of the banns seems the unfeeling response of a pedantic adherent to form. The reader may also recall that prayer is a favorite resource of Pamela; and indeed the gospel of Barnabas, who concludes by inculcating a reliance on grace, which is in turn to be attained "by Prayer and Faith," is a simulacrum of the religion of Richardson's heroine. It is a measure of the extremity to which Fielding carries his "demotion" of Adams that he should pair him with a preacher who mouths these passwords of Methodism and even briefly affiliate Adams himself with that "useful and truly religious doctrine" for which the misguided Parson Tickletext in *Shamela* recommends Richardson's novel: "for he preached nothing more than the Conquest of . . . [the Passions] by Reason and Grace."

The falseness of Adams' position is made unmistakably clear in a broadly contrived reversal of the situation in the bedpost scene. The parson's distraction at the supposed loss of his son (occurring just after he declaims "Had *Abraham* so loved his Son *Isaac* as to refuse the Sacrifice required, is there any of us who would not condemn him?") radiates comic ironies in a widening circle from the immediate context of his sermon against the passions to his observation in the earlier scene that "it must require infinitely more Learning" than Joseph possesses to withstand the first onslaughts of grief. When Joseph attempts to console him with "Arguments . . . out of his own Discourses," the grief-stricken father who earlier rebuked the distraught lover for not accepting consolation ("Would you take Physic . . . when you are well, and refuse it when you are sick?") tells him not "to go about Impossibilities"; the parson who censured the "indulger" in immoderate grief as "not worthy the Name of a Christian" draws no solace from the promise of a heavenly reunion with his child. Although the incident is similar in structure to Fielding's unmaskings of hypocrisy, the paradox of Adams' behavior is not that he is worse than he pretends to be but that he is better than he knows. The wellspring and primary manifestation of his extraordinary goodness is not "Learning," secular or sacred, nor "Reason," which he tells Joseph "it is the Business of a Man and a Christian to summon," but those impulsive human feelings against which he inveighs. Hence the reader is expected to approve Adams' paternal fondness and to share his joy at the boy's delivery;[17] but when he obliviously resumes his inculcation of stoicism, our sympathies are entirely with the long-suffering Joseph, who at last drops the deference which he has consistently maintained and angrily confronts his mentor with the discrepancy between his preaching and practice.

From here it is only a short step to the strange meeting in Fanny's bedroom, where Adams is wholly on the defensive and Joseph, following the pattern of his father's earlier response,

[17] Hence the ironic reference in the chapter title to "some Behaviour of Mr. *Adams,* which will be called by some few Readers, very low, absurd, and unnatural." For discussion of Fielding's rhetoric in this scene, see below, pp. 278–80. For its conformity with the views expressed in his essay "Of the Remedy of Affliction for the Loss of our Friends," see n. 12 above.

views him with suspicion that mellows into indulgent superiority. With this image of the younger man standing in judgment of his former teacher, the process of realigning the protagonists, which began as they were approaching the house of Mr. Wilson, is completed just before Joseph is revealed as that gentleman's son. But in his concern with working out this pattern and placing Joseph in the terminal role of romantic hero smiling at his comic sidekick, Fielding may for once have miscalculated his effect. Despite the increasing emphasis on Adams' less amiable behavior, in this scene he is only a strayed lamb, and the reader may feel with some justice that it is "unnatural," even in the immediate circumstances and against the background of the perpetual threats to Fanny's chastity, that the two good-natured young people should suspect "the best Creature living" of any villainous design. This faint false note is not sufficient, however, to disturb for long the prevalent good feeling of the final pages, from which even Fanny's new sister is not excluded. Nor does it diminish our sympathetic satisfaction in the happy consummation of that love which Adams says "savours too much of the Flesh," as Fielding in a final fling at *Pamela* concludes his novel with a celebration of the conjugal sex which Richardson's figleaf morality excluded from his rendition of the perfect marriage.

The ordering, emphasis, and articulation of the narrative noted in the preceding analysis indicate that at some stage of the novel's composition Fielding arrived at a clear intuition of its distinctive form, which his many particular artistic choices seem designed to realize. The most obvious manifestations of an overall plan are visible in the mechanics of plotting; the anticipation of a return encounter between the initial antagonists, fostered at the close of the first episode and sustained by recurrent reminders through the middle of the narrative; the planting of Wilson and the peddler at the center of the book and the establishment of the probability of their subsequent reappearances in the parish; and the various other devices by which the reader's knowledge of events, persons, and relationships is controlled to make surprising yet credible the major turns in the unfolding story. Compared to the intricate devisings of a modern detective story, this level of Fielding's composition is rather crude. The peddler, for example, is palpably a a walking plot device. But something of the ingenious manipulation of fallible signs in *Tom Jones* is already present in the handling of this device. The peddler first appears as an incidental figure, another of the good-hearted "low" persons, like the postilion and chambermaid in book 1, ironically contrasted with the selfishness of the prosperous "respectable" world (personified in this instance by Trulliber). And when he is reintroduced in book 4, the grinding of machinery is muffled by his appearance as the rescuer of Adams' son, at a moment when attention is concentrated on the comic disparity between the parson's sermonizing and his sentiment. In its immediate context, the facetious display of "learning" with which his providential relief of the travelers is heralded seems to be only one of the narrator's playful digressions. In retrospect, however, the observation "That when the most exquisite Cunning fails, Chance often hits the Mark, and that by Means the least expected" is a wittily apt way of introducing the character whose coinciding acquaintance with Fanny's early history and meeting with the travelers are pivotal to the resolution of the story.[18]

It should by now be apparent, however, that Fielding's sense of the form of his novel went beyond this substratum of material plot organization and the representational strategy by which the reader's apprehension of it is influenced, even as it penetrated beneath the external narrative arrangement. There is evidence throughout the novel of his cognizance of its unique

[18] The typography of the early editions, in which the apothegm is set off in block capitals, may have been part of the joke.

dynamic structure and his awareness of the problems entailed in preserving its comic character while developing an affecting and morally satisfying story of the perils and rewards of a pair of virtuous lovers in a hostile world. Equally manifest is his sensitivity to the more delicate problem of adversely differentiating one of his protagonists from the other without confusing their amiable comedy with the surrounding antipathetic ridiculous, or impairing the reader's active affection for the generous-hearted man of mistaken notions.

Fielding's awareness of these problems is graphically demonstrated in two of the more substantial revisions he made in the last stage of the journey when he prepared the second edition. In the original version, when the captain attempts to persuade Fanny to acquiesce in the will of his wicked master (3:12) by describing the "Splendor and Luxury" which should make her "despise that pitiful Fellow" (Joseph), she replies in the vein of romantic heroine that "the Riches of the World could not make her amends for the Loss of him; nor would she be persuaded to exchange him for the greatest Prince upon Earth." In the second edition, her response is quite different:

> She answered, She knew not whom he meant, she never was fond of any pitiful Fellow. "Are you affronted, Madam," says he, "at my calling him so? but what better can be said of one in a Livery, notwithstanding your Fondness for him?" She returned, That she did not understand him, that the Man had been her Fellow-Servant, and she believed was as honest a Creature as any alive; but as for Fondness for Men . . . .

By introducing this bit of affectation, Fielding not only made Fanny's behavior consistent with her similar pretense to Adams earlier (2:10), but he also insured that the abduction would remain within the realm of the comic, even as it reached its most desperate point.

A few pages later, in the most extended addition he made to the novel, Fielding delayed the "Procession" to Booby Hall with a dispute over transportation between Joseph and Adams, designed to counterbalance the effect of their previous disagreements and to head off an unsympathetic response to the recently emphasized exposure of the Parson's less attractive side. Joseph's respectful refusal to be mounted, "no not even to ride before his beloved Fanny, till the Parson was supplied," is emphasized by contrast with the whispered suggestion of one of the servants that he "suffer the old put to walk if he would," to which he responds "with an angry Look and a peremptory Refusal." To underscore the more fundamental moral differentiation which might be obscured in the developing distinction between the two good men, the narrator then explicitly contrasts their earnest reciprocal insistence on yielding place with the conventional insincerity of the world's *Alphonse-et-Gastonerie.*

The intentions demonstrable in these revisions, the awareness of the novel's form implicit in the details of its composition, are reflected in numerous other instances.[19] The kind of formal integration Fielding achieved in *Joseph Andrews* had not been previously attained in what we now call the novel. Yet it remains essentially an episodic narrative, a "series of actions, all tending to produce one great end." Much of its power derives from the quality of these several actions, and much of its art resides in their conception, construction, and representation. In composing the elements of his narrative, as in designing its "main end or scope," Fielding drew upon and modified the precedents of Cervantes and the other continental comic *romanciers.* Further light may be thrown on his achievement and its relation to the tradition if we supplement analysis of the novel's form with an assessment of his indebtedness and innovation in the construction of its "Circle of Incidents" and the fashioning of its narrative "Dress."

[19] See below, pp. 207–19 and 263–67.

II

Imitation and Invention: The Art of the Parts

Character and Action: Some Representative Adaptations

FIELDING is traditionally praised for his achievements in the depiction of character, an emphasis encouraged in *Joseph Andrews* by the apparently flimsy causal substratum of its plot, and by Fielding's own editorial preoccupation with this aspect of his and related works. In his Preface, he defined Hogarth's art as the depiction of the thoughts and affections of men and traced the comic essence to its source in the discrepancy between true and feigned character. Again in the opening chapter of book 3, he discussed his novel and its predecessors almost exclusively in terms of their portrayal of universal figures of human nature. Yet Aurelien Digeon's description of *Joseph Andrews* as "not a novel of action, but a character-novel" is quite misleading. If Fielding did not concentrate his invention on a succession of materially "curious" or sensational events like many earlier writers of fiction, he was rarely content "merely to place the characters into situations wherein their qualities will be displayed."[1] His characteristic

[1] *The Novels of Fielding* (London, 1925), p. 58.

tendency was to generate comic actions out of character in a way that belies Digeon's simple dichotomy.

This can be seen most clearly when Fielding's practice is compared with that of Lesage. The part of *Joseph Andrews* most closely resembling *Gil Blas* is Wilson's history. The pattern of Wilson's pursuit and rejection of the world's vanities resembles Gil Blas's corruption and reformation, but like Lesage's hero, he is less a character whose fortunes interest us than a device for displaying the town's follies and injustices in summary review—an aim reflected in the topical satiric organization discernible beneath the surface of his story. Within the framework of its sketchy reformation plot, or rather pseudoplot, Fielding's dissolute youth is conducted through a remarkably well-ordered life. An exposition of the life of the beau is followed by a section on sexual vices and foibles; in the third section Fielding covers a representative range of the town's social groups—tavern roisterers, a "philosophic" freethinkers club, poets and players, and gamesters; the survey concludes with an examination of the contemporary writer's hard lot. Within each of these sections, as in the movement from one to the next, the sequence of episodes is determined by the author's program of subjects more than by any internal principle of development within the story. Proceeding systematically in his tabulation of some common types of vicious sexual behaviour, Fielding juxtaposes the naïve Wilson's betrayal by his first case-hardened mistress to his own heartless seduction of an innocent young girl, then contrasts his frustrated pursuit of that "*Ignis Fatuus*," the coquette, with the opposite but equally unsatisfactory affair with an insatiable cit's wife. Having run through a brief permutative analysis of the subject, he terminates the sex life of the hitherto concupiscent Wilson to move on to his next topic. With similar arbitrariness, he institutes the literary phase of his satire by planting in his head "the strangest Thought imaginable . . . and what was this, but to write a Play?" And when he has carried his London Rasselas through a sufficient range of the town's activities to warrant the conclusion that "the Pleasures of the World are chiefly Folly, and the Business of it mostly Knavery; and both, nothing better than Vanity," he contrives a comparably mechanical conclusion to his advenures, extracting him from debtors prison and transforming him into a model of sober diligence and conjugal fidelity through the agency of a newly minted heiress for whom Wilson has "long conceived a violent Passion" (though he has given no hint of her existence before she descends from the machine).[2]

The same employment of mimetic means in the service of an essentially rhetorical or didactic conception is evident in the story's incidents. The response of the flirtatious Saphira to the proposal of the young man she has led on—"She wondered what I had seen in her Conduct, which could induce me to affront her in this manner"—is not, like comparable righteous outbursts from Lady Booby and Leonora (see below, pp. 158–

[2] Gil Blas's rambling autobiography exhibits a similar, although more loosely ordered, topical procedure, as the protagonist moves through various walks of life; and he also retires from the world's vanities to rural domesticity after his release from prison. There is a more particular resemblance between Wilson's writing love letters to himself and the fatal folly of Don Mathias de Silva (*Gil Blas* 3 : 8). As Wilson remarks, this pretense occurs in a number of stage comedies, and it may only be a coincidence that both Lesage's and Fielding's episodes turn upon the resultant challenge to a duel. If Fielding did have Lesage's incident particularly in mind, his redirection of it is another indication of the satiric conception of Wilson's tale. Lesage focuses on the individual folly of the *petit-maitre;* his death in the duel which he approaches as mindlessly as he has previously persisted in taunting the defender of defamed virtue is the product of his own extravagance. Fielding deflects the point of his attack from the relatively innocent beau to the vicious town. When Wilson's casual defamation is given the lie by an officer, he does not overreach himself, like the foolish Don Mathias, but prudently withdraws—and finds himself a social outcast. Then an "honest elderly Man" in "Compassion for my Youth" explains his crime, encourages him to "shew the World I was not such a Rascal as they thought me to be" by issuing a challenge to the man who has checked his libel, and volunteers to deliver it "out of pure Charity."

161 and 188), a surprising comic development so much as an illustration of the "particular kind of Folly, I . . . endeavour to describe." Surprise is precluded by an extended analysis of the coquette, the type of which Saphira is a representative instance, *preceding* the event. Similarly, the point of Wilson's experience with the "Rule of Right" club is not the comic discovery of the discrepancy between these gentlemen's theory and their practice, but satiric exposure of the fallacy of a moral system governed solely "by the infallible Guide of Human Reason." In analogous fashion, the account of the young girl's ruin and the record of Wilson's later misfortunes are not conceived as particular actions evoking pathos or indignation but as representative instances of the town's corruption and of the modern author's painful dependence on elusive patrons, whimsical managers, and Grub Street exploiters for his uncertain livelihood.

Only in the unparticularized incidents of these illustrative adventures—where epitome and abstraction serve to generalize the world's imperfect state as Adams' simplicity is being brought into critical contrast with his friends' circumspection, without obtruding excessively on the primary narrative—does Fielding approach the simple exposition of foibles to be found in two of the episodes he cited as instances of Lesage's biographical veracity. Having invented that earnest fraud, Dr. Sangrado, Lesage devised no more for him to do than expatiate intermittently on his absurd aquatic doctrines. Still more static and undeveloped are the successive discrtete portraits in which the members of "Le Bureau des Ouvrages d' esprit" (4:8) pass in review. Fielding, on the other hand, usually puts his most incidental characters to work, involving them in some larger comic action, as when the false wit of the Italianate traveler embellishes Adams' hogsblood drenching (2:5), or a country parson's feigned learning performs a key function in the unfolding farce of Adams' arraignment (2:11). The literary and theatrical satire of Lesage's surveys of green room and tavern are incorporated in a dynamic interaction between a poet and a player (see below, pp. 165–66). Even in what appears to be a pause in the action, Fielding's inclination to develop clearly structured comic actions transmutes exposition of Adams' background and incidental political satire into a neatly turned little three-act ironic comedy, dramatizing through the parson's account of his electoral "successes" (2:8) his equal innocence of his neighbors' insincerity and his own misplaced vanity.[3]

Fielding's stagecoach episode at first appears to answer Digeon's description: as the passengers successively react to Joseph's plight with affected modesty, fear of robbery, and apprehension of legal culpability, they seem arbitrarily placed in a situation in which their unsympathetic traits may be mechanically displayed. But, in contrast to Lesage's static group portraits, these divergent attitudes quickly draw the passengers into a four-way conflict with the coachman over the injured man's fate, a dispute which culminates in the irony of his being rescued out of a singularly unattractive complex of motives—

[3] In the course of his unfolding political career, Adams persuades his alderman nephew to support three consecutive winning candidates and is successively rewarded with the loss of his curacy; its restoration together with eight pounds "to buy me a Gown and Cassock, and furnish my House"; and the unkept promise of a living. His first candidate runs against the court party on the cry "the *Church* . . . in Danger," but once elected takes up town residence and "never so much as goeth to Church," and after getting a Place he campaigns for the very court candidate he previously defeated. Yet Adams numbers the loss of his curacy in support of this gentleman among the "Opportunities" he has "not been without" of "suffering for the sake of my Conscience." The parson's second choice, "a worthy Man, and the best Friend I ever had," vows to "sacrifice every thing to his Country; and I believe he would, except his Hunting, which he stuck so close to, that in Five Years together, he went but twice up to Parliament." His third favorite, the late Sir Thomas Booby, is "a very fine Parliament-Man," for "he made Speeches of an Hour long"—but "could never persuade the Parliament to be of his Opinion." Yet Adams can conclude by envisaging the possibility that his son (whose ordination Sir Thomas "and the other honest Gentlemen my Neighbours" have promised "these five Years") may "be of as much consequence in a public Light, as his Father once was," assuring the patriot that "he will use his Talents as honestly as I have done."

the fare-grudging coachman yielding to the lawyer's self-serving threat of prosecution and the old man's mischievously actuated bounty, while the suddenly unprotesting lady confines herself to holding the "Sticks of her Fan before her Eyes."

In the next turn of the episode, Digeon's formulation and Fielding's theory coincide. To the waggish gentleman's suggestion that she offer Joseph some spirits to warm him, the lady resentfully replies "she never tasted any such thing"; a moment later the coach is stopped by the highwaymen, and "the Lady, in her Fright, delivered up a little silver Bottle, of about a half-pint Size, which the Rogue, clapping it to his Mouth, and drinking her Health, declared held some of the best *Nantes* he had ever tasted." Such a peremptory unmasking might be expected from a writer who observed that the comic effect is produced "in higher and stronger Degree" when we "discover any one to be the exact Reverse of what he affects." But this character exposure does not set Fielding's work off from earlier fiction, as Digeon would have it. The ironic catastrophe of Gil Blas's faithful service to the Archbishop of Granada (7:4) similarly discloses the power of the prelate's vanity over his own self-regarding effort to outwit it. The sequel of this episode and a parallel incident in *Marianne* are more precisely anticipatory of Fielding's unmasking formula and the kind of ethical matter in which he embodied it. A priest whom Gil Blas has restored to favor effuses gratitude and offers of service until the former secretary informs him of his own fall from episcopal grace, whereupon "il devint froid et rêveur," and hastily departs. The prioress who is all tender compassion for the maiden seeking sanctuary executes a similar *volte face* when she learns she is a penniless orphan: "il n'y eut plus ni de ma belle enfant, ni de mon ange; toutes ces douceurs furent supprimées."[4]

In reducing these precedents to the formulary outline of the lady passenger's unmasking, Fielding may have been clarifying

[4] *Marianne*, p. 153.

their basic structure in keeping with his notion of the surprising discovery of affectation;[5] but it was not as a paradigm that he set it before the reader at the outset of his central comic journey. Rather it establishes a kind of bench mark against which to measure the diversity of his comic invention. Recognizing that the formal, almost academic, clarity of an incident so transparently drawn to fit his theory would soon make the discovery of affectation predictable rather than surprising, he created only two more of its kind, and in each of these he endeavored to disguise the mechanism of the formula exposed by the very brevity of the prude's unmasking. Between the fire-eating patriot's initial display of pugnacity (2:7) and the discovery of his cowardice (2:9), Fielding diverts attention to Adams' political history. The prevailing fraudulence of political catchwords in that chronicle may suggest that the shooter's blustery contempt for anyone who won't "sacrifice his Life for his Country" is of the same order, but the apparent function of his remarks as the occasion for Adams' dissertation—a surmise Fielding fosters by postponing the discovery for some time after the gentleman has ended his heroic rant—throws the reader off the track. The event precipitating this discovery (Fanny's screams) proves to be no simple contrivance designed for that end but a major surprise in itself and the beginning of a sustained chain of incident. Similarly, the unmasking of the snobbish "Miss *Grave-airs*" a few chapters earlier (2:5) is embedded in a matrix of action that propels the incident unexpectedly

[5] Marivaux undercuts the potential surprise of his reversal by having Marianne describe the nun's true character at the beginning of the scene. The reversal in the archbishop episode does not turn upon the discrepancy between the prelate's assumed and real character. Having attained his position of special trust by flattering the very weakness which brings his downfall, Gil Blas anticipates that his master may react precisely as he does, and the ticklish choice between this likelihood and disinheritance for neglecting his charge is at the center of the comedy. The unexpected turn comes in the archbishop's reason for dismissing his secretary: "Je ne trouve point du tout mauvais que vous me disiez votre sentiment. C'est votre sentiment seul que je trouve mauvais" (*Gil Blas* 2 : 30–31).

beyond its formulaic ending: instead of being pleased at the discovery that her haughty antagonist is an ex-postilion's daughter, as Adams encourages the reader to anticipate, the prudent Slipslop is alarmed, for the daughter of a great family's steward is more to be feared than a modestly situated gentlewoman.

The patriot's exposure is the only one of these incidents to occupy more than a passing moment in the narrative. If Fielding did not produce any more of them, it may also have been because the simple discovery of affectation in itself did not offer enough scope for the development of an extended action. When he did generate one of his principal incidents out of the nucleus of character exposure, he broke out of the simple reversal formula found in Lesage and Marivaux. Parson Adams' encounter with the liberally promising squire (2:16) is particularly revealing of the characteristic direction of Fielding's invention, as well as of the complexity of his imitation. One of the members of the Marquise de Chaves' salon is a bishop who "fait des offres de service à tout le monde, et ne sert personne."

> Ce Prélat est d'un caractere assez plaisant: il a quelque crédit à la Cour; mais il voudroit bien persuader qu'il en a beaucoup. . . . Un jour il recontre chez le Roi un Cavalier qui le salue; il l'arrête, l'accable de civilités, et lui serrant la main: Je suis, lui dit-il, tout acquis à votre Seigneurie. Mettez-moi, de grâce, à l'épreuve; je ne mourrai point content, si je ne trouve une occasion de vous obliger. Le Cavalier le remercia d'une maniere pleine de reconnoissance; et quand ils furent tous deux séparés, le Prélat dit à un de ses Officiers qui le suivoit: Je crois connoître cet homme-là: j'ai une idée confuse de l'avoir vû quelque part.[6]

Out of what Lesage dispatched in an anecdote, Fielding evolves a carefully structured extended action. Mindful that his reader, now halfway through the novel and having the immediately preceding encounter with Trulliber freshly in mind, is not easily to be surprised by a new disclosure of insincerity, he first

[6] *Gil Blas* 1 : 319.

skillfully draws him into sharing Adams' favorable view of the gentleman. His "courteous and obliging . . . Answer, accompanied with so smiling a Countenance" to Adams' request for directions is a pleasant contrast to the curse which answered the Parson's previous inquiry of this kind; his offer of a friendly glass appears to be a continuation of the good fortune the travelers have just had in the unexpected benevolence of the peddler; his approval of Adams' attitude toward his young charges contrasts with Slipslop's recently witnessed hostility; and his denunciation of a proud priest who might be another Trulliber, has, except for one tell-tale phrase (which I have bracketed) the very ring of Fielding's own rhetoric:

I am sorry to say the Parson of our Parish instead of esteeming his poor Parishioners as a part of his Family, seems rather to consider them as not of the same Species with himself. He seldom speaks to any unless some few of the richest of us; nay indeed, he will not move his Hat to the others. [I often laugh when I behold him on *Sundays* strutting along the Church-Yard, like a Turky-Cock], through Rows of his Parishioners; who bow to him with as much Submission and are as unregarded as a Sett of servile Courtiers by the proudest Prince in *Christendom*. But if such temporal Pride is ridiculous, surely the spiritual is odious and detestable: if such a puffed up empty human Bladder strutting in princely Robes, justly moves one's Derision; surely in the Habit of a Priest it must raise our Scorn.

But beyond this care in making the promiser's fraudulence unexpected Fielding gives the whole episode a fresh turn from the predictable pattern of its simpler antecedents. For here the reader's discovery of the promiser's true character is only the preliminary to the real comedy of the incident. When the gentleman, on the strength of a few minutes' acquaintance, offers the penurious Adams a three hundred pound living, the reader suspects he is a fraud. His subsequent purely suppositional offers of a chaplaincy (if Adams were not married) and a farm (if his wife could manage a dairy) amusingly confirm this suspicion. Thus informed of the imposture, the reader can enjoy the process of Adams' extraordinarily slow discovery of the same fact.

The structure of that process, and the overall shape of the episode, in which the prospective recipient of wealth and patronage is by stages reduced to vainly soliciting his benefactor for three half crowns, may have been suggested by the hungry Sancho Panza's colloquy with an innkeeper whose hearty proffer of "Fish or Flesh, Butcher's Meat or Poultry, Wild-Fowl . . . Whatever Land, Sea, and Air afford" dwindles sequentially with the guest's successive selections to "a delicate Pair of Cow-heels that look like Calves Feet, or a Pair of Calves Feet that look like Cow heels" (pt. 2, chap. 59). The way the publican's chapter of accidents—chickens devoured by kites, pullets gone to market, veal eaten by the last guest—and his assurance that "by next Week we shall have enough to spare" anticipate the gentleman's pretexts and protestations strongly suggests that Fielding consciously adapted the serial structure of this brief vaudeville turn to amplify the process of Adams' discovery for maximal effect. The predictable formulaic ending might have come with the departure of the promiser at the close of the episode's primary scene. His last-minute withdrawal of proffered hospitality on the excuse of his housekeeper's having locked up his rooms offers a natural occasion for the discovery of his true character. Again, his reneging on the substitute offer of horses seems to afford a logical conclusion. It is now the "morning after," and the travelers have had time to reflect on his behavior. The anticipatory dispute between Joseph and Adams over their use of the horses looks designed to heighten the climax of their nonappearance. And the pretext for this disappointment—the gentleman's whole stable have been physicked without his knowledge—is so patly contrived and similar to the previous excuse that even Adams might be expected to see through it. Instead he is so concerned for the gentleman thus victimized by his servants that Joseph is required to remind him of the practical exigencies of their own situation, whereupon the episode approaches the last rungs of the ladder of diminishing beneficence. Still Fielding manages to defer the inevitable. When the messenger sent to request the money needed for their reckoning returns, after an ominous delay, to report the gentleman's absence, Adams confidently redispatches him to await his appearance. Even when the lad again returns with the implausible news that their suppositious patron has gone on a long journey, Adams rebukes Joseph's knowledgeable suspicion and must be finally disabused by the host. In thus suspending Adams' inordinately slow "take" past several points at which the inference would seem inescapable, Fielding demonstrates vividly the extent of his comic hero's innocent good nature, not by creating a situation in which it may be displayed, but by developing an effectively teasing structure of comic action.

Fielding's distinctive interest in constructing comic actions is illuminated in another way when one compares his practice with its antecedents in the kind of comic romance incident most conspicuously answerable to the name of action—the numerous fights and other disturbances to be found in *Don Quixote* and *Le Roman comique*. Although Cervantes, as part of his ridicule of the chivalric romances, thrust his decrepit warrior into "battles" with a frequency exceeding that of *Amadis de Gaul*, he put principal emphasis on his hero's capacity for finding challenges in the most innocent circumstances, and hence upon the bizarre conception of the battle more than the battle itself. Occasionally he burlesques the hyperbolic renditions of romantic combat, but in the fights with the windmills and the sheep, as in most episodes of this kind, the actual combat is less important than the knight and squire's discussions of the event. A grosser vein of physical comedy, exemplified in Sancho's blanket tossing, his master's bout with the wineskins, the emetic catastrophe of "Fierabrass's balsam," and the battle royal in the innyard, was broadened by Scarron to the confusion and grotesque spectacle of his fracases and melees. The "surprizing and bloody Adventures" punctuating Fielding's narrative bear general resemblances to the practice of both writers. Adams' assault by the hunting party (3:6) is reminiscent of Quixote's encounters with even stranger opponents, and the kitchen battle in which he is doused with hogsblood (2:5) and the night scene at Lady Booby's (4:14) both contain echoes of *Don Quixote* and *Le Roman comique*. But Fielding's primary interest in the construction of these scenes of comic violence is in neither the oddity of their conception nor merely their confusion and spectacle, but, characteristically, in their structural development as unfolding comic actions. In particular, those incidents which appear to be directly inspired by earlier scenes are written as if to improve upon his models, enriching their material by infusing the hurly-burly with character comedy, and forming them into complex comic structures.

Thus, although the movement of Fielding's first inn battle (2:5) generally resembles that of Scarron's "combat inégal" (*Roman comique* 2:7) in a similar setting, the two episodes are conceived quite differently. Starting as a quarrel between Rancune and the widow of the dead innkeeper whose corpse he has used in a practical joke, Scarron's scene progressively expands to include the other players and a reinforcement of neighbors to support the landlady's cause, until it becomes a pitched furniture battle. Fielding's incident begins with the hostess attending to Joseph's injured leg, and in rapid succession the host, Adams, the hostess, and Slipslop are drawn into conflict, until the scene concludes with the tableau of the host laid out, Adams doused in hogsblood, and Slipslop triumphantly holding aloft a handful of her opponent's hair. But Fielding does not bring his characters into the action to swell the hurly-burly. Instead, he creates a kind of tag match, in which the duel passes from one pair of antagonists to another until it amusingly comes full circle: the host damns his wife for helping Joseph; his inhumanity arouses Adams; when he knocks out her husband, the hostess drenches the parson; Slipslop then retaliates; and the host upon reviving damns his wife for wasting the puddings. Adams' bizarre blood bath is but one of the surprising comic turns in the unfolding process of the fight, in which the men are successively rendered *hors de combat* and the women take over the battle, with Slipslop unexpectedly cast as Adams' avenger and the hostess rising to the sanguine defense of her despotic spouse, only (like Trulliber's wife) to be damned for her effort.

The character of Scarron's disputants is largely undifferentiated and contributes little or nothing to the comedy of his battles. His fights usually arise out of simple accidents or his characters' general predisposition to quarrel. Even in the previously mentioned incident, where the cause is more specific, the fact that his mock hero is a rogue capable of body snatching for a prank and that his opponents are the dead man's mourners has no significance beyond providing the occasion for the fight. But from the initial contrast between the hostess' care for Joseph's injury and her husband's flippant suggestion of amputation Fielding develops an interaction whose course is determined by the diverse dispositions of its participants. The host is a "surly Fellow, who always proportioned his Respect to the Appearance of a Traveller," the hostess "a better Wife than so surly a Husband deserved." There is more than a shade of difference between her uxorial "assistance, or rather . . . revenge" and the not altogether generous impulse of the aggressive Slipslop, who, "not being of a Temper so extremely cool and patient as perhaps was required to ask many Questions on this Occasion [her discovery of the gory Adams]; flew with great Impetuosity" at the hostess, "giving her . . . several hearty Cuffs in the Face, which by frequent Practice on the inferiour Servants, she had learned an excellent Knack of delivering with a good Grace." The comedy of violence is thus merged with the comedy of character, and the amusement of the fight itself is supplemented by our sense of the wry injustice by which "the poor Woman" whose charitable act precipitated the conflict "had indeed fared much the worst."[7]

The other episode in which Fielding approaches most closely the characteristic comic mayhem of Scarron, the fight preceding the abduction of Fanny (3:9), involves no admixture of this ironic comedy.[8] But even in this simple physical action the gross details are effectively subordinated. For Fielding the chamber pot is not the fountainhead of humor, but a "low" element which lends itself effectively to his burlesque of Homer.[9] And, though he follows the splashing of its contents in the captain's face with Adams' receipt of a filthy mop in his, neither of these events is treated as the climax of the incident, as it might be for Scarron, and neither is allowed to stop the onward movement of the battle, nor to distract Fielding from his primary interest in revealing its course in detail:

> Hitherto Fortune seemed to incline the Victory on the Travellers side, when, according to her Custom, she began to shew the Fickleness of her Disposition: for now the Host entering the Field, or rather Chamber, of Battle, flew directly at *Joseph*, and darting his Head into his Stomach (for he was a stout Fellow, and an expert Boxer) almost staggered him; but *Joseph* stepping one Leg back, did with his left Hand so chuck him under the Chin that he reeled. The Youth was pursuing his Blow with his right Hand, when he received from one of the Servants such a Stroke with a Cudgel on his Temples, that it instantly deprived him of Sense, and he measured his Length on the Ground.

[7] For the relation of this incident to one in *Don Quixote*, see below, p. 190.

[8] The fight itself, however, is preceded by the sardonic pseudocontrast between the poet, "who prudently retreated down Stairs, saying it was his Business to record great Actions, and not to do them" and the Captain, who "was no sooner well satisfied that there were no Fire-Arms, than bidding Defiance to Gunpowder, and swearing he loved the Smell of it, he ordered the Servants to follow him."

[9] See below, p. 245.

Significantly, it is in his specifically mock-epic "battles"—this preabduction fight, Adams' and Joseph's defenses of Fanny's virtue (2:9 and 4:7), and the "Hunting Adventure" (3:6)—that Fielding's interest in clearly outlining the movement of the action itself, as compared to Scarron's emphasis on spectacular confusion and Cervantes' preoccupation with the fantastic conception of his hero's combats, emerges most strikingly. In each of these incidents, he traces the seesaw course of an exciting contest in which one side is first in the ascendancy and then the tide is dramatically reversed. In thus constructing his miniature battles, Fielding apparently had his eye on neither Cervantes nor Scarron, but the "great Original" whose narrative mannerisms he burlesques in these incidents. If one compares these incidents with the duel between Hector and Ajax (*Iliad* 7:244–75), for example, it is apparent that Fielding has ingeniously applied Homer's circumstantial account of the grand actions and counteractions of heroic spear combat to the homely maneuvers of rough and tumble fistfighting, making vivid and distinct each stroke and counter while preserving, as Homer does, the overall sense of movement in the contest. This transfer of manner adds to that special amusement of "the classical Reader" to which Fielding referred in the Preface, but it also provided him with the means of constructing dramatic slow motion, fast action battles. This unique mixture of mock-heroic and straight excitement is particularly well suited to the seriocomic treatment of the "dangers" to the lovers required by the form of the novel.

The "Hunting Adventure" appears to be of a different order from these lesser fights. Here, if anywhere, we might expect to find that "diminution of the reader's belief in the authenticity of . . . the action" which, according to Ian Watt, "occurs whenever the usual tenor of Fielding's narrative is interrupted by the stylistic devices of epic."[10] But even when Fielding indulges in

[10] *The Rise of the Novel* (Berkeley, 1957), p. 255.

burlesque to the top of his bent, his interest in the unfolding action of battle and concern for the movement of the incident as a whole are discernible, as can be seen most clearly by comparing the dogs' battle with its closest analogue in *Don Quixote*. This is not Quixote's battle with the sheep, nor his demolition of a puppet show (pt. 2, chap. 26), nor his fight with a bag of belled cats (pt. 2, chap. 46), despite the similarity of materials. In the sheep and puppet incidents, the comedy resides chiefly in the mad conception of the battle; in the cat fight, primarily in the chaotic din of the struggle in the dark. The genius of Fielding's incident does not lie simply in the idea of a battle between men and dogs, nor in the spectacle of the contest, though each of these contributes something, but in the brilliant fusing of this idea with a parody of the *Iliad*. Hence the formal analogue to Fielding's dog battle is Cervantes' most fully developed parody of the chivalric duels in *Amadis de Gaul* and its like, the "stupendous combat between the brave Biscayan and the valorous Don Quixote" (pt. 1, 1:8–2:1). This is the most extensively represented of Quixote's combats, for as part of his burlesque Cervantes spreads this exchange of three strokes over two chapters bridging a book division, distending the narrative with hyperbolic descriptions of the wrath of Quixote, the resolution of the Biscayan, the terror of the onlookers, and the exact career and consequence of each stroke, and then humorously suspending the action with the combatants' swords poised to strike while the author goes off in search of the continuation of his supposedly incomplete manuscript.

Now Fielding's hunting adventure is even more inflated with the machinery of epic narration, and the fact that it too contains an extended digression midway through the incident suggests that Fielding may have had his eye on Cervantes' episode. But Fielding's lengthy epic pause does not break the movement of the battle, as Cervantes' deliberately does. It separates its preliminary phase, in which Adams is hounded into flight, from the mock-heroic battle proper, which begins with the introduction of Joseph into the field, with all the paraphernalia which accompanies the long-awaited entrance of Achilles in the *Iliad*. Whereas Cervantes' interruption makes a joke of the notion of suspense, leaving his combatants preposterously poised for several pages, Fielding builds comic suspense by having his narrator try to get on with the action, only to keep tripping over his epic conventions. After his burlesque invocation, he launches into the formula for rapid action: "No sooner did *Joseph Andrews* perceive the Distress of his Friend . . . than he grasped his Cudgel in his right Hand"—but the hero's weapon must be described, including the scenes *not* depicted thereon. After this delay, the narrator again tries to move ahead: "No sooner had *Joseph* grasped his Cudgel . . . than . . . the heroick Youth . . . ran with the utmost speed to his Friend's assistance"; but in his determination to get on in his "Description, which should be *rapid* in this Part," the narrator formally eschews the simile and thus manages to delay the commencement of the action once more. In contrast to Cervantes' journey into the Arab quarter in search of manuscript, this little comedy of the writer's difficulties does not take us out of the action completely but builds up the reader's expectancy for the battle and heightens, by contrast, its vivid impression of furious action. Thus, even when indulging his burlesque bent to the full, Fielding never loses sight of the overall shape of the battle as an action. And Joseph's ensuing slaughter of the pack, for all its parody of the wrath of Achilles, is at the same time a more vivid and detailed account of the action of a fight than one finds in Cervantes or Scarron.[11]

The culmination of Fielding's physical comedy is reached at the close of the novel in the "several curious Night-Adventures,

[11] Compare the whirlwind catalogue of Joseph's victims with the *Iliad* 22 : 455–90. For further discussion of the mock-heroic vein of the narration see below, chap. 9.

in which *Mr. Adams* fell into many Hair-breadth 'Scapes" (4:14). In making this the climactic comic episode of the book, Fielding seems to be deliberately reminding the reader of the broad tradition in which he is writing. Even the "mere *English* Reader" would be likely to recognize "the mistake in the night" as a commonplace of earlier comic fiction. In *Le Roman comique* alone there are three such incidents. La Rappinière, waking to find his wife absent, jealously follows her supposed footsteps, falls, and is discovered grappling with a nanny goat (1:4); Ragotin, staggering about in a drunken stupor, takes the wrong turn and goes to sleep in a crude straw bed instead of his own (1:11); when a peddler mistakenly returns to the wrong room from the privy, Rancune takes advantage of his error to steal from his pack (3:4). Didapper's mistaking of Slipslop's room for Fanny's, and Adams' wrong turn in leaving the same chamber obviously relate to these incidents in a general way, but there is a more striking resemblance between Fielding's episode and a scene in *Don Quixote* (pt. 1, 3:2).[12] While the injured knight lies fantasying that the "Daughter to the Lord of the Castle" (the innkeeper), "strangely captivated with his graceful Presence and Gallantry, had promis'd him the Pleasure of her Embraces," the "kind-hearted" Maritornes, grotesque ancestor of Fielding's warm-natured Betty, passes his bed on her way to keep an assignation with a mule driver. Under the spell of his romantic fantasy, Quixote embraces the wench. Her effort to disengage herself rouses her lover, who beats Quixote. When her master comes to quell the disturbance, Maritornes hides in Sancho's bed and they are soon exchanging blows. The scene culminates in "a strange Multiplication of Fisticuffs and Drubbings" in the dark. "The Carrier pommell'd

[12] Ehrenpreis, pp. 29–30, refers to Cervantes' scene along with others from *Guzman de Alfarache* and *Pamela* (Mr. B. "dressed as a girl and bedded with Pamela"), but seems to regard a very different kind of episode from Marivaux's *Pharsamon* as the closest analogue of Fielding's incident.

Sancho, Sancho mawl'd the Wench, the Wench belabour'd the Squire, and Inn-keeper thrash'd her again."

The parallels between this incident and Fielding's episode are too numerous and particular to be accidental. Cervantes' scene begins with Quixote madly mistaking the servant girl for a princess ("Her Breath, that had a stronger *Hogoe* than stale Venison, was to him a grateful Compound of the most fragrant Perfumes of *Arabia*. . . . He thought he had no less than a balmy *Venus* in his Arms, while he hugg'd a fulsome Bundle of Deformities, that would have turn'd any Man's Stomach but a sharp-set Carrier's"); Fielding's with Didapper's taking Slipslop for "his Angel," the delicious Fanny ("A Savour now invaded his Nostrils which he did not expect in the Room of so sweet a young Creature, and which might have probably had no good effect on a cooler Lover"). Adams enters the struggle in response to Slipslop's cries as the muleteer intervenes in behalf of his love. The exchange of blows amidst the bedsheets between the parson and Slipslop corresponds to that between Sancho and Maritornes, with Adams taking his opponent for a devil and then a witch, even as Sancho believes his antagonist to be "the Night-Mare." In Cervantes' episode Maritornes' master enters to dispel the darkness; in Fielding's it is Slipslop's mistress who enters with a light. As Maritornes departs from Quixote's bed, the arena of the first part of the action, to curl up "round as an Egg" in Sancho's bed, which then becomes the center of the fray, so Fielding's narrative follows Adams as he departs from Slipslop's bed, the original battleground, to curl up at the foot of Fanny's. And as Quixote, in the aftermath of his adventure, attributes his misfortune to the work of enchanters, so Adams at the close of Fielding's episode attributes his predicament to witchcraft.[13]

[13] The hypothesis is strengthened by the similarities between the descriptions of Maritones and Slipslop (see below, p. 232). Fielding may even have been inviting the reader familiar with *Don Quixote* to watch him outdo his

These close parallels between the two scenes afford a special opportunity to compare Fielding's comic art with that of Cervantes. Cervantes' incident is itself richer and more amplified than the kind of simple night mistakes found in Scarron. It stems not from a simple mistake but from the convergence of Maritornes' visit with the knight's fantasy. The discrepancy between Quixote's idealized vision and the gross facts of reality is nowhere more vividly and amusingly dramatized. This specific Quixotic comedy reaches its climax in the absurd romantic "interview" in which the faithful servant of Dulcinea gallantly begs the "lady's" forgiveness for not being free to fulfill her desires, all the while clasping the struggling wench to him. When this passage of romantic love is terminated by his drubbing at the hands and feet of the muleteer, the usual formula of Don Quixote's "adventures" is complete. Cervantes' continuation of the episode builds its physical comedy to a wild climax, but in another sense the structure of the episode is anticlimactic. The comic hero (and with him the specific comedy of character) drops out with the collapse of his bed in the middle of the action, and the generic rough-and-tumble humor is inevitably less interesting.

Fielding extends his episode in very different fashion. As if deliberately to outdo Cervantes as well as Scarron, and to have some fun with the stock night accident, he incorporates within his scene no less than three such mistakes in succession, each of which gives the action a surprising new comic turn. The first

---

master as he brings his "imitation of Cervantes" to a close. For such a reader there would be an added amusement in the ironic variations worked upon the details of his model. Whereas Maritones is only stung by Sancho's blows into "forgetting the Danger she was in, and her dear Reputation," Slipslop, with "wonderful Presence of Mind," seizes upon the invasion of her bed as "an Opportunity to heal some Wounds, which her late Conduct had, she feared, given her Reputation." Consequently, in place of the enamored knight detaining the struggling girl, in Fielding's episode it is the burly gentlewoman who holds the disabused seducer fast. And Adams, coming to the aid of the damsel in distress, delivers the effeminate ravisher from his whiskered victim.

phase of the action, Didapper's unfortunate mistaking of Slipslop's room for Fanny's and their comic tussle, might have sufficed Scarron as an incident, but this is only the preliminary to Fielding's main bout, which begins when Adams mistakes the sex of these combatants. Again, Scarron, or Cervantes, might have been content to terminate the tussle between Slipslop and Adams with the simple introduction of light and the resultant recognition between the disputants. But Fielding's lady with the lamp is no undifferentiated incidental figure, employed as a device for ending the scene, and so we have the ironic comedy of the novel's comic villainess and principal sexual hypocrite indignantly denouncing the perfect innocent for "chusing her House for the Scene of his Debaucheries." After this climax, when Adams is exonerated and the confusion resolved, the reader might well expect that these "several curious night adventures" are at an end. But Adams takes the wrong turn and ends up in Fanny's bed. Again, this little action might in itself have sufficed Scarron for a comic incident, which he might have completed, as he did Ragotin's nocturnal error, with the simple discovery of the situation and his attribution of it to supernatural causes. These elements are present in Fielding's scene, but the bed into which the parson has wandered is not merely a filthy one or that of some indifferent figure, nor is the person who discovers him a mere amused spectator, and so to the irony of Lady Booby's denunciation of Adams is added that of his being suspected by his young friends and charges.

Thus, in clear contrast to the movement from the central comedy of Quixote's mania to the scufflings of Sancho and three incidental characters, Fielding, applying the lesson of Cervantes' own improvement upon the central sequence of part 1 (see above, pp. 39–40), commences with the peripheral comedy of Didapper's mistake and goes on to involve the comic protagonist with the other four principal characters of the novel. This is not merely a physical interaction, but, as in the earlier inn battle, an interplay of divergent personalities, and the reader's full appreciation of the comedy is dependent on his awareness of the relations of these characters and their actions to the previous actions of the novel. While building an effectively sustained sequence of comic surprises from the stock materials of the night mistake, Fielding summarizes the comic actions of the novel in successive tableaux depicting the bizarre misunderstandings of the comic hero with the two comic villainesses and with the young lovers, and all this without any sense of contrived arrangement.

As against the simple and rather mechanistic one-character comedy of the unmasking, the traditional episodes of uproar and accident obviously afforded dramatic action. Yet even under Fielding's transmutation they offered only a comparatively limited role for character. His first major "violent Scene," the Tow-wouses' row (1:17), indicates the direction in which he was to develop his most singular kind of comic action. There the comic wonder and physical turmoil of Cervantes' and Scarron's comparable dramatic interruptions[14] are supplanted by a largely verbal uproar, with Mrs. Tow-wouse declaiming like the injured matron in a restoration tragedy,[15] and the unfortunate Betty patiently enduring "Slut," "Trollop," and "Whore," but suddenly incensed at the appellation "Bitch." In the less violent and more extended "Interviews" at the heart of his comedy, Fielding found a way of "naturally" exposing affectation while exploiting the unrealized possibilities of dynamic development in a kind of action that would not appear to war-

[14] The offstage eruption of Quixote's battle with the wineskins breaks in upon the narration of "The Curious Impertinent" (pt. 1, 4:8). The wild free-for-all of the *Combat de Nuit* (*Roman comique* 1:12) similarly interrupts Destin's history just as it is underway.

[15] Fielding also manages to incorporate a jesting glance at *Pamela*: "O you damn'd Villain, is this the Return to all the Care I have taken of your Family? This the Reward of my Virtue? Is this the manner in which you behave to one who brought you a Fortune, and preferred you to so many Matches, all your Betters? To abuse my Bed, my own Bed, with my own Servant. . . ."

rant the name. If, as George Sherburn has suggested, the "real art" of *Joseph Andrews* "lies not in the puppet-like manipulation of the persons but in their psychology,"[16] that psychology is most trenchantly realized and skillfully employed in the dramatic dialogue of innocence and affectation.

[16] *A Literary History of England*, ed. A.C. Baugh (New York, 1948), p. 956.

Dialogue as Action

THE basic device of Fielding's second parody of *Pamela*—the transposition of sexual roles—is such a classically simple stroke of comic inspiration that it may seem invidious to remark that there are a number of obvious analogues of the scenes between Joseph and Lady Booby to be found in the continental comic romances.[1] But the fact that Fielding's con-

[1] Besides the incidents discussed below, young Jacob flirts with his mistress, whom he finds at her *toilette* "dans un certain desordre assez piquant" (*Le Paysan parvenu,* pp. 14–16), and a priest in Girault's third part of *Le Roman comique* recounts the provocative bedside advances made by his mistress when he is a young servant (*Roman comique*, pp. 383–84). By the early eighteenth century, the situation was sufficiently familiar to enable Lesage to play upon the stock expectation to heighten the surprise of one of his hero's most amusing reversals (4 : 1–2). Shortly after entering the service of Don Vincent de Guzman, Gil Blas notes that his young mistress favors him over the other servants. When Aurore smilingly welcomes him to a midnight rendezvous in her boudoir "en déshabillé" and tells him her favor will be demonstrated by "la démarche que je fais cette nuit," his erotic expectations seem to be realized and he throws himself at her feet, "comme un heros de théâtre qui se met à genoux devant sa Princesse"—only to be told that she has selected him as her confidential agent in her amorous pursuit of another man. Anticipations of Fielding's episode are even to be found in *Don Quixote.* Maritornes' appearance in the knight's bedchamber is preceded by a fantasy

ception, which at some stage of his invention obviously drew upon the biblical paradigm, may have been nourished by his acquaintance with earlier comic seduction episodes does not detract from the imaginative brilliance of his application of this formula to the ridicule of Richardson. On the contrary, comparison of the bedside interviews with their possible antecedents reveals Fielding's distinctive development of these common materials, a development which set the pattern for the half-dozen major comic dialogues in *Joseph Andrews.*

A work more than once cited as a possible source of Fielding's seduction scenes is *Le Paysan parvenu.*[2] Among the numerous intimate interviews between its lowly young hero and various amorous ladies his senior in age and station (his career is little more than a series of such meetings), those which have been singled out—the scenes with Mme de Fécour—are surely the least likely to have influenced Fielding's composition. Mme de Fécour is an uncomplicated sensualist "bonne convive, plus joyeuse que spirituelle à table, plus franche que hardie, pourtant plus libertine que tendre," inhibited by neither "orgueil ni modestie." The superficial similarity between her first private interview with Jacob (pt. 4) and Joseph's first conversation with his mistress only serves to bring out the difference between the two incidents. When Lady Booby, feigning inadvertence, reveals "one of the whitest Necks that ever was seen," Joseph

in which he imagines himself in danger from the landlord's comely daughter, "but at last his Virtue overcame the powerful Temptation, and he firmly resolv'd not to be guilty of the least Infidelity to his Lady Dulcinea del Toboso, tho' Queen Genever her self, with her trusty Matron Quintaniona should join to decoy him into the alluring Snare" (p. 99). Near the end of part 2, the pretended passion of the duchess's fair handmaiden Altisidora makes him "apprehensive of the Danger to which his Fidelity was exposed, but yet firmly determin'd to withstand the powerful Allurement" (p. 734); and he is moved to expostulate like Joseph (see n. 12, chap. 3 above): "Why, (said he, with a Sigh heav'd from the Bottom of his Heart) why must I be so unhappy a Knight, that no Damsel can gaze on me without falling in Love?" (p. 736).

[2] Erich Bosdorf, *Entstehungsgeschichte von Fieldings "Joseph Andrews"* (Weimar, 1908), pp. 41–43; Cross 1 : 322; Digeon, p. 52 n.

blushes with embarrassment; when Mme de Fécour unabashedly confronts Jacob with "une des plus furieuses gorges que j'aie jamais vu," he responds with an appreciative stare. In contrast to Lady Booby's frustrated effort to intimate her inclination indirectly, this jolly lady chucks her "belle jeunesse" under the chin, and tells him to be more forward with her in the future.[3]

A truer prototype of the conduct of Lady Booby is the behavior of Mme de Fécour's friend, Mme de Ferval, whose relations with Jacob are a more prominent part of the novel. Pretending to be a devout recluse, but privately less austere, this hypocritical widow is taken with Jacob's good looks and encourages him to flirt. During their second interview she receives him reclining half-undressed on a sofa, managing to display her charms while affecting modesty. She is concerned that their meetings may be discovered and sounds out the lad's ability to keep a secret. Having arranged a private rendezvous where they may pursue their amorous conversation with more freedom, she affects astonishment and alarm when they are locked in an apartment and resists, but not too strenously, Jacob's efforts to press his suit home.

This is obviously nearer to the vein of Fielding's action, but Marivaux's comedy is more diffused and ambivalent, and essentially different in form. Commingled with the satiric exposure of the lady's pretense is a sympathetic interest in the delicate nuances of *tendresse*. Her coyness is closer to conventional feminine reticence than the affected prudery of Lady Booby. In contrast to the simplicity of Lady Booby's appetite, she, like Jacob's other conquests, initially befriends the lad out

[3] Even further from the vein of Fielding's episode is the scene cited by Bosdorf (n. 2 above) from part 6 of *Le Paysan parvenu*, not by Marivaux and published two years after Fielding's death: "En prononçant ces mots, elle avança ses bras vers moi; j'allai au-devant, et je lui imprimai ma bouche sur cette grosse gorge, dont je ne pouvais me détacher, quand un bruit imprévu m'obligea de me retirer" (pp. 310–11).

of genuine kindness as well as vanity and concupiscence. If she initiates the flirtation, his complaisant gallantry is responsible for its progress. In their first interview he is the principal hypocrite, pretending not to love his intended bride to please his new patroness. Although the climactic interruption of their secret tête-à-tête involves a major comic embarrassment for her (the acquaintance who finds the austere devotee in this compromising situation also recognizes her "nephew" as plain peasant Jacob), in the sequence of the action as a whole her stratagems and discomforts are a secondary source of amusement. The comedy of the sequence is primarily the comedy of Jacob's temporary success and eventual frustration and embarrassment.

A truer analogy and more likely inspiration of Fielding's scenes has not been previously noted, perhaps because it is to be found in a less expected place. In *Le Roman comique* (2:10), Mme Bouvillon, a portly widow, arranges a private supper with Destin and attempts to seduce him. The clarity of her intention, and her comic effort to intimate it while affecting to deny it, is much closer to Lady Booby's manner than the behavior of either of Marivaux's ladies, and the young thespian's demeanor is more like Joseph's than Jacob's. Humbly deferential to the lady's superior years and station, he is timidly tongue-tied during the meal and passively defensive throughout the scene. Their postprandial dialogue exhibits the very pattern of Fielding's.

La Bouvillon, qui crut peut-être que Le Destin y avait pris garde, lui dit: Voyez un peu cette étourdie qui a fermé la porte sur nous! Je l'irai ouvrir, s'il vous plaît, lui répondit Le Destin. Je ne dis pas cela, répondit la Bouvillon en l'arrêtant, mais vous savez bien que deux personnes seules enfermées ensemble, comme (elles) peuvent faire ce qui leur plaira, on en peut aussi croire ce que l'on voudra. Ce n'est pas des personnes qui vous ressemblent que l'on fait des jugements téméraires, lui repartit Le Destin. Je ne dis pas cela, dit la Bouvillon, mais on ne peut avoir trop de précaution contre la médisance. Il faut qu'elle ait quelque fondement, lui repartit Le

Destin; et pour ce qui est de vous et de moi, l'on sait bien le peu de proportion qu'il y a entre un pauvre comédien et une femme de votre condition. Vous plaît-il donc, continua-t-il, que j'aille ouvrir la porte? Je ne dis pas cela, dit la Bouvillon en l'allant fermer au verrou; car, ajouta-t-elle, peut-être qu'on ne prendra pas garde si elle est fermée ou non; et, fermée pour fermée, il vaut mieux qu'elle ne se puisse ouvrir que de notre consentement.

Like Joseph, Destin answers the lady's wishes-disguised-as-fears with pious assurances of her exceptional reputation and the unbridgeable gulf between their stations. Like Lady Booby, Mme Bouvillon finds her affectations of modesty taken literally and must amusingly reiterate "je ne dis pas cela." If this part of the episode resembles Joseph's interviews with Lady Booby, Mme Bouvillon's more direct procedure after her hints have failed might be the antecedent of his encounter with Slipslop, (1:6) even down to the mock-heroic manner:

L'ayant fait comme elle l'avait dit, elle approcha du Destin son gros visage fort enflammé et ses petits yeux fort étincelants, et lui donna bien à penser de quelle façon il se tirerait à son honneur de la bataille que vraisemblablement elle lui allait présenter. La grosse sensuelle ôta son mouchoir de col et étala aux yeux du Destin, qui n'y prenait pas grand plaisir, dix livres de tetons pour le moins.

"Le pauvre garcon" is rescued from the ensuing ticklish battle at close quarters ("Il fallait combattre ou se rendre") by Ragotin's pounding on the door in the same way that "poor Joseph" is rescued from the "violent amorous Hands" of the "hungry Tygress" Slipslop by Lady Booby's ringing.

The characteristic Scarronesque turn in the latter part of this scene differentiates it most clearly from the interviews between Joseph and Lady Booby, and from the distinctive pattern of Fielding's extraordinary comic dialogues. Having engaged predator and prey in a brief dialogue, Scarron soon descends to gross physical humor, bringing the scene to a slapstick conclusion:

Le Destin tira sa main du dos suant de la Bouvillon pour aller ouvrir à Ragotin . . . et, voulant passer entre elle et la table, assez adroitement pour ne la pas toucher, il rencontra du pied quelque chose qui le fit broncher et se choqua la tête contre un banc, assez rudement pour en être quelque temps étourdi. La Bouvillon cependant, ayant repris son mouchoir à la hâte, alla ouvrir à l'impétueux Ragotin qui, en même temps, poussant la porte de l'autre côté de toute sa force, la fit donner si rudement contre le visage de la pauvre dame qu'elle en eut le nez écaché et de plus une bosse au front grosse comme le poing.

If Fielding took some hints from this scene, he also improved upon its essentially anticlimactic structure, avoiding its mechanical termination by developing the comedy of faulty communication to an internal resolution. Each of his bedside parleys is brought to a climax by an explosion from within, less spectacular but more dramatically effective than Scarron's uproar. The second interview between Joseph and Lady Booby (1:8), where the parody reaches its climax in the footman's proclamation of his virtue, is perhaps the more flamboyant, but the first (1:5) offers a clearer model of Fielding's comedy of characters speaking at cross purposes. The lady is trying to initiate a lovers' parley in the accepted manner of amorous intrigue, but Joseph puts her out by persistently adhering to the role of a servant addressed by his mistress. Failing to elicit anything but expressions of obedience and respect through her prudent queries concerning Joseph's love life and his discretion, and her bolder strip-tease tactic, the poor lady is reduced to conducting the amatory chess game with herself:

"No," says she, "perhaps you may not call your Designs wicked, and perhaps they are not so."—He swore they were not. "You misunderstand me," says she, "I mean if they were against my Honour, they may not be wicked, but the World calls them so. But then, say you, the World will never know any thing of the Matter, yet would not that be trusting to your Secrecy? Must not my Reputation be then in your power? Would you not then be my Master?"

When Joseph fails to respond to this combination of moral reassurance and temptation, the lady conjectures "perhaps you may fear I should prosecute you" and asks, still reassuringly, "Tell me *Joey*, don't you think I should forgive you?" Joseph's innocent response to this question brings the interview to its climax.

"Indeed, Madam," says Joseph, "I will never do anything to disoblige your Ladyship." "How," says she, "do you think it would not disoblige me then? Do you think I would willingly suffer you?" "I don't understand you, Madam," says *Joseph*. "Don't you?" said she, "then you are either a Fool or pretend to be so, I find I was mistaken in you, so get you down Stairs, and never let me see your Face again: your pretended Innocence cannot impose on me."

What happens here is in a sense obvious: frustrated in her attempts to get through to her obtuse footman, the lady amusingly takes advantage of Joseph's innocuous remark to disengage herself by taking offense at an implication he never intended. But this sudden turn is unexpected; her reaction is not triggered by anything so patently provocative as Joseph's later testimonial to his virtue. Behind the expiration of her patience at this remark, apparently indistinguishable from Joseph's other courtesies, is one of those "curious Productions of Nature" Fielding hopes "will be observed by the slower and more accurate Reader" (2:1). The fatality of Joseph's reply is that it seems to Lady Booby to mock her hypocritical aversion to that which she is actively soliciting. To the town-bred lady whose mind is on sex, the servant's routine politeness sounds like the boastful innuendo of a gallant. The vehemence of her reaction is increased by her unconscious recognition of the truth of his remark, and she ends by projecting onto Joseph the sexual aggressiveness which she herself has exhibited throughout the scene. Having thus humorously made poor Joseph the villain of the episode, she pounces on his conventional apology ("I have always endeavoured to be a dutiful

Servant both to you and my Master") drawing the affectation of suffering widowhood about her exposed concupiscence ("O thou villain, . . . Why did'st thou mention the Name of that dear Man, unless to torment me, to bring his precious Memory to my Mind").

The general pattern established in this first dialogue is exhibited in varying form in each of Parson Adams' major colloquys with a hypocrite—with Trulliber (2:14), with Peter Pounce (3:13) and with Lady Booby herself (4:2). In each of these incidents, as the innocent and the hypocrite interpret each other's motives and attitudes on the basis of their own, the comedy turns on the ingenuous or disingenuous misconstruction of remarks.

Adams' interview with Lady Booby near the end of the novel (4:2) appears to involve less dramatic development than the scenes between Joseph and his mistress; Adams and the lady are opposed from the outset of the conversation, and their interchange only confirms their respective stands. Yet within this apparent deadlock Fielding builds their interaction to a climax through a sequence of comic turns. As part of her disinterested moral pose, and to make Joseph out the greater villain, the lady remarks in passing that she has no objection to Fanny. Adams, eager out of good nature and respect to find common ground with the lady, assures her with characteristic enthusiasm of his own high opinion of the girl, naïvely adding to his praise of her character what he regards as a point of no great significance, that she is "the handsomest Woman, Gentle or Simple, that ever appeared in the Parish." The preacher's casual parenthesis of amplification wounds the lady's vanity, and in reaction she drops the pretense of impartiality. From this point on, Joseph, the original target of her attack, is virtually forgotten, as she recurs with obsessive sarcasm to the object of her jealousy.

It is mighty becoming truly in a Clergyman to trouble himself about handsome Women, and you are a delicate Judge of Beauty, no doubt. A Man who hath lived all his Life in such a Parish as this, is a rare Judge of Beauty. Ridiculous! Beauty indeed,—a Country Wench a Beauty—I shall be sick whenever I hear Beauty mentioned again. —And so this Wench is to stock the Parish with Beauties. . . . *Slipslop* tells me how her Head runs on Fellows; that is one of her Beauties, I suppose. . . . he shall not settle here, and bring a Nest of Beggars into the Parish; it will make us but little Amends that they will be Beauties. . . . Since you understand yourself no better . . . nor the Respect due from such as you to a Woman of my Distinction. . . . then you and the greatest Beauty in the Parish may go and beg together. . . . I will suffer no Parsons who run about the Country with Beauties to be entertained here."[4]

[4] Ironically, this tirade may have had its origins in the ranting of Lady Davers, whose characterization Fielding singled out for criticism at the end of *Shamela*. Late in *Pamela I* she abuses her brother's new bride, or, as she insists, mistress, in a lengthy and vivid scene that culminates in her sarcastic commentary on the absent Mr. B's note to Pamela (Richardson's italics indicate the text of the letter):

"*I beg of you, therefore, my dear*"—*My dear!* there's for you! I wish I may not be quite sick before I get through—"*What I beg of you therefore, my dear . . . is, that you will go in the chariot to Sir Simon's, the sooner in the day the better,*"—Dear heart! and why so, when WE were not expected till night? why, pray observe the reason—Hem! . . . "*because you will be diverted with the company;*"—Mighty kind, indeed!—"*who all*"—Jackey, mind this—"*who all so much admire you.*" . . . "*Who all so much admire you,*" . . . I must repeat that—Pretty Miss!—I wish thou wast as *admirable* for thy virtue, as for that baby-face of thine! . . . But now comes the reason why this LITTLE absence, which, at the same time, is so GREAT AN ABSENCE, is so *tedious*: for "*I am,*" ay, now for it! "*with the* UTMOST *sincerity, my dearest love*" —Out upon DEAREST love! I shall never love the word again! Pray bid your uncle never call me Dearest Love, Jackey!—"*For ever yours!*"—But, brother, thou knowest thou liest. And so, my good Lady Andrews, or what shall I call you? your *dearest love* will be "*for ever yours!*" And hast thou the vanity to believe this?—But stay, here is a postscript. The poor man knew not when to have done to his *dearest love*. He's sadly in for't, truly! Why, his *dearest love,* you are mighty happy in such a lover! [Everyman ed. 1 : 353–54]

In Lady Booby's speech, Fielding's memory of this scene seems to have coalesced with a more characteristically Richardsonian passage near the end of *Pamela II* (2 : 427):

Miss Goodwin is highly delighted now with my sweet little Pamela, and says, she shall be her sister indeed! "For, Madam," said she, "Miss is a beauty!—And we see no French beauties like Master Davers and Miss."—"Beauty! my dear," said I; "what is beauty, if she be not a good girl? Beauty is but a specious, and, as it may happen, a dangerous recommendation . . . .

Despite this unmasking of the lady's real feelings, Adams, as innocent of feminine psychology as of malice and envy, characteristically assumes he is engaged in rational discourse and that he need only explain the situation to dissuade the lady from her intention. When she answers his legal arguments with the flat assertion of her will, he naïvely appeals to her charity:

Surely the Parties being poor is no Reason against their marrying. G—d forbid there should be any such Law. The Poor have little Share enough of this World already; it would be barbarous indeed to deny them the common Privileges, and innocent Enjoyments which Nature indulges to the animal Creation.

Here poor Adams again unwittingly enrages the lady, in much the same manner that Joseph innocently precipitated her explosion at the end of the first interview. To Lady Booby's inflamed imagination, the parson's little sermon presents a picture of Joseph and Fanny copulating. Projecting her vision onto his text, in one of the funniest turns of the novel, she rebukes him for affronting her with "such loose Discourse."

At this point the scene appears to be falling into the pattern of Joseph's first interview with Lady Booby: after the innocent's well-intentioned responses provoke the hypocrite's rage, she seizes on an innocuous remark to affect outrage, and place him on the moral defensive. But in this scene Fielding adds to the amusement of this ironic turn the moral satisfaction of another. The persistently conciliatory and deferential Adams is at last provoked by the lady's threat of depriving him of his cure to correct the error under which the lady has proceeded throughout the interview:

I know not what your Ladyship means by the Terms *Master* and *Service*. I am in the Service of a Master who will never discard me for doing my Duty: And if the Doctor . . . thinks proper to turn me out from my Cure, G—— will provide me, I hope, another. At least, my Family as well as myself have Hands; and he will prosper, I doubt not, our Endeavours to get our Bread honestly with them.

Whilst my Conscience is pure, I shall never fear what Man can do unto me.

The reader's pleasure in this climactic rebuff does not preclude amusement at the fact that Adams in the end is as unaware of the psychology of his opponent as he was at the beginning: "I am assured, when you have enquired farther into this matter, you will applaud, not blame my Proceeding."

Here as in the seduction scene the innocent infuriates the hypocrite by trying to agree with her pretended attitudes. This comic irony is the mainspring of Adams' exploding interview with Peter Pounce (3:13), but Fielding evolves a more complex structure from the paradox of Peter's character. The miserly steward would hypocritically deprecate his wealth, for, reading others' characters by the light of his own, he is fearful of their avarice and envy, and he is conscious of society's demands upon the rich; but at the same time he is vain of his wealth and would have the world acknowledge it. In the course of the dialogue, the former of these motives, uppermost at first, is overcome by the latter. At the beginning of the scene, Peter the hypocrite says, "I thank God I have a little . . . with which I am content, and envy no Man: I have a little . . . with which I do as much good as I can." Adams, oblivious to hypocrisy, and misconstruing Peter's meaning of "doing good," concurs in his sentiments (or so he thinks) by observing that "Riches without Charity were nothing worth." This launches Peter into an ingenious invective against the demands of charity, concluding with an even more deprecatory view of his estate: "I do assure you I expect to come myself to the Parish in the end."

Now begins the comic reversal which brings the scene to its climax. When the land-poor Peter hypocritically invites Adams' compassion, the parson with characteristic generous sympathy assures him he has never shared the neighbors' exaggerated estimates of his wealth. Without realizing it, Adams has already crossed Peter's vanity, but Fielding delays the explosion, first allowing the parson to glance innocently on the touchy question of how Peter amassed his wealth and the irritating distinction between acquired riches and inherited position, then having him compound his error: interpreting Peter's frown at his report of the general estimate of his fortune in the light of his earlier hypocritical deprecations, Adams hastens to assure him that *he* has always maintained it was less. With this Peter's vanity bursts forth, and the man who began the scene by expressing his contentment with his "little," jealously accuses Adams of attempting "to undervalue me in the Country," and reveals his envy of the inherited gentry.

Fielding's fullest realization of the comic possibilities of an exchange between innocence and hypocrisy is the interview between Adams and Trulliber (2:14). Expectation for this scene is built up by the preliminary comedy of Adams in the pigsty and Trulliber at table. The interview itself combines the misunderstandings observed in other dialogues with a prolonged slow discovery by Adams, both of these ingredients arising from the fact that, although the two men speak the language of their calling, only Adams believes in what he professes. Adams begins the interview with the innocent expectation that a fellow clergyman will be pleased to aid him. But before he can reveal the point of his "Embassy" Trulliber contributes to his own subsequent discomfort. Ill-naturedly interpreting Adams' innocuous reference to his curacy as disparagement of his clerical standing, he must intrude a vain boast of his wealth. The first comic turn follows immediately, when Trulliber learns that Adams wants money. His predicament is the reverse of Peter Pounce's: having bragged of his wealth, he wishes he could play it down.

The center of the interview consists of Trulliber's successive attempts to escape, each comically frustrated by Adams' persistent misunderstanding of his intention. First he retreats behind a screen of pious platitudes, prudently withdrawing his boast along the way ("I thank G—— if I am not so warm as some, I am content"). Fastening on Adams' gospel figure, he tries to turn it to his own advantage: "Lay up my Treasure! what matters where a Man's Treasure is, whose Heart is in the Scriptures? there is the Treasure of a Christian." Like the Roman priest's discourse against earthly riches (3:8), these words are intended to suggest to the needy petitioner that as a Christian *he* should not be concerned with money. But to the good-hearted Adams, they are an echo of his own charitable sentiments, and he is overjoyed at his brother's beneficence. When he asks that the loan which he thinks has been granted be made quickly, Trulliber, with half-feigned misunderstanding, counters by interpreting the request as an order to "stand and deliver." Irritated at Adams' obtuseness, he refuses more bluntly, professing suspicion of Adams' calling. Poor Adams, proceeding under the doubly false assumption that he is in rational discourse with a fellow Christian, argues that his being no clergyman does not exempt his colleague from the obligation of common charity. This further infuriates Trulliber, who is accustomed to preaching rather than being preached at; when he tells Adams that he knows what charity is, the comedy suddenly takes a doctrinal turn. Still not grasping his opponent's meanness, Adams pedantically lectures him: "I must tell you, if you trust to your Knowledge for your Justification, you will find yourself deceived, tho' you should add Faith to it without good Works."

This initiates the sequence of rapid turns concluding the dialogue. Seizing the high moral ground, Trulliber denounces Adams for disparaging faith and scriptures; poor Adams seems to put himself further on the defensive by crying "Name not the Scriptures"; but then, forbearing no more, the hero turns the accusation of disbelief back upon his opponent, pronouncing him no Christian. The pattern resembles that of the conclusion of Adams' interview with Lady Booby, but the final turn is more amusing and surprising because of the rapidity of revolutions in this last exchange. Though Adams' practical mission has failed, his moral victory is underscored by the image of the good parson departing with a smile as the exasperated hypocrite threatens to prove with his fists that he is a good Christian.

In these lively dialogues between innocence (feigned or real) and affectation, the errors and embarrassments of Joseph and Adams are laughable, but they are secondary to the frustrations and discomfitures of the hypocrite. Whether the innocent has a kind of moral victory in the end or is driven off in bewilderment, the paramount effect or net result is the comic suffering of the hypocrite, whose self-love and sensitivity to exposure make it impossible for him or her to be easy.[5] Another source of the comic pleasure in these incidents derives from the actual movement of the dialogue as it evolves through unexpected turns and accidents to a dramatic climax. Fielding's special conception of the very structure of the dialogue as comic, apparent in the Peter Pounce interview, where the hypocrite is brought to oppose his own initial assertions, is most fully realized in two scenes in which neither participant is an innocent.

The first of these is the dialogue between the poet and player (3 : 10). Its progress from an amicable beginning through two sharp comic turns to a disagreeable conclusion results not from the difference between the characters, but from their common disingenuity and vanity. In the first stage of the dialogue, each defends his own profession and finds fault with the other's. But before this can lead to a hot dispute, their vanities are disengaged by mutual assurances that the other is excluded from the general disparagement of his fellows. Now the two continue to

[5] In the Trulliber episode, this effect is enhanced by the browbeaten Mrs. Trulliber's efforts to support her husband. Given his low opinion of her and his despotic conception of domestic relations, her attempted assistance is at once an insult to his capacity to handle Adams and a distracting insurrection from the rear.

disagree, but they have completely changed loyalties—each inveighs *against* his own colleagues, while they vie in according each other encomiums. The second unexpected reversal by which the fraudulence of this little love feast is exposed comes about with the same "naturalness" as the explosions in Fielding's other dialogues. Carried away by his passionate contempt for his fellows, the player sails into a speech from Lee's *Theodosius* and the poet vainly asks him to "repeat that tender Speech in the third Act of my Play which you made such a Figure in." But the player has forgotten it, and this mortal injury initiates a chain of mutual recrimination about the failure of the play in question, until the true feelings of the two emerge. Though the scene is broken off with the poet, "whose Fury was now raised," about to explode, Fielding has, of course, completed his little comic structure. Each of the two characters, initially affecting loyalty to his own profession, then admiration for the other, and by implication his profession against his own, in the end shows himself to be only for himself.[6]

Fielding's fullest development of the comedy of hypocrisy occurs in the longest and most convoluted of the dialogues in *Joseph Andrews*, the bedtime scene between Lady Booby and Slipslop near the end of the novel (4 : 6). Here the backfiring attempt to accommodate the hypocrite takes another form: unlike Joseph or Adams, Slipslop is governed only by her desire to say what her mistress wishes to hear, but her efforts are hampered by her own inadvertencies and by the agitated conflict of desire and hypocrisy within Lady Booby.

The servant gets off to a poor start by failing to catch her mistress' first invitation to attack Pamela and praise Joseph; to make up for this lapse, she dutifully assents to her mistress' as-

[6] Digeon (p. 90 n.) remarks a similarity between this scene and the dialogue of Trissotin and Vadius in Moliere's *Les Femmes savantes*. If these two poets' progress from mutual compliment to mutual vilification provided Fielding with a model, the scene lacks the dramatic complexity of his incident, and its single reversal is brought about more artificially, and more expectedly.

sertion that Joseph's low rank disqualifies him as the object of "a Woman of Fashion," only to be rebuked for being "always one's Echo." When the lady argues Joseph's superiority in "real Merit" to the fashionable matches decreed by the "Tyranny of Custom," Slipslop reads the signs correctly, but sins against her mistress' hypocrisy by two clearly identifying her as the lady in the case. When Lady Booby angrily withdraws to the safety of the hypothetical vein she employed in her first interview with Joseph, poor Slipslop is again too quick to agree:

"Me," said the Lady, "I am speaking, if a young Woman of Fashion who had seen nothing of the World should happen to like such a Fellow. —Me indeed; I hope thou dost not imagine—" "No, Ma'am, to be sure," cried *Slipslop.* —"No! what no?" cried the Lady. "Thou art always ready to answer, before thou hast heard one."

Having salved her injured propriety, the lady ingeniously contrives to revive Slipslop's advocacy of Joseph, feigning grief over her late husband whose loss has ended "all Thoughts of Men" and then, inconsequently, inviting "some of thy Nonsense to turn my Thoughts another way. What dost thou think of Mr. *Andrews*?" The servant's argument (a repetition of the lady's own attack on the tyranny of custom) is now perfectly acceptable, but in assenting to the direct question, "If you was a Woman of Condition, you would really marry Mr. *Andrews*?," Slipslop (perhaps momentarily imagining herself in the coveted role) unthinkingly appends the conventional "If he would have me" and provokes the wrath of her mistress' injured vanity. When she tries to mend this error with the assurance that only Fanny bars the lady's path to Joseph's heart, she only frightens her with the thought that her compromising legal actions against Fanny are no secret. To counteract this imagined exposure, Lady Booby reverts to her most exalted hypocritical puritanism and, as the reader has come to expect in these dialogues, indignantly blames Slipslop for the outrageous insinuation that she might tolerate the vile passion of love and fix it "on such an Object, a Creature so much beneath my Notice."

Down-to-earth Slipslop, understanding nothing of the lady's qualms about acknowledging her dealings with Scout, is now as genuinely baffled as Joseph or Adams might be, and if the scene were to end here its structure would parallel that of the original interview between the Lady and her footman. But the most unexpected turn is yet to come. When the lady denounces her servant as a "low Creature, of the *Andrews* Breed . . . a Weed that grows in the common Garden of the Creation," Slipslop, comically mistaking the botanical metaphor for a slur upon her virtue, angrily abandons her efforts to be agreeable and denounces the lady's hypocritical qualms in a passionate speech. Delightful as it is to see Slipslop at least break into the clear after stubbing her toes so often, and to hear the long-subservient waiting woman at last tell off her haughty mistress, it is a more amusing irony to perceive that her version of Adams' delayed outburst tells the lady exactly what she wants to hear. The event twice before approached in the scene but missed through comic accident—the lady's open acquiescence in the dream she secretly cherishes—is thus brought about by unanticipated means just when the two women appear to be farthest apart. And though this is a kind of happy ending for the comic villainess, since Slipslop's outburst permits her to favor her passion without injuring her pride, it is still satisfying to the good-natured reader because of the surprise with which this serpentine colloquy is brought to a harmonious close, an outcome all the more welcome because this final comic interview is the first to end amicably.[7]

[7] Fielding's consciousness of his achievement in this most elaborate of his dialogues may be reflected in his chapter title ("Of which you are desired to read no more than you like"), reminiscent of the similarly ironic complaint of Cervantes' narrator at the commencement of Sancho's government (see above, p. 40). For his contemporary reader, the amusement of the scene may have been enhanced by the consciousness of Pamela's preoccupation with marriage across social classes.

The special character of these half-dozen dialogues may be clarified by comparison with another scene that resembles them. The dialogue between Adams and his host at the end of the first volume (2 : 17) is a kind of conversation at cross-purposes: the parson and the man of trade fail to understand one another because each views the world from the vantage point of his own interests and background; the literal-minded host mistakes Adams' metaphors and even suspects him of writing for the *Gazetteers;* and, because the vanity of each is involved, the conversation which begins amicably grows into a warm dispute. But the vital germ of ill-natured hypocrisy is missing, and the misconstruction of meanings does not set off a succession of sudden and surprising turns. Though there is an amusing development in the course of the scene, as the relatively disinterested dispute over the merits of learning versus experience evolves into a battle of personal and professional vanities, there is nothing like the tautly structured interaction found in the previously considered dialogues.

These differences illuminate the peculiar conception of dialogue-as-action embodied in Fielding's interviews involving hypocrites. Beneath the meandering surface of a conversation to pass the time of a journey or the gossip between a lady and her maid at bedtime, Fielding builds a carefully shaped comic action in which the speeches are events, and the dramatic plot-in-miniature, developing in a straight line or through one or more reversals to a climactic conclusion, turns upon the slightest accidents of expression. Joseph or Adams or Slipslop frustrates or embarrasses the hypocrite by failing to grasp his or her intention or by unconsciously touching some sore point; characteristically, the ill-natured person construes the innocent remarks of the other as malicious or insinuating; these mutual misinterpretations sooner or later produce an explosion of wounded vanity or frightened hypocrisy which may be the climax of the scene, as in Joseph's first interview with Lady Booby, or only the beginning of further comic complications, as in Adams' interview with Trulliber or Slipslop's scene with her mistress. Whatever the structure of the individual scene, the dialogue is usually not completed without the hypocrite, with characteristic shrewdness and self-love, contriving to put the innocent or his counterpart (Slipslop) in the wrong, an ironic turn which qualifies the predominant comic satisfaction at the hypocrite's discomfiture. Part of that satisfaction stems from seeing the hypocrite driven to self-exposure. Provoked by Adams' reference to Fanny's beauty, Lady Booby drops her disinterested pose and reveals her jealousy; under Adams' innocent goadings, Pounce forgets his tactic of affected penury and screams out his wealth; exasperated by Adams' exposure of the gap between his profession and conduct, Trulliber reveals his "Christianity" by threatening to beat his suppliant; the poet and the player are each unmasked in the course of their conversation; even in the final dialogue, Lady Booby, in offering no resistance to the rhetoric of her "comical Creature," in effect drops her pretense and tacitly acknowledges her real feelings.

It would be plausible to attribute these dramatic dialogues to Fielding's playwriting experience. Yet there are no comparably structured conversations in any of his theatrical comedies. The absence of any such incidents in *Tom Jones* strengthens the hypothesis that he derived this conception from the books he had before him in composing *Joseph Andrews.* Besides the abortive precedent of Destin's interview with Mme de Bouvillon, anticipations of the distinctive form he imposed on the dialogue with hypocrisy are indeed to be found in the continental writers preoccupied with the comedy of pretense, Lesage and Marivaux.[8]

[8] The leisurely discourses of Quixote and Sancho, reflecting their amiable delight in conversation for its own sake, are far removed from Fielding's tightly drawn little comic dramas; there is no dialogue of misunderstanding, and they rarely approach a sharp conflict of wills.

Two incidents in *Gil Blas* are rudimentary prototypes of Fielding's dialogues. In the first of these (2 : 7), the young barber Diego naïvely presumes upon the affection of a rich uncle. The older man, vain of the social rank he has reached through his poetry, wants no poor relation about to recall his lowly origin; to rid himself of the lad, he affects an interest in him and advises him to tour the country to perfect his vocation, even offering a little money to speed him on his way. Misreading this hypocrisy, the lad decides that he might do better staying in Madrid and solicits his uncle's assistance in obtaining a place in one of the noble households he frequents. Whereupon the vain poet, disguising his own motive and transferring the blame in the manner of Lady Booby, angrily denounces the "petit libertin" for wishing to give up his profession and abandons him "aux gens qui te donnent de si pernicieux conseils." In the other incident (8 : 13) Gil Blas himself is cast in the unsympathetic role. After his accession to power has turned his head, one of the secretary's country acquaintances comes to see him at court and runs head on into his inflated vanity. When Gil Blas does not recognize him, the man reminds him that they played together as children, to which the courtier haughtily replies: "Je n'ai . . . qu'une idée très-confuse des amusemens de mon enfance; les soins dont j'ai été depuis occupé m'en ont fait perdre la mémoire." When the provincial heartily congratulates him on his good fortune and says he will joyfully relate the news to his parents, the factotum is embarrassed into making a perfunctory inquiry after their health, and the coldness of his interest prompts the bluff grocer to chide him for neglecting his needy family. This good-natured endeavor backfires like those of Joseph and Adams ("Au lieu d'être touché de la peinture qu'il me faisoit de ma famille, je ne sentis que la liberté qu'il prenoit de me conseiller, sans que je l'en priasse"), and Gil Blas angrily terminates the interview by denouncing his countryman: "Allez . . . ne vous mêlez que de ce qui vous regarde. . . . Il vous convient bien de me dicter mon devoir. Je sçai mieux que vous ce que j'ai à faire dans cette occasion."

Both of these incidents contain the germ of Fielding's comic dialogues—the encounter between the naïve and the affected ending in an angry explosion. But in the first the principal source of amusement is the young fool's misfortune and not the hypocrite's embarrassment; and even in the second there is nothing like Fielding's delightful buildup to the explosion through an extended exchange between the parties. In both instances, Lesage dissipates the dramatic quality which Fielding cultivates, presenting the incidents largely through narration rather than in dialogue. This is more than a technical difference. The distinctive effect of Fielding's scenes derives from the fact that the mental process behind the character's remarks is never made explicit; it is to be inferred by the reader from the surprising and amusing turns of the conversation itself. But Lesage reveals the uncle's motivation before each of his speeches and allows Gil Blas to disclose the psychology behind his explosion before the explosion itself, thereby weakening its comic impact.

Closer to the form of Fielding's dialogues is a scene in *Le Paysan parvenu.* The climax of the opening episode is an interview between Jacob and his master, who tries to persuade the servant to marry the maid Genevieve to provide a screen for his own affair with the girl. Like Lady Booby, the gentleman begins by lightly sounding out Jacob's relations with the female servants, and like Joseph (but unlike himself in his interviews with ladies) Jacob affects not to understand what the master is talking about. Coming to the point, the master, pretending a kindly interest in his servants, offers to underwrite their immediate marriage. The middle of the interview differs from Fielding's scenes, for Jacob frankly tells the master he sees through his hypocrisy, and the master, with equal frankness, argues that it will be in Jacob's best interest to accept his proposal. The conclusion is again in Fielding's vein. When Jacob bluntly refuses, alluding to his family tradition of marrying virgins, he is angrily denounced for villainously trifling with the poor girl's affections. Affecting compassion for the girl, but in fact fearful of his own exposure, the master attacks Jacob in advance for spreading "cette impertinente idée-là" of the maid's unchastity and piously laments: "et c'est moi, c'est ma simple bonne volonté pour elle qui serait la cause innocente de tout le tort que vous pourriez lui faire."[9] This outburst of the fearful hypocrite's pretended righteousness is in the very manner of Lady Booby.

The closest structural prototype of Fielding's dialogues at cross-purposes is found in *Marianne*. In part 3, M. de Climal's seduction campaign culminates in a long scene between the hypocritical old lecher and the young girl, who, like Joseph, pretends to understand less than she does. Assuming that he is dealing with a naïve and slightly coquettish child, the old man tries to persuade the girl to become his mistress while preserving his pose of virtuous benefactor. When Marianne frustrates his efforts at insinuation by playing dumb and embarrassingly recurring to his religion and virtue, he openly declares his love, though he still hypocritically conceals its real nature. To frighten the girl into accepting his proposal, he dwells on her helplessness and her potential fate as the cast-off mistress of some fickle young lover like his nephew. When Marianne weeps at the cruelty of this rhetoric, de Climal misinterprets her response as signaling the success of his strategy and reassures her by proposing to make her a handsome settlement. Now Marianne gently tries to make clear that she understands the true character of his proposal and will have no part of it, complaining that he is not the *honnête homme* she thought him to be; but the old man, still underestimating the girl, thinks this only a conventional qualm to be overcome by the sophistry that his love is the instrument of Divine Providence.

[9] *Le Paysan parvenu*, p. 30.

The dialogue is interrupted at this point by the intrusion of Valville, who takes in the scene of his pious uncle kneeling as a suitor and disdainfully departs. Marianne wants to tell the nephew she is innocent, but the old man, still caught up in his passionate scheme, assures her that she will never have to think about Valville again. With this, Marianne casts aside deference, bemoans her lost reputation, curses the day she met her patron, and denounces "toutes ces hypocrisies-la."

The old man cannot misunderstand this. Taking cover behind the ambiguity of his earlier discourse, he turns the blame upon Marianne:

> Petite ingrate que vous êtes, me répondit-il en pâlissant, est-ce là comme vous payez mes bienfaits? A propos de quoi parlez-vous de votre innocence? Où avez-vous pris qu'on songe à l'attaquer? Vous ai-je dit autre chose, sinon que j'avais quelque inclination pour vous, à la vérité, mais qu'en même temps je me la reprochais, que j'en étais fâché, que je m'en sentais humilié, que je la regardais comme une faute dont je m'accusais, et que je voulais l'effacer en la tournant à votre profit, sans rien exiger de vous qu'un peu de reconnaissance? Ne sont-ce pas là mes termes? et y a-t-il rien à tout cela qui n'ait dû vous rendre mon procédé respectable?[10]

But this only leads him into a trap; good-naturedly accepting his protestations, Marianne points out that he can have no objection to correcting Valville's mistaken impression, and that if he will not go to him, she will. The exasperated hypocrite, fearfully misinterpreting this naïve offer as a threat to expose him, drops all pretense and announces his intention of abandoning the girl.

Considerably longer than any of Fielding's dialogues, this scene resembles them in its pattern of persistent misunderstanding building to a breakup when the parties at last understand each other, in the hypocrite's characteristic mistaken fear of exposure and his defense by impugning the innocent, and in

[10] *Marianne*, p. 122.

the many amusing turns of dialogue along the way. But Marivaux is less interested than Fielding in the dialogue as an internally developed dramatic structure. The climax of the incident is an interruption from without the scene, and, while this is an effective comic surprise (especially in the context of the uncle's earlier discovery of the nephew in the same posture), it obscures the shape of the dialogue itself, breaking its momentum just as it is reaching a climax. More basically, in its conception and effect Marivaux's scene is a curiously left-handed version of Fielding's characteristic incident. As Mme de Ferval is the secondary figure in her interviews with Jacob, so here the suffering of the hypocrite is secondary to that of the heroine. Though the old man is frustrated by Marianne's feigned innocence as Lady Booby is by Joseph's, for the greater part of the scene it is the hypocrite who misinterprets and misunderstands, and it is he who must have his eyes opened at last, while the sympathetic figure is frustrated in her efforts to "get through" and at last explodes. Because the scene is focused primarily on the suffering of the girl, and because the amusement at her backfiring efforts to dissuade de Climal is overlaid with more serious discomfort, the effect is a strange mixture of comedy and pathos peculiar to Marivaux and distinct from the punitive pleasure of Fielding's scenes.

When Fielding began to contemplate the opening episode of *Joseph Andrews*, the thought of *Pamela* could have led by a natural train of association to this scene of another dependent maiden resisting her powerful patron's advances and the analogous confrontation between Jacob and his seducing master. Either of these might have stimulated his memory of Jacob's interviews with Mme de Ferval which in turn might have recalled Destin's *tête-à-teton* with that other hypocritical widow, Mme de Bouvillon. Whether his reflection actually followed any such course, or whether he arrived at his inversion of Richardson's situation without conscious recollection of any of these scenes—once he had created his first dramatic conversation between the lady and her footman, he recognized in it a structure which could be adapted to the interactions of other characters and made one of the basic formulas of his system of comic actions. If a few approximate precedents and clear prototypes of Fielding's formula are to be found in the continental comic romances, none of his predecessors seems to have had his precise conception of the dialogue of affectation as a paradigm to be developed through a series of variations. Only Marivaux approaches his ingenuity in fully dramatizing the interaction of personalities and bringing out the hypersensitivity of the hypocrite by making the course of the conversation turn upon the slightest accidents of expression. And not even he had so clear and consistent a sense of the climactic form to be built from a conversation at cross-purposes. Though he may have drawn some ideas for his dramatic dialogues from Lesage, Scarron, and Marivaux, Fielding forged them into a kind of incident peculiarly his own, creating some of the most memorable scenes in comic fiction.

The History of the World in General Satirically Revised

FIELDING'S first examples of the "biographer's" truthfulness are drawn from three of Cervantes' interpolated stories.

> For tho' it may be worth the Examination of Critics, whether the shepherd *Chrysostom*, who, as *Cervantes* informs us, died for Love of the fair *Marcella*, who hated him, was ever in *Spain*, will any one doubt but that such a silly Fellow hath really existed? Is there in the World such a Sceptic as to disbelieve the Madness of *Cardenio*, the Perfidy of *Ferdinand*, the impertinent Curiosity of *Anselmo*, the Weakness of *Camilla*, the irresolute Friendship of *Lothario;* tho' perhaps as to the Time and Place where those several Persons lived, that good Historian may be deplorably deficient.[1]

The choice is a curious one not only because Quixote and Sancho are passed over for a group of peripheral figures. Although Fielding's catalogue of frailties suggests that these characters come within the specific satiric vision of fictional truth implicit in his intention to "hold the Glass to thousands in their Closets," they are not cut from the same cloth as the subsequent

[1] *Joseph Andrews*, p. 186.

characters he cites: Lesage's Sangrado and archbishop, and his own coach passengers and innkeepers. Their stories, like many of the tales inserted in the continental comic romances, are of a different order of literary reality from that of their narrative context.

Most of the interpolations of Cervantes, Lesage, and Scarron are melodramatic or pathetic love stories.[2] The commonest plot formula, developed most extensively in the interlocking stories of Cardenio, Lucinda, Dorothea, and Ferdinand in part 1 of *Don Quixote* and reproduced a dozen times by Cervantes and Lesage, is as ancient as the Greek romances. A pair of faithful lovers are separated, often on the eve of marriage, through accident, family interference, or the machinations of a jealous rival; after a period of trial the suffering lovers are happily and permanently reunited in the denouement. Alongside these tragicomic stories are some with unhappy endings, perhaps the best known of which is Cervantes' first interpolation, the pathetic pastoral romance of Chrysostom, a young gentleman who turns shepherd to pursue his indifferent mistress and pines away when she spurns him.

It is not only their departure from the predominant comic vein which sets these tales off from their parent narratives. Chrysostom's story embodies in extreme form the romantic conventions of character and sentiment prevalent in varying degrees in most of the "novels." The passion that leads Ferdinand to betray his friend Cardenio and subsequently drives

[2] Of the twenty-nine more or less independent narratives incorporated in the five novels Fielding cited in book 3, chap. 1, only a handful can be considered in some sense comic or satiric. Excluded from the following generalizations and from subsequent references to the conventional or traditional tale are: Lesage's five rambling picaresque autobiographies, generally resembling their parent narrative; the lengthy and incomplete nun's story which takes over the last three parts of *Marianne* and preserves with less comic coloration the satiric vision of the main story; and the accounts of a litigious couple and of a sexual confidence game near the end of Marivaux's portion of *Le Paysan parvenu*.

Cardenio mad is strong enough in "The Curious Impertinent," the third Cervantean story alluded to by Fielding, to overpower the wisdom and scruples of Lothario, the perfect friend, and the chastity of Camilla, the model wife, eventually proving as fatal to this adulterous couple as to the unrequited Chrysostom. For the typical hero or heroine, as for Chrysostom, love transcends all other considerations and knows no alteration this side of the grave. In part 1 of *Don Quixote* (4 : 12–14), a Moorish maiden, smitten at a distant glance, betrays her people and forsakes Islam to contrive the escape of a Spanish captive; complementarily, in part 2 (chap. 58) a Spanish gentleman follows a banished Morisca into exile. Lucinda may submit to her parents by wedding powerful Ferdinand, but she will prove her fidelity to Cardenio by killing herself after the ceremony. Cardenio may mistakenly think he has been betrayed by Lucinda, but he is no more capable of terminating or transferring his love than is the dear object of his concern.[3]

The contrast between this conventional romantic psychology and the prevailing satiric realism of the comic romances was mordantly expressed by Marivaux in the passage leading up to Marianne's enumeration of the "little difficulties" her lover had to overcome to remain constant (see above, p. 64). Distinguishing her "histoire véritable" from "un roman," she anticipates Fielding's reasoning in book 3, chapter 1:

> Un héros de roman infidèle! on n'aurait jamais rien vu de pareil. Il est réglé qu'ils doivent tous être constants; on ne s'intéresse à eux que sur ce pied-là, et il est d'ailleurs si aisé de les rendre tels! il n'en coûte rien à la nature, c'est la fiction qui en fait les frais.
>
> . . . Mais . . . Je vous récite ici des faits qui vont comme il plaît à l'instabilité des choses humaines, et non pas des aventures d'imagination qui vont comme on veut. Je vous peins, non pas un coeur

[3] Three of Lesage's characters (bk. 4, chap. 10; 8 : 1; 9 : 6), seek their death when their love is balked. One of them kills himself when his elderly inamorata reveals she is his mother—not out of horror or shame, but disappointment.

fait à plaisir, mais le coeur d'un homme, d'un Français qui a réellement existé de nos jours.[4]

Although it was not until ten years after the publication of *Joseph Andrews* that Fielding characterized "the Stories of Cardenio and Dorothea, Ferdinand and Lucinda, &c." as episodes in which Cervantes "approaches very near to the Romances which he ridicules" (see above, p. 34), he evidently recognized the applicability of Marivaux's remarks to elements of his own tradition when he wrote the novel. He could hardly have thought that Cervantes intended his reader to view Chrysostom as a "silly Fellow": in so describing him he intimated that he himself might be the skeptic whose existence he questioned. Claiming, and perhaps believing, that even the most conventionally romantic "novels" of his predecessors were more "natural" than *The Grand Cyrus* or the works of Mrs. Manley, he recognized that they might be rendered still truer to human nature, which "every where furnishes an accurate Observer with the Ridiculous."

At least this is the clear implication of the interpolated narratives in *Joseph Andrews*. The accommodation to the satiric vision of the novel apparent in the use of Wilson's history for the wholesale display of vice and folly took a subtler form in Fielding's two more "literary" tales, "The History of *Leonora*, or the Unfortunate Jilt" (2 : 4–6) and "The History of two Friends" (4 : 10). In these two little stories he created an ironic counterpoint to his own comic adaptation of the Greek romance formula in the story of Joseph and Fanny, sardonically reworking in the first the conventions of the love intrigue in general and in the second a particular story of Cervantes. Together, they offer a special insight into the complexity of the relationship behind the description of his work as an imitation of Cervantes. While proclaiming *Don Quixote* "the History

[4] *Marianne*, pp. 375–76.

of the World in general . . . from the time it was first polished to this day . . . and forwards, as long as it shall so remain," he took pains to correct or modernize that history by satirically rewriting portions of it. Yet he evidently drew the germinal ideas and structural suggestions for his ironic versions from Cervantes' models.

A minor episode in Cervantes may have suggested to Fielding the basic idea of making his interpolations comic variations of their prototypes—as well as the specific direction of his first variation, the story of Leonora. At the end of part 1 (4 : 24), the goatherd Eugenio tells a story which appears to be conceived as a parody of another goatherd's tale near the beginning of *Don Quixote*, the tale of Chrysostom and Marcella. As in the earlier story, the heroine's beauty attracts suitors from near and far, and she will have none of them. But at the point where the proud and chaste Marcella decides to turn shepherdess and forsake society the foolish Leandra, having put off all meritorious suitors, elopes with a braggadocio peasant-soldier newly returned from abroad "all gay and glorious, in a thousand various Colours, bedeck'd with a thousand Toys of Crystal, and Chains of Steel . . . but all false, counterfeit and worthless." After the girl is robbed and abandoned by this swindler and has retired to a convent, her former suitors become shepherds, "giving vent to our Passions" and making "Complaints to Heaven on our Misfortune," just as Marcella's victims pursue her in pastoral guise, filling the countryside with their "doleful Ditties" and "woful Complaints." But "this Tragedy," as Eugenio calls it, can hardly be viewed as one by the reader. If the melancholy inclination of the two former contenders for the foolish girl's hand seems disproportionate to their loss, the same action taken by many others "in imitation of us" is clearly ridiculous: "So far does this Extravagance prevail, that here are those who complain of her Disdain who never spoke to her; and others who are jealous of Favours which she never granted to any."

The image of a landscape of lamenting lovers, an object of wonder in the first story, here becomes ludicrous, as the burlesque rhetoric of Eugenio's description makes clear: "There is not a hollow Place of a Rock, a Bank of a Brook, or a shady Grove, where there is not some or other of these amorous Shepherds telling their doleful Stories to the Air and Winds. Echo has learnt to repeat the Name of *Leandra*, *Leandra* all the Hills resound, the Brooks murmur *Leandra*, and 'tis *Leandra* that holds us all Inchanted, hoping without Hope, and fearing without knowing what we fear."

Whether or not Cervantes intended this second goatherd's tale to be a comic revision of his first, it might well have been seen as such by the man who called Chrysostom a "silly fellow."[5] The substitution for the nobly chaste Marcella of a girl whose behavior is attributed to "the Levity and Vanity of Mind, natural to Womankind" clearly prefigures Fielding's own conversion of the traditional faithful heroine into an "extreme Lover of Gaiety," whose "greedy Appetite of Vanity" feeds on masculine admiration. There are obvious parallels be-

[5] The comic tone of the tale is suggested by the manner of its introduction, in which Eugenio's harangue "in his familiar Dialect" of a nanny goat for female waywardness is the object of the travelers' amusement. The "Rustical and Unpolish'd" goatherd's melodramatic inference that the conclusion of his story, "tho' depending, yet may easily be perceiv'd likely to be unfortunate," is neither presaged by this "low" opening nor borne out by the event. Although "the manner of his relating it" has "more of a Scholar and Gentleman, than of a rude Goat-herd," this impression is immediately canceled by Eugenio's engagement in a low comedy brawl with Quixote and Sancho. The comic revision of pastoral is foreshadowed two hundred pages earlier when the lovelorn Cardenio is overheard singing in the wilderness. In an aside which anticipates Fielding's remarks in book 3, chapter 1, the narrator comments: "For though the Poets are pleas'd to fill the Fields and Woods with Swains and Shepherdesses, that sing with all the Sweetness and Delicacy imaginable, yet 'tis well enough known that those Gentlemen deal more in Fiction than in Truth, and love to embellish the Descriptions they make, with Things that have no Existence but in their own Brain" (p. 209). The hypothesis that Eugenio's story is intended as an ironic echo of Chrysostom's is supported by the generally recapitulative character of the closing chapters of part 1.

tween the foolish Leandra's story and that of "the unfortunate Leonora." Each is beguiled by a meretriciously glamorous and boastful stranger, fresh from his travels, whom she prefers to the worthier local suitor or suitors. As Leandra is promptly deserted once she has been tricked into delivering her father's money, Leonora is jilted when the fortune-hunting Bellarmine fails to obtain the expected dowry. But, whereas in Cervantes' tale the ridicule is directed at the true and false suitors, Fielding focused his on the heroine. Employing a strategy similar to that of *Shamela*, he simply altered the character of the conventional heroine while retaining the standard complications of her story (the separation of lovers on the eve of marriage, the appearance of an imposing stranger who fixes his sights on the heroine, the parent or guardian impressed by the second suitor's magnificence, the persuasions of a confidante in his behalf, the dilemma of the heroine beset by rival lovers, and the duel between these rivals) to develop the hint of Cervantes' little sketch into a sustained comic reworking of the traditional romantic tale.[6]

Perhaps to invite the reader's comparison of the story with its conventional counterparts, Fielding began "The Unfortu-

[6] Alan D. McKillop (*The Early Masters of English Fiction* [Lawrence, Kans., 1956], p. 112) remarks that Leonora's story is "deliberately filled with the stock formulas of the current love tale or 'novel'." Although the pattern of Leonora's story is probably based on an amalgam of clichés absorbed from his reading of "novels" both inside and outside the Cervantean tradition, Fielding might possibly have had the outlines of three of his predecessors' interpolations more immediately in mind. Lucinda and Cardenio exchange love letters, they are separated when he is sent away on the scheming Ferdinand's trumped-up business, and their betrothal is prevented when the girl's parents accept the powerful Ferdinand as a better "catch." In "Le juge de sa propre cause" (*Roman comique* 2 : 14), the heroine and her devoted Don Carlos are on the verge of matrimony when an Italian count sees the girl at a ball, and her father quickly accepts his proposal. In the story of Don Gaston de Cogollos (*Gil Blas* 9 : 6), the hero and his beloved Doña Helena are separated on the eve of their nuptials when he must flee after killing a rival in a duel. During his exile, the girl's father and her maid persuade her, by means of a counterfeit report of her lover's infidelity, to accept a wealthy suitor.

nate Jilt" as if it were to be a serious tale. "Yonder lives the unfortunate *Leonora*, if one can justly call a Woman unfortunate, whom we must own at the same time guilty, and the Author of her own Calamity," his lady storyteller artificially exclaims. Though not so solemn as this introduction would imply, the action of the first part of the tale seems to be essentially that of a conventional love story. In a courtship complete with exchange of love letters, the upright hero woos and wins the beauteous and high-spirited heroine, and their happy union awaits only his return from the brief session of the local assizes, Fielding's down-to-earth revision of the traditional lover's protracted banishment to a distant land.[7] It is with Horatio's departure and the arrival of Bellarmine, the point at which the crisis of the traditional story would begin, that Fielding's tale becomes unmistakably sardonic. In the conventional love tale, a heroine may be unwillingly forced or unwittingly tricked into forsaking a lover who has been absent for years or is presumed dead.[8] But no sooner has Horatio departed than Leonora's head is turned by the mere glimpse of a coach-and-six. Instead of the

[7] Even in these opening pages there are, in addition to the initial satiric characterization of the heroine, comic touches indicating that the tale is not to be the conventional episode it seems. Horatio's proposal can be read as a sustained bawdy double entendre, and there is an excess of delicacy and ingenuity in the love letters. The joking with the epistolary convention itself is more obvious. The lady coach passenger has not only "got by heart" the elaborately phrased letters of Horatio and Leonora but also "can repeat *verbatim*" three others from Bellarmine and Lindamira; and when she observes the decorum of asking leave to recite the first letter, the question must be "put to the Vote"!

The hero's enforced absence is the initial complication in the history of Donna Mencia de Mosquera (*Gil Blas* 1:11) and "Les deux freres rivaux" (*Roman comique* 2:19), as well as in the stories of Cardenio and Don Gaston de Cogollos.

[8] Doña Mencia de Mosquera must be endlessly "obsédée, importunée, tourmentée" by her whole family before she accepts an advantageous match, though she has had an eyewitness report of the death of the husband she has not heard from in seven years. "Mais les coeurs constans ne sçauroient, avoir qu'une passion" (*Gil Blas* 1 : 54).

conventional nobleman or foreign dignitary,[9] the threat to the lovers' happiness is a direct descendant of Leandra's tinseled soldier, a preposterous Frenchified beau whose courtship consists of speeches in praise of the cut of his own clothes. "[The] most uneasy of all the Situations I can figure in my Imagination," Leonora self-congratulatingly writes Horatio in response to his love letter, is that "of being led by Inclination to love the Person whom my own Judgment forces me to condemn." These words are still ironically echoing in the reader's mind when the heroine succumbs to this formidable gallant—or rather to his equipage.

There follow three scenes of comic suffering in which the pathos and melodrama of the conventional heroine caught between the demands of inclination and judgment, or love and honor, are turned to humorous effect. The first of these, Leonora's internal debate over the conflicting claims of her two lovers, is reminiscent of Lady Booby's conflicts of passion and principle. In "arguing with herself," Leonora reasons in part in the fashion expected of the traditional heroine. Her ostensible concern is with her obligations to Horatio and with the hurt she must inflict on one or the other of her lovers. But her very expression of the romantic clichés in the form of questions ("what signifies it that I have seen him [Bellarmine] . . .? Is not *Horatio* my Lover? almost my Husband? . . . But did not I no longer ago than yesterday, love *Horatio* more than all the World?") invites the reader to note the disparity between the behavior of this heroine and her conventional sisters. Intermingled with her "proper" sentiments, and implicit even in her dwelling on the disastrous effects of her loss upon the unlucky suitor ("May he

[9] Ferdinand is the son of a duke "whose Quality and Merit entitl'd him to the lawful Possession of Beauties of the highest Rank" (*Don Quixote*, p. 214). Doña Mencia's second suitor is a Marquis, Doña Helena's a rich visitor from a distant province. For the closest ironic analogue to this aspect of Leonora's story, see the remark on "Le juge de sa propre cause," n. 6 above.

not in despair break his Heart if I abandon him?"), is an incipient vanity which emerges as her true dominant motive in a torrent of "reasons" which turn the seesaw argument into a rout:

Did not the dear Creature [Bellarmine] prefer me to every Woman in the Assembly, when every She was laying out for him? When was it in *Horatio's* power to give me such an Instance of Affection? Can he give me an Equipage, or any of those Things which *Bellarmine* will make me Mistress of? How vast is the Difference between being the Wife of a poor Counsellor, and the Wife of one of *Bellarmine's* Fortune! If I marry *Horatio*, I shall triumph over no more than one Rival; but by marrying *Bellarmine*, I shall be the envy of all my Acquaintance. What Happiness!

By intimating in advance that Leonora has already decided in favor of Bellarmine (she has previously referred his proposal to her father "who, she knew, would quickly declare in favour of a Coach and Six"), Fielding reduces this "agony" to a mere affectation of moral conflict, a process by which she may rationalize (absurdly) her inclination. By the same token, the following scene between Leonora and her aunt becomes a caricature of the conventional situation in which the duenna or relative argues for the more materially advantageous match against the inclinations of the faithful heroine. Again beginning in conventional fashion, in response to her aunt's adjuration "not [to] withstand your own Preferments," Leonora, "sighing, 'begged her not to mention any such thing, when she knew her Engagements to *Horatio*.' " But as she amusingly shifts the ground of her objection—from the pretended sense of obligation to the fear of the world's opinion to the technical problem of discarding her fiancé gracefully—it is evident that her resistance is only put on to draw from the older woman some external justification for her conduct. Having thus adroitly elicited "the world's" support for her own previously determined sentiments, she can, a few pages later, when Bellarmine is reported killed, play the betrayed virtuous maiden, blaming her "adviser" for her predicament: "You seduced me, contrary to my Inclinations, to abandon poor *Horatio* . . . it was you, who got the better of my Youth and Simplicity, and forced me to lose my dear *Horatio* for ever."

The climax of this central sequence, the scene in which Horatio unexpectedly breaks in upon a tête-à-tête between Leonora and her new lover, is a comic version of Lesage's dramatic nocturnal confrontations among members of a romantic triangle. One of his heroines, having been tricked into marrying by a false report of her fugitive lover's infidelity, meets his later reproachful and passionate addresses with a firm refusal to put inclination above virtue; when the desperate lover attempts suicide, her husband unexpectedly emerges from concealment to deter him.[10] A similar midnight interview between another virtuous victim and her erstwhile royal suitor is disrupted by the intrusion of her husband, and the resultant violence ends in the deaths of both husband and wife.[11] Like these heroines, Leonora is caught between the claims of two lovers, and like them she adheres to her later commitment in the face of the appeal of her former lover. The nature of Horatio's disappointment, however, is radically different from that of his heroic brethren: whereas they are balked by the conventional heroine's noble affirmation of fidelity to her marriage vows against the promptings of her own undying love, Horatio learns that "nothing more extraordinary had happened in his three days Absence, than a small Alteration in the Affections of *Leonora*." At the conclusion of his conversation at cross-purposes with his fiancée, who affects only a "common Acquaintance" with him, the bewildered Horatio, like the girl's

[10] The story of Don Gaston de Cogollos, *Gil Blas* 9 : 6.

[11] "Le Mariage de vengeance," *Gil Blas* 4 : 4. For the reader familar with such scenes of passionate declamation and violence, the absurdity of Bellarmine's empty oaths and belligerent hat-cocking is heightened by implicit contrast.

aunt a few pages later, and like the innocents in the main actions of the novel, finds himself unaccountably the guilty party, as the abused heroine tearfully wonders "what Reason she had given him to use her in so barbarous a Manner."

With her response to the conventional romantic calamity of the duel that follows,[12] the ironic contrast between Leonora and her traditional prototypes is completed. The news of Bellarmine's supposed death first produces a lament which dwells characteristically on the "cursed Charms" that have destroyed "the most charming Man of this Age." Then, compounding her violation of the heroine's code in the preceding scene, she indulges in regrets and recriminations at having picked the loser and finds her "feelings" for "my dear *Horatio*" conveniently reviving. But when the accelerating process of her alternating affections is given still another turn by the news that Bellarmine lives, the parodic comedy is at an end, and the story enters a new phase. In deciding to go to the wounded Bellarmine's bedside against her aunt's advice, Leonora behaves foolishly, but for the first time she acts out of an impulse other than personal vanity and against the kind of worldly prudential considerations that have previously governed her conduct.

By interrupting the tale at this point, Fielding facilitates the shift from the unsympathetic comedy of the complication to a denouement in which the anticipated punitive satisfaction at seeing the jilt herself jilted is qualified by a measure of compassion for "the unfortunate *Leonora*." When the tale is resumed after the comic battle between Adams, Slipslop, and the innkeepers, the center of narrative attention shifts from Leonora, whose actions are continually before us in the first installment,

[12] Lesage was particularly fond of the duel as a threat to the happiness of his lovers. Doña Mencia's husband and Don Gaston de Cogollos both are forced to flee abroad after killing their respective rivals, and Don Alphonse's blossoming romance with "la belle Seraphine" is blighted by the discovery that he has killed her brother (4 : 10).

to the machinations of two more antipathetic comic figures, the girl's ill-natured father and the envious prude Lindamira. By keeping his heroine offstage from the time her fortunes begin to decline and her motives to improve, Fielding allows the impression of her silly vanity to fade. As we see her attacked by the jealous gossip and made the football of economic maneuvering between her lover and her father, our recognition that the self-indulgent girl's fate is the product of her own folly is softened. Thus Fielding could make Leonora's story the vehicle of his satiric treatment of the romantic conventions and still conclude it on a note of sentiment consistent with the tone of the storyteller's introduction, carrying the lesson of her folly home more feelingly and restoring to his ironic inversion the guise of a conventional tale. In keeping with this modification, he made only one additional play on the conventional formulas in the second part of the story, but he made it central to the climax of the action. The comic aspect of the catastrophe is heightened by the satiric transformation of the traditional prudent father seeking a worthy alliance into an old miser whose selfishness and hypocrisy overmatch Bellarmine's.[13]

If material hints for "The Unfortunate Jilt" were offered by the goatherd's tale, its formal prototype is to be found in "The Curious Impertinent." Like Leonora's history, this "novel" of Anselmo's perverse insistence that his friend test his wife's chastity is a punitive apologue in which the protagonist undoes his own present good fortune by pursuing an *ignis fatuus.* ("Was ever Man so unhappy as *Anselmo*, who industriously

[13] In addition to the stories of Cardenio and Don Gaston de Cogollos and "Le juge de sa propre cause," the motif of faithful lovers separated by paternal preference of a richer or more "suitable" suitor is prominent in "Le Mariage de vengeance"; the story of Basil, Quiteria, and Camacho (*Don Quixote*, pt. 2, chaps. 19–21); and the prior's story in Girault's sequel of *Le Roman comique* (3 : 13).

contriv'd the Plot of his own Ruin and Dishonour? . . . He that aims at Things impossible, ought justly to lose those Advantages which are within the Bounds of Possibility," exclaims Cervantes' narrator, prefiguring the qualified compassion of Fielding's storyteller.) Cervantes' story exhibits, in more sharply differentiated form, the overall structural pattern of Fielding's tale. Beginning as a sober warning against a morbid marital pride and jealous curiosity, the story turns to comedy when the foolish husband succeeds in cuckolding himself and is at last certain of his wife's fidelity when it is no more. After this comedy reaches a climax in a mock-tragic charade of matronly innocence resisting violation, staged by the adulterous couple for their eavesdropping victim's benefit, the narrative is interrupted by Don Quixote's somnambulistic battle with a "giant." In its brief sequel, the tale departs more sharply than Fielding's from its dominant vein, returning to its initial seriousness with a vengeance. The accidental discovery of his dishonor and folly so affects "the unfortunate Anselmo" that he is "struck with Death almost that very Moment," to be followed shortly by his remorseful friend and grief-stricken wife. "This was the unhappy End of them all proceeding from so impertinent a Beginning."

Recognizing Cervantes' division of the story as a technique for articulating the awkward transition from the central comedy to this rather perfunctory moralizing conclusion, Fielding adapted it to a similar but more subtle function in working out the structure of Leonora's story. As a kind of acknowledgment of his indebtedness for this procedure and the larger formal pattern in which it is employed, he made the comic fight that occurs between the two sections of his story a homelier English version of the culinary "battle" that intrudes upon "The Curious Impertinent." The image of Don Quixote's duel with the sacks of wine, in which Sancho "saw . . . Blood run all about the House," is revived in the incarnadine spectacle of Adams "all over covered with Blood" after his drenching with the pan of hogs puddings.[14]

One can see why Fielding (who described Mrs. Tow-wouse' discovery of her husband in bed with her maid as "a Catastrophe, common enough, and comical enough too, perhaps in modern History, yet often fatal to the Repose and Well-being of Families") might naturally have turned to "The Curious Impertinent" in seeking a model for his own first story. It clearly lies closer to his own mode of comic realism than the other stories whose authenticity he maintained in book 3, chapter 1. The fall of the peerless wife and extraordinarily devoted friend may be "Proof that Love is a Power too strong to be overcome by any thing but flying," but theirs is not the ethereal passion that inspires Chrysostom; unlike the noble Cardenio and Lucinda, Camilla and Lothario are human enough to fall. Indeed, the explicit premises of the tale—that "the Nature of Women is, at best, but weak and imperfect" and that the "Virtue [which] may pass through the fiery Trial of vigorous Solicitations and Addresses" is "that which is not to be found in Nature"—run directly counter to the convention of romantic fidelity that Fielding inverted in "The Unfortunate Jilt."[15]

[14] Cross may have had these structural resemblances in mind when he cryptically alluded to the two tales as "exact parallels" (1 : 322), but the context suggests that he probably had reference to their function in the movement of the narrative as a whole. The inference that Fielding was following the pattern of "The Curious Impertinent" is strengthened by the fact that in no other tale in the tradition is the conclusion so set off from the story's main body.

[15] Fielding probably also would have appreciated two details of Cervantes' story. Attribution of the subversion of Camilla's chastity to "The Weakest Part of Woman, her Vanity," would strike a responsive chord. The mock-melodramatic declamations of Lady Booby and Mrs. Tow-wouse are prefigured by her performance in the climactic "formal Tragedy of . . . ruin'd Honour": "*Avaunt* false Thoughts. Revenge is now my Task, let the Treacherous Man approach, let him come, let him die, let him perish; let him but perish, no matter what's the fatal Consequence. My dear *Anselmo* receiv'd me to his Bosom Spotless and Chaste, and so shall the Grave receive me from his Arms" (p. 298).

It is not surprising, then, that he should have based the second of his inserted tales, the story of Paul and Leonard, even more directly on "The Curious Impertinent." What is unexpected, given the affinity of this story with Fielding's satiric vision, is the form his imitation took. Instead of serving as a formal model, Cervantes' tale here provided a material paradigm, a basic plot situation to be subjected to another of Fielding's satiric transformations. Having played ironically upon the complications of the conventional love intrigue in Leonora's story, in his briefer tale near the end of the novel he amusingly questioned the assumption of wedded bliss underlying all romantic happy denouements (including his own) by drawing a sardonic "true" picture of the marital state. In doing so, he wittily put himself "one up" on his master by revising the most realistic of his tales in keeping with his own vision of "the nature of things." "Here," he seems to say, "is the story of two friends and a wife as it might take place in contemporary 'real life.'" Transferring the action from the traditional novella setting of Florence to an English country house and replacing its amorous intrigue with squabbling over woodcocks and waistcoats, he fashioned a tale whose pointedly sexless domestic bickering is so remote from Cervantes' morbid jealousy and adulterous passion that the connection between the two stories has never been noted, though Fielding himself hinted at it in his title. "The History of two Friends" echoes the opening sentence of "The Curious Impertinent," which introduces a phrase that occurs like a refrain in Cervantes' story: "*Anselmo* and *Lothario* . . . were so eminent for their Friendship, that they were called nothing but the *Two Friends*."[16]

[16] The phrase is repeated when the newly wed Anselmo tells his decorously reticent friend "that he would never for the idle Reputation of a cautious Husband, suffer so tender and agreeable a Name to be lost, as that of *The Two Friends*" (p. 270), and again at the close of the story when Anselmo hears a stranger recount the news of his shame: "No Man could ever suspect such a Crime from a Person engag'd in so strict a Friendship

Fielding begins his tale in similar fashion, informing us that "Leonard and *Paul* were two Friends" whose mutual affection was "so deeply fixed in both their Minds" that it survived fifteen years' separation to be "revived in all its Force" on their chance reunion. Like "The Curious Impertient," Fielding's story recounts what happens to this undying attachment when the ingredient of a wife is added. But the recipe is satirically altered. The thesis of Cervantes' tale is that Anselmo's married state would be blissful were it not for his perverse curiosity. Leonard is not so fortunate. The figure of his wife bears the same relation to the initially modest and devoted Camilla as Fielding's Leonora does to the traditional noble maiden. "Tho' her Person was of that kind to which Men attribute the Name of Angel," this lady, remembered by Paul in her single state as one who "always appeared to be of a most agreeable Temper," is "in her Mind . . . perfectly Woman," most notably in possessing "a great degree of Obstinacy." Hence Leonard's ostensibly happy marriage is a perpetual dispute, and instead of being ensnared by his hostess' charms Paul desires only a little quiet.

Like his Cervantean counterpart, Fielding's bachelor is a person of superior prudence and wisdom. As Lothario argues systematically against Anselmo's crazy intention, so Paul preaches magnanimity to each of the disputants in turn; and, like Lothario in the first part of Cervantes' story, he is drawn into an innocent kind of double-dealing with both husband and wife. For a time his policy of persuading both partners to give way by privately agreeing with each brings peace to the house, but as Cervantes' tale culminates in Anselmo's discovery of his betrayal, so Fielding's reaches its climax when the bickering couple discover their common deception and turn on the unlucky bachelor. Thus the story of Paul and Leonard,

with *Anselmo*, as *Lothario* was; for they were call'd the *Two Friends*" (p. 309).

like "The Curious Impertinent" (and "The Unfortunate Jilt"), is a comic apologue which makes its point through an ironic reversal of the protagonist's fortunes. As Anselmo, in satisfying his compulsion to certify his wife's chastity, manages to undo them both, Paul, in attempting to pacify the conjugal quarrelers, achieves an equally bitter success, uniting them in a bond of hatred toward himself.

But, while both stories might thus have as their moral "it is better to leave well enough alone," Fielding made the effect of this outcome in his story pointedly different from that of Cervantes. Anselmo's double betrayal is a just retribution for his own persistent folly, as Leonora's abandonment is the fitting consequence of her "greedy appetite of vanity." But if Paul, like Anselmo, may be said to "aim at things impossible," this is no imputation of fault on his part but Fielding's satiric reflection on "the nature of things" in his world. Paul's naïve presumption in attempting to meddle in a marriage (the apparent object of the "useful Lesson" which, according to the facetious chapter title, the story "may afford . . . those Persons, who happen to take up their Residence in married Families") is mitigated by his scrupulous effort to ignore the controversy until his friend actively solicits his opinion. Though it ultimately backfires, his "doctrine of submission" is a sensible and good-natured marital philosophy. His appeal to the love each spouse is supposed to feel for the other implies a generosity of impulse in marked contrast to the pettiness of his hosts. His simultaneous support of both quarrelers, considering the triviality of their differences and the fact that it does put them on a better footing, is a mild and wholesome deception. The real source of their fury on discovering his imposition is not that they have have been dealt with dishonestly but that he has trifled with the cherished certainty of each in the rightness of his or her opinion. In contrast to the division arduously wrought between Cervantes' "Two Friends" by the sustained power of perversity and passion, the friendship of Paul and Leonard is an easy sacrifice on the altar of vanity.

Both the mock homiletics of Fielding's chapter title and the fact that his tale is read from a schoolbook suggest that it will be brought to the same kind of moral conclusion Cervantes appended to "The Curious Impertinent." Instead, in a characteristic literary jest, he unexpectedly disrupts the story's narration and leaves it ostensibly incomplete while in fact bringing its peculiar ironic form to an effective climax. By interrupting the tale in the midst of the mounting quarrel between the two friends, Fielding leaves the reader with a vivid comic impression of what has happened in the course of his brief tale to the affection "so deeply fixed in both their Minds." By breaking off just after the "injured" husband charges the poor peacemaker with having caused most of the couple's quarrels and, in an ironic echo of Cervantes' story, having almost "been the Occasion of their Separation," he brings the unfinished story to a characteristically wry conclusion. In pointed contrast to the retributive justice of Cervantes' ending, the moral universe is turned upside down, and, instead of the punitive satisfaction entailed in Anselmo's victimization by his own contrivance, amusement is mixed with a sense of comic injustice.

In presenting this sardonic vignette of married life (preceded and followed by Mrs. Adams' uxorial ministrations to the good parson) a few chapters before the end of the narrative, Fielding may have intended to cast a shade of comic skepticism over its romantic consummation, as the tale of Eugenio and Leandra reflects on that of Chrysostom and Marcella. But along with Leonora's story, "The History of two Friends" also produces an opposite effect. In the first of these stories, the heroine's love proves to be a mere form easily sacificed to the whim of vanity; in the second, conjugal communion is reduced to opinionated rivalry. In reaction to this peculiarly sterile composite picture of love and marriage in which neither romantic sentiment nor carnal passion obtains, the reader may sympathize more with the innocent Joseph and Fanny and derive more satisfaction from their union, in which these aspects of love are harmonized. Although marital antagonism is as prevalent in *Joseph Andrews* as medical fraud in *Gil Blas*, and true sexual love as scarce as Christian love for one's neighbor, this rhetoric carries a special force in these independent stories, where even Fielding's "mere English reader," familiar with the conventions of the ubiquitous "novel," might anticipate actions of a very different order.

One would not expect to find in Mr. Wilson's history anything like the comic revisions of earlier tales observed in these two detached formal stories. Like the episodic autobiography from which it derives (see above, pp. 130–32), it makes its satiric points directly; so far from rewriting the clichés of the conventional love tale, it culminates in a baldly contrived romantic denouement whose unabashed sentimentality is not even given the kind of comic attenuation allotted the story of Joseph and Fanny. Yet it furnishes collateral evidence that in devising these two stories Fielding had his eye on their prototypes in the continental comic romance tradition, and particularly those of Cervantes. For the context in which it is introduced is based on an episode in *Don Quixote*, and when these are compared even this least "literary" of Fielding's interpolations divulges an apparently calculated ironic contrast.

The episode of Wilson's hospitality to the weary travelers at the midpoint of *Joseph Andrews* is clearly modeled on Don Quixote's meeting with "the Knight of the Green Coat," Don Diego de Miranda, which occurs at a comparable point in Cervantes' narrative (pt. 2, chaps. 16–18). Like Fielding's trio at the Wilson's, Quixote and Sancho are hospitably but unostentatiously entertained by Don Diego and his family. For each set of travelers the sojourn is a kind of idyll, a tranquil respite from "adventures." Don Diego is one of the rare characters who do not make fun of Don Quixote, and Wilson is virtually the only person Adams meets outside his parish who does not treat him with duplicity, hostility, or contempt. Like the "sober gentleman of La Mancha," the mature Wilson is a sensible man of good will whose prudent tending of his own garden serves as a norm of good conduct and foil for the ludicrously erring yet extraordinarily good comic hero. Fielding's "description of Mr. Wilson's way of living," with its familial round of simple rural pleasures and domestic duties extending outward in acts of neighborly charity, is an anglicized version of the retired life espoused by Cervantes' model Christian gentleman. After hearing a description of "the Gentleman's way of Living," Sancho Panza proclaims him "the first Saint on Horse-back I ever saw in my born Days." Adams' evaluation of "Mr. Wilson's way of living"—"that this was the Manner in which the People had lived in the Golden Age"—is comparably hyperbolic.

The conclusion that Fielding was consciously imitating Cervantes' episode is borne out by a still more precise and idiosyncratic resemblance. Don Diego's son is a poet, and his literary aspirations are the principal topic of discussion during Quixote's visit. As Wilson is suspicious of Adams until his dissertation on Homer converts his misgiving to warm admiration, so Don Diego's doubts about his guest's sanity are overwhelmed by Quixote's eloquent discourse in defense of the son's vocation:

> For . . . the Art of Poetry . . . is none of those that disgrace the ingenious Professor. Poetry, Sir, in my Judgment, is like a tender Virgin in her Bloom, Beautiful and Charming to Amazement. . . . But this Virgin must not be roughly handl'd, nor dragg'd along the Street, nor expos'd to every Marketplace, and Corner of great Men's Houses. . . . She must not be Mercenary, though she need

> not give away the Profits she may claim. . . . She is not to be attempted by Buffoons, nor by the Ignorant Vulgar, whose Capacity can never reach to a due Sense of theTreasures that are lock'd up in her. . . . But whoever shall apply himself to the Muses with those Qualifications, which . . . are essential to the Character of a good Poet, his Name shall be Famous, and valu'd in all the polish'd Nations of the World. . . . And when Kings and Princes see the wonderful Art of Poetry shine in prudent, virtuous, and solid Subjects, they honour, esteem, and enrich them.

The satiric point of Fielding's imitation now begins to emerge. In the light of the detailed analogy between the two episodes, it is surely no coincidence that the bitterest phase of Wilson's town experience and the lowest point in his descent, short of imprisonment, is reached when he enters upon the literary life. Only two chapters after defining *Don Quixote* as the history of that part of the world "which is polished by Laws, Arts and Sciences . . . from the time it was polished to this day," Fielding presents an image of his own vocation which is a studied inversion of Cervantes' lofty vision of a disinterested and honored calling. It is not the inspiration of the muse but "Poverty and Distress with their horrid Train of Duns, Attorneys, [and] Bailiffs," that drive Wilson to literature. In wry rebuttal to Quixote's noble suggestion that the poet should not be mercenary, Wilson exclaims, "Happy indeed would be the State of Poetry, would these Tickets pass current at the Bakehouse, the Ale-House, and the Chandler's-Shop." However true Quixote's observations may be for "the world in general," in Fielding's "true history" the "tender Virgin" is more "roughly handl'd" than the young girl whom Wilson debauches. She is indeed "expos'd to every Marketplace, and Corner of great Men's houses," as the young playwright in search of patronage haunts "the cold Parlours of Men of Quality" where no beneficent "Kings and Princes" are to be found: "After seeing the lowest Rascals in Lace and Embroidery, the

Pimps and Buffoons in Fashion admitted, I have been . . . told . . . that my Lord could not possibly see me this Morning."

When the "utmost mortification" of occasionally receiving a "Guinea from a Man of Quality, given with as ill a Grace as Alms are generally to the meanest Beggar," is followed by the managers' casual scuttling of his play, Wilson has yet to experience fully how "the Character of a . . . Poet" is "valu'd" in his "polish'd Nation." Far from winning him honor and esteem, "the Reputation of a Poet" proves his "Bane," hindering access even to the lowly employment of an attorney's scribe; and the very name of Cervantes' "ingenious Professor" is reduced to a derisive epithet: "Whenever I durst venture to a Coffee-house . . . a Whisper ran round the Room, which was constantly attended with a Sneer—*That's poet Wilson.*"

The diverse disenchantments wrought in Fielding's reshaping of the materials provided by Cervantes and his fellow "biographers" furnish vivid illustration, in places one would least expect to encounter it, of the more Swiftian satiric direction he gave the tradition of comic realism to which he made himself heir. In the tale of Leonora, the romantic love and fidelity of the conventional heroine are replaced by a "greedy appetite of vanity"; in the story of Paul and Leonard, the stormy sexual passion and intrigue of Cervantes' triangle are superseded by the petty domestic bickerings of two more vain creatures; and, in the corrupt world of Wilson's history, Cervantes' noble "Art of Poetry" is regarded as if it were indeed a "disgrace to the ingenious Professor." In thus bringing the realism of his predecessors up to date, Fielding implicitly disparaged the quality of life in his own society. The satiric point of Wilson's authorial plight would be clear to the reader who has never heard of Don Quixote, much less Don Diego de Miranda, and the primary comic impact of the two shorter tales is independent of their ironic reference to specific or particular antecedents. But for the reader aware of the parallels the amusement of these tales is heightened, as Fielding's bitter vision of the estate of letters is sharpened, by its ironic contrast to Cervantes' ideal picture, and the more general derogation of the complacently "civilized" world of mid–eighteenth century England is pointed up by the satiric departures of all three "true" episodes from their fictional antecedents.

Incident into Sequence: The Parts and the Whole

WALTER ALLEN identified a distinctive aspect of Fielding's art when he remarked his ability "to cap absurdity of situation on absurdity of situation in a single scene, and to go on doing it beyond what we expect to be the climax."[1] If, as Allen says, this is "the prerogative of great comic writers," Fielding's predecessors were not much inclined to exercise it. Of the continental writers he had before him, Cervantes offered the most precedents for this kind of construction; yet, of the hundred or so adventures in *Don Quixote*, those which are carried beyond their expected or immediate conclusion can be exhaustively enumerated here.[2] After the free-for-all touched off by Quixote's amorous parley with Maritornes has subsided, the apparently concluded episode is briefly resuscitated (pt. 1, 3:3) when the knight's haughty response to an officer's solicitous inquiry earns him a final knock on the head. His glorious rout of a

[1] *The English Novel* (London, 1954), p. 49.

[2] I exclude from consideration such running jokes as the enchantment of Dulcinea and its consequences or the Micomicona hoax, not to mention that "unincremental repetition" which Northrop Frye sees at the heart of Cervantes' comedy (*The Anatomy of Criticism* [New York, 1966], p. 168).

funeral procession (pt. 1, 3:5) is followed by the knight's solemn cross-examination of a priest pinned beneath his mule, in which the madman blandly attributes the disaster he has visited on the mourners to their error of appearing "with your white Surplices, bearing Torches and sable Weeds, like Ghosts and Goblins, that went about to scare People out of their Wits." An unexpected twist is added to the comedy of the Micomicona hoax (pt. 1, 4:4) when the long-forgotten servant lad who was the unlucky beneficiary of the hero's first noble deed unexpectedly returns and the knight is prevented by his "Engagement" to the make-believe princess from fulfilling his promise of justice.

Cervantes' most remarkable development of this kind, and perhaps the most strikingly sustained sequence in the continental comic romances, is the exploding series of actions in the innyard at the climax of part 1 (4:16–18). The three-ring fracas precipitated by the attempted departure of two non-paying guests and the arrival of the pursuers of a young runaway lover while Quixote is dangling in a *strapado* of Maritornes' mischievous devising is just quieting down when the unexpected reappearance of the itinerant barber initiates a new chain of events. His fight with Sancho over his stolen equipage leads to the solemn adjudication of the question of Mambrino's helmet, and the humorous decision in favor of Quixote's fantasy results in turn in a battle royal "so that the whole House was a Medley of Wailings, Cries, Shrieks, Confusions, Fears, Terrors, Disasters, Slashes, Buffets, Blows, Kicks, Cuffs, Battery, and Bloodshed," which is terminated by Quixote's conceit that he is "involv'd in the Disorder and Confusion of King *Agramant's* Camp." When he persuades the curate and the judge to reenact the roles of the peacemaking kings in this romantic episode, the sequence again appears to have reached its conclusion, but now another of Quixote's heroic deeds comes home to roost—the officers attempt to arrest the knight for freeing the galley slaves

—and a fourth and final battle erupts before order is at last restored.

Scarron's extended incidents are cruder versions of this episode, with more emphasis on the accumulation of violence and accident than on the humorous conjuncture of persons and unexpected consequences of presumably closed episodes. His most effectively sustained comic sequence occurs in the episode of the landlord's ghost (2:7), in which the usual formula of an outcry from Ragotin followed by discovery of the trick played on him is expanded into a more complex episode. Ragotin's panic at Rancune's supposed death is followed by the landlady's discovery that her husband's corpse has disappeared and the maid's finding of the body under a bed. The "mystery" of these events is resolved by the disclosure of Rancune's grisly practical joke, but this precipitates the wild "combat inegal" into which all the inn residents and neighbors are drawn (see above, p. 140). The settlement of this row appears to bring the episode to a close, "Mais la Discorde, aux crins de couleuvre, n'avait pas encore fait dans cette maison-là tout ce qu'elle avait envie d'y faire," and Ragotin's new outburst carries the company upstairs, where the little man is found stuffed in a trunk; he tries to retaliate against the maid who put him there, has his breeches pulled down and is spanked, and, in trying to escape this assault, gets his feet caught in a chamber pot, with which Scarronesque predicament the episode concludes. Cruder than this sequence or the briefer but structurally similar "Combat de Nuit" (1:12) is the succession of misfortunes befalling drunken Ragotin near the end of part 2, which proceeds by simple accumulation without the sense of a complex set of nearly simultaneous actions.

Neither Lesage nor Marivaux built such chain reactions of comic violence. In keeping with his tendency to concentrate on the static display of foibles, Lesage rarely carried an incident past its expected conclusion. But the ironic sequence in which the comic catastrophe of Gil Blas's dismissal by the archbishop is capped by the desertion of the two-faced priest prefigures Fielding's characteristic practice more precisely than any other compounded incident in the tradition. Relying for his incidental effects on the extended dramatic scene and the unexpected interruption or confrontation, Marivaux also rarely fused one comic incident onto another. The most noteworthy exception occurs in the fifth part of *Le Paysan parvenu*, where the frustration of Jacob's tryst with Mme de Ferval leads into a scene in which the hypocritically proper lady is amusingly brought by carefully graduated degrees from her initial self-righteous embarrassment to the acceptance of the intruding gentleman as her suitor, at which point the inadvertent exclamation of the eavesdropping Jacob disrupts his rival's progress even as that gentleman did his.[3]

What is occasional practice for his predecessors is habitual with Fielding. He may heighten the effect of an incident by protracting it, as in the latter part of the promiser episode, or embellish it with an ironic subaction, as in the same incident, where he arranges to have Joseph and Adams engaged in a "fierce Dispute . . . whether *Fanny* should ride behind *Joseph*, or behind the Gentleman's Servant" when "a Servant arrived from their good Friend, to acquaint them, that he was unfortunately prevented from lending them any Horses." He gives Joseph's mock-heroic triumph over Didapper's servant (4:7) a completely unexpected erotic turn as the sight of Fanny's uncovered bosom, "more capable of converting a Man into a Statue, than of being imitated by the greatest Master of that art," comically transfixes her rescuer. He will use the aftermath of an incident to bring out the ways of the world, as he does in the

[3] The climactic interview between Marianne and M. de Climal leads into a scene centering on the girl's linendraper landlady's humorous reaction to her abandonment; one might also consider the ironic reversal of roles between de Climal and Valville a delayed continuation of the comedy of the hypocrite's discovery of the two young people together.

hogsblood battle, where the beau back from the grand tour uses poor Adams' gory state as a pretext for displaying his garbled Shakespeare and faulty Italian, and the two lawyers try to get the parson and his host to continue their battle vindictively in the courts. He may even hammer home an already implicit comic point, as he does by having Adams *resume* his lecture to Joseph after displaying his own disregard of his preachments in response to his son's supposed drowning.

Of the dozen or so extensions in the tradition, only a few involve some kind of ironic development either in relation to the basic incident or other parts of the narrative. Fielding's extensions usually involve some comic irony, like the resumption of the lecture. To the irony of Lady Booby's censure of Adams' debauchery is added the irony of his suspicion by Joseph and Fanny. To the internal irony of the drowning episode is added the ironic reversal of the roles of Joseph and Adams in the earlier scene of Joseph's grief (3:11). Even the extension of Leonora's story beyond the conventional catastrophes threatened by the duel and by Lindamira's effort to prejudice Leonora's father against the marriage serves to bring out the irony of its denouement. While the action seems to be progressing past these obstacles toward the heroine's union with Bellarmine (a fitting comic punishment in itself), her fate is actually worsening, for neither of these externally caused breaches would be as wry a reversal as the ultimate humiliation of the jilt's being herself jilted.

Two special instances of Fielding's delight in compounding irony are Adams' encounter with the Roman priest (3:8) and the aftermath of the justice scene (2:11). In the first of these, what appears to be a simple, if magnified, unmasking when the grave gentleman concludes his eloquence in contempt of earthly riches by requesting a loan becomes a wry reversal of the earlier encounter with the promising gentleman when Adams discovers his money is stolen. The irony of the benevolent parson suspected of false charity by a priest whose otherworldliness is apparently calculated sham is heightened by the reader's recognition that his behavior, as it must appear to the shrewd papist, closely resembles that of the false-promiser: after joining in pious exhortations against earthly goods, he enthusiastically offers his petitioner much more than he asks for, then protests that he is prevented from carrying out his good intention by circumstances beyond his control. After the farce of the arraignment is ended by the intervention of a spectator who recognizes Adams, a quarrel between the parson's captors over the division of the reward they might have received if he had been a robber prompts Adams to sermonize against the tendency to dispute over unreal issues, and he tells a comic anecdote of the rivalry between two unsuccessful aspirants for his clerkship over which of them would have been chosen if their successful rival had not. Amusing as these elements are in themselves, they are only preliminary to the doubly ironic climax of the episode, in which Adams and the justice are drawn into a dispute over the already settled case, with Adams, who argued during the hearing against his commitment, now arguing pedantically that by law he should be jailed!

Profiting from the example of Cervantes' innyard sequence, Fielding extended or complicated a number of his incidents with an eye to their place or function in his overall narrative scheme. The most obvious of these is the climactic night scene, but some lesser instances are indicative of his habitual concern with the shape of his story.[4] Cervantes' "bloody" interruption of "The Curious Impertinent" is as brief as his subsequent conclusion of the tale is perfunctory. But Fielding's version of the encounter with the wine sacks touches off a chain of comic developments:

[4] McKillop, *The Early Masters of English Fiction*, p. 114, notes that the "method of the scene is essentially that which Cervantes uses in his important inn scenes, with various characters and themes converging."

after the continental traveler and the lawyers have added their footnotes to the battle, the quarrel between Slipslop and "Mrs. Grave-Airs" over admission of humble Joseph to the coach is capped by the exposure of that "lady's" low position which is in turn topped by Slipslop's unexpected reaction. By prolonging this comic sequence, Fielding widens the gap between the parodic comedy of the first part of Leonora's tale and its comic-pathetic denouement, facilitating and disguising this modification. At the same time the beau's resemblance to Bellarmine serves to recall the interrupted story, and Fielding playfully heightens the reader's anticipation of its completion: "Every thing being now adjusted, the Company entered the Coach, which was just on its Departure"—when each of the passengers recollects some possession left at the inn. Even after the coach departs, the ladies must sharpen their claws on the departed snob before Leonora's story is finally resumed.

Another kind of structural use of incident development is seen in Fielding's parallel treatment of the two episodes which serve as milestones marking the beginning and conclusion of Adams' wandering adventures in book 2. The first of these, Adams' confrontation with the contradictory testimony of the two lawyers (2:3), has as its core the classic three-part structure of a comic anecdote. One lawyer presents the local gentleman as a thorough villain; his companion paints him as a saint; when puzzled Adams turns to the host, he explains that neither view is correct. The incident builds to a clear climax as the host, canceling out the opposing views on several parts of the gentleman's conduct, at last reaches the "punch line":

"Aye, aye," says *Adams*, "and how doth he behave as a Justice, pray?" "Faith, Friend," answered the Host, "I question whether he is in the Commission: the only Cause I have heard he hath decided a great while, was one between these very two Persons who just went out of this House; and I am sure he determined that justly, for I heard the whole matter." "Which did he decide it in favour of?" quoth *Adams*. "I think I need not answer that Question," cried the Host, "after the different Characters you have heard of him."

This is the "natural" conclusion of the incident, but Adams' refusal to believe that "Men should arrive at such a Pitch of Wickedness, to be-lye the Character of their Neighbour from a little private Affection, or what is infinitely worse, a private Spite" leads to a discussion in which the contrast between Adams' Christianity and that of his host is amusingly set forth:

"Out of love to your self, you should confine yourself to Truth," says *Adams*, "for by doing otherwise, you injure the noblest Part of yourself, your immortal Soul. I can hardly believe any Man such an Idiot to risque the Loss of that by any trifling Gain, and the greatest Gain in this World is but Dirt in comparison of what shall be revealed hereafter." Upon which the Host taking up the Cup, with a Smile drank a Health to Hereafter: adding, "he was for something present." "Why," says *Adams* very gravely, "Do not you believe another World?" To which the Host answered, "yes, he was no Atheist." "And you believe you have an immortal Soul?" cries *Adams*: He answered, "God forbid he should not." "And Heaven and Hell?" said the Parson. The Host then bid him "not to prophane: for those were Things not to be mentioned nor thought of but in Church." *Adams* asked him, "why he went to Church, if what he learned there had no Influence on his Conduct in Life?" "I go to Church," answered the Host, "to say my Prayers and behave godly." "And dost not thou," cry'd *Adams*, "believe what thou hearest at Church?" "Most part of it, Master," returned the Host. "And dost thou then tremble," cries *Adams*, "at the Thought of eternal Punishment?" "As for that, Master," said he, "I never once thought about it: but what signifies talking about matters so far off? the Mug is out, shall I draw another?"

This continuation of the incident integrates the episode into the narrative more effectively than would a simple termination with the departure of the original comic subjects such as Lesage might have fashioned. But more significantly, by shifting from the "special case" of the lawyers to the good-natured host, who is no extreme figure like Mrs. Tow-wouse or the stagecoach passengers or Barnabas, but perhaps a better than average citizen of his world, Fielding emphasizes at the outset of Adams' sally the discrepancy between his ideal expectations and the realities of human nature. Similarly, at the end of book 2, the prolongation of the promiser episode through Adams' dialogue with another wordly host is an added twist to the comedy of the parson's delayed discovery, for after his own experience is confirmed by the host's account of the gentleman's villainies, the parson still sees evidences of a sweet Christian disposition in the rogue's face. But the dispute between the man of learning and the man of trade also serves to summarize the central comedy, leaving the reader with a vivid impression of Adams' relation to the world through the irony of his vehement defense of physiognomy and learning as the sources of ethical knowledge, an irony which has the greater impact because it follows immediately upon the two episodes (Trulliber and the promiser) in which Adams' inordinately slow discovery of the character of his opponent is at the heart of the comedy.

In the longest comic scene of the novel (3:7), Fielding dramatically epitomized the larger process of modifying the view of Adams, in the midst of which it is placed, by carrying the reader through a skillfully articulated reversal in attitude toward his "roasting." During the first stage of this little comedy, as unfunny pranks and lame witticisms accumulate, the reader wonders, as in the encounters with Trulliber and the promiser, when Adams will catch on, but there is also a mounting comic indignation as these contemptible persons tease the good parson. The first major turn comes when the dancing master's mocking invitation and the captain's firecracker at last stir the good-natured man's wrath. When he begins his sober denunciation, the incident seems to be following the formula of the Trulliber scene and anticipating the interview with Lady Booby a few chapters later:

> Sir, I am sorry to see one to whom Providence hath been so bountiful in bestowing his Favours, make so ill and ungrateful a Return for them; for tho' you have not insulted me yourself, it is visible you have delighted in those that do it, nor have once discouraged the many Rudenesses which have been shewn towards me; indeed towards yourself, if you rightly understood them; for I am your Guest, and by the Laws of Hospitality entitled to your Protection. One Gentleman hath thought proper to produce some Poetry upon me, of which I shall only say, that I had rather be the Subject than the Composer. He hath pleased to treat me with Disrespect as a Parson; I apprehend my Order is not the Object of Scorn, nor that I can become so, unless by being a Disgrace to it, which I hope Poverty will never be called. Another Gentleman indeed hath repeated some Sentences, where the Order itself is mentioned with Contempt. He says they are taken from Plays. I am sure such Plays are a Scandal to the Government which permits them, and cursed will be the Nation where they are represented. How others have treated me, I need not observe; they themselves, when they reflect, must allow the Behaviour to be as improper to my Years as to my Cloth.

The reference to "Laws of Hospitality," the naïve expectation of the final sentence, and the formal manner of the whole discourse are idiosyncratically, and humorously, Adams'; the thought (except the implied approval of the Licensing Act) is Fielding's, and the sentiments are the reader's.

But this is only the first turn of the incident. As the speech continues, Adams appears increasingly ridiculous—vainly boasting the possession of a half guinea, disclaiming the boast ("I do not shew you this out of Ostentation of Riches"), then reasserting it ("you see I am not very poor"); pedantically inflating the squire's invitation to dine into "an Honour which I did not ambitiously affect"; and reasoning about his mistreatment as if he were before a solemn judge of a canonical court ("I endeavoured to behave towards you with the utmost Respect; if I have failed, it was not with Design, nor could I, certainly, so far be guilty as to deserve the Insults I have suffered"). This serious-turned-comic address might have provided a climax for the incident, which could end effectively with Adams' little triumph over the braggart captain, whose cowardice and stupidity he neatly exposes. But it is in fact the transition to the climactic third stage of the incident, in which the shrewd doctor, deducing Adams' character from the pedantic bent of his speech, succeeds where the dancing master and the squire have failed, drawing him into actively making a fool of himself. Like Cervantes' duke and duchess, he skillfully plays upon the hero's "blind side." Putting himself forth as the parson's equal in pious gravity, he offers a bait which could not be better designed to appeal to Adams' foibles. With the mention of a philosophic amusement recorded in "an old *Greek* Manuscript" as a "favourite Diversion of *Socrates*," calling for "some grave Speech, full of Virtue and Goodness, and Morality," Adams' love of the classics, his moral solemnity, and above all his vanity are engaged. An invitation to present one of his treasured sermons would be welcome in any circumstances; to do so in the role of Socrates before an imaginary royal court (one recalls his political autobiography) is irresistible. Thus the parson's discourse against the mischievous pranks generates his participation in the most elaborate and preposterous joke of all; and the episode which begins as an attack on "the present Taste" for "Roasting" (and perhaps a derisive "real-life" deflation of the elaborate machinations of the "witty" duke and duchess) ends in unabashed indulgence in such humor. In the chapter following his defiance of "the wisest Man in the World to turn a true good Action into Ridicule," Fielding graphically demonstrates the psychology of the comic response described in the Preface, at the stage of the narrative where it is most relevant to the reader's changing view of Adams. As affectation is capable of transforming "the Misfortunes and Calamities of Life" so that objects "which at first moved our Compassion, tend only to raise our Mirth," so here Adams is turned from an object of sympathy to one of amusement by his own vain seeking after what proves to be the comic catastrophe. The two-edged episode serves the overall structure by first strengthening the desire for an end to Adams' abuse and then showing the less amiable side of his character.

Another revealing instance of Fielding's amplification of an episode with an eye to improving its comic structure as well as its place in the movement of the novel as a whole is his revision of the justice scene (2:11). In the first edition of the novel, the preliminary vulgar jokes against Fanny and the baiting of Adams by the Latin tagmaster overshadow the very brief comedy of the arraignment itself, which is presumably the core of the episode. The justice's peremptory order to commit the accused is followed by a short colloquy in which Adams' protests are comically overruled by the justice, after which a spectator recognizes Adams and the justice is instantaneously converted from a presumption of guilt to a presumption of innocence. Amusing as this sharp reversal is, the device by which it is brought about is a rather unsophisticated contrivance for Fielding, who usually finds internal means of resolving his scenes. Because of the brevity of the arraignment and the external mechanism of its resolution, the reversal lacks the dramatic impact produced by the unexpected final turn of the previous sustained interaction between Adams and the local "wit," in which the forbearing parson, after allowing the man of false learning his series of triumphs, at last loses patience and excoriates his opponent's ignorance, only to be comically defeated by his inability to match a wager, sufficient proof to the company that Adams "must go a little longer to School, before he attempted to attack that Gentleman in *Latin*." In the second edition, by adding the farce over Adams' *Aeschylus*, Fielding brings the arraignment itself to an internal comic climax, as the crisscrossing conversation between the justice, the clerk, Adams, and the local parson culminates in a perfectly timed convergence of misunderstanding:

> . . . the Justice looking at it, shook his Head, and turning to the Prisoner, asked the Meaning of those Ciphers. "Ciphers!" answer'd *Adams*, "it is a Manuscript of *Aeschylus*." "Who? who?" said the Justice. *Adams* repeated, "*Aeschylus*." "That is an outlandish Name," cried the Clerk. "A fictitious Name rather, I believe," said the Justice. One of the company declared it looked very much like *Greek*. "*Greek!*" said the Justice, "why 'tis all Writing." "Nay," says the other, "I don't positively say it is so: for it is a very long time since I have seen any *Greek*. There's one," says he, turning to the Parson of the Parish, who was present, "will tell us immediately." The Parson taking up the Book, and putting on his Spectacles and Gravity together, muttered some Words to himself, and then pronounced aloud—"Ay indeed it is a *Greek* Manuscript, a very fine piece of Antiquity. I make no doubt but it was stolen from the same Clergyman from whom the Rogue took the Cassock." "What did the Rascal mean by his *Aeschylus*?" says the Justice. "Pooh!" answered the Doctor with a contemptuous Grin, "do you think that Fellow knows any thing of this Book? *Aeschylus*! ho! ho! ho! I see now what it is.—A Manuscript of one of the Fathers. I know a Nobleman who would give a great deal of Money for such a Piece of Antiquity.—Ay, ay, Question and Answer. The Beginning is the Catechism in *Greek*.—Ay,—Ay,—*Pollaki toi*—What's your Name?"—"Ay, what's your Name?" says the Justice to *Adams*, who answered, "It is *Aeschylus*, and I will maintain it."—"O it is," says the Justice; "make Mr. *Aeschylus* his *Mittimus*. I will teach you to banter me with a false Name."[5]

This addition makes the mechanical resolution by recognition less palpable and also less significant, since the judge's reversal is now transformed from the pivotal comic event to an added comic irony. The result is a scene which mounts successively through three interchanges, the baiting of Fanny, the Latin

[5] The interpolated interchange amounts to a full page in the Wesleyan edition, roughly the length of the Latin tag match and about a fourth of the incident in its finished form.

contest, and the accelerating farce of the arraignment itself to the climactic "make Mr. *Aeschylus* his *Mittimus*."

In thus improving upon the form of this scene, as in his earlier extension of it with the ironic postmortems described above, Fielding apparently had clearly in mind the importance of this episode as the climax of the rapid-fire chain of comic events making up Adams' second sally. His sense of the larger problems of form is also illustrated by the function of the sequence more immediately encompassing this scene in shaping the reader's response to the close of the first half of the novel. From the point of the ravisher's reversal of roles with Adams and Fanny (2:10), there is a mounting feeling of comic indignation which reaches its apogee in the successive interactions of the justice scene. In contrast to the roasting scene, where the reader draws some satisfaction from the final immersion of the perverse squire, the resolution of the justice scene offers no compensatory satisfactions beyond the passing embarrassment of the local parson whose false learning is exposed. This effect is deliberate on Fielding's part; his consciousness of it is reflected in his decision to bring back the magistrate at the close of the novel to report that the ravisher had been dealt justice, a unique and singularly conspicuous tying up of a forgotten loose end. By building up and leaving unresolved this kind of comic pain, Fielding amplifies the reader's satisfaction at the subsequent reunion of Joseph and Fanny, thereby contriving to make this meeting between a boy whom the reader has seen mostly in a humorous light and a girl whom he has scarcely seen at all an effective romantic happy ending to the first half of the novel, prefiguring the joyous conclusion of the denouement.

Other evidences of Fielding's cognizance of the novel as a whole in his construction of episodes are his concentration of the display of affected persons in the middle of book 1 as a preliminary to Adams' adventures in the world; his avoidance of anticlimax by varying and complicating such recurrent kinds of incident as the unmasking, the battle, and the dialogue at cross-purposes in the course of the narrative; and his development of ironic relations between an incident and something which has gone before. Even the slightest elements are made to serve more than an immediate function. As the Italianate traveler serves to keep in mind the suspended tale of Leonora, so Slipslop's unexpected fearful response to the exposure of Miss Grave-airs offers a "natural" means of reminding the reader of the suspended comic drama to be resumed at the close of the novel: "She wished she had not carried the Dispute so far, and began to think of endeavouring to reconcile herself to the young Lady before she left the Inn; when luckily, the Scene at *London,* which the Reader can scarce have forgotten, presented itself to her Mind, and comforted her with such Assurance, that she no longer apprehended any Enemy with her Mistress."

Fielding seems to have been unusually aware of an intermediate level of structure between the individual incident or episode, be it simple, compound, or complex, and the novel as a whole. More consistently than any of his predecessors, he combined his incidents into effectively shaped comic sequences. Having examined his forming of some of the longer sequences in chapter 4, I confine myself here to a few observations on the art of the kidnapping sequence (3:9–12) and the two sequences which make up most of book 1. In interrupting the account of Fanny's abduction to dwell on the dialogue of the poet and player and Adams' bedpost sermon to Joseph in his hour of trial, Fielding seems to have adapted the technique employed by Cervantes in suspending the battle with the Biscayan, for the interruption is not determined by the course of events, as in the Leonora episode, but by the "perverse" decision of the narrator to follow one set of characters rather than another. This creates a kind of artificial suspense where there might be none, since Fanny is rescued almost immediately, but as in Cervantes' incident the very artifice of the interruption as well as the substance of the intervening scenes invites the reader's laughter. The ordering of the two scenes again reflects Fielding's calculation. The natural route would be for the narrator to remain with the protagonists at the scene of their defeat, then proceed downstairs, where the colloquy of poet and player would be interrupted by the arrival of the rescue party. Reversing this order heightens the reader's sense of humorously arbitrary digression, and prepares him to laugh at the spectacle of the hero's "suffering." By developing from the incidental satiric comedy to a climax in the comic interaction of the two protagonists, the sequence emphasizes this important event in the process of their changing relationship. And the apparently clumsy interposition of the bedpost dialogue between the undisclosed "accident" interrupting the downstairs scene and its explanation serves to reassure the reader while playfully teasing him further with a digression within the digression.

The two consecutive scenes between Parson Adams and Parson Barnabas (1:16–17) are the only such between a principal character and the same incidental figure. This anomaly is part of a pattern of expectation by which Fielding builds the loose Tow-wouse inn sequence to an effective climax. Shortly after the emptiness of Barnabas' Christianity is exposed in his flustered efforts to find the substance behind the cliché of Christian forgiveness, Adams appears on the scene. Encouraged by the dialogue with the "learned" surgeon immediately upon his arrival, the reader anticipates a similar comic scene between the true and false parsons. But Fielding delays this event for the better part of two chapters, passing up the chance to have Adams and Barnabas meet during the dispute over Joseph's precious bit of gold; and when the two are introduced their first conversation proves to be amusingly amicable, turning upon their common vocational interest. The comic suspense is sustained right through the second scene: the two parsons' common opposition to Methodism leads Adams to expound his latitudinarian views with no demurrer from Barnabas, but as the scene goes on Barnabas' silence changes its meaning, and the long-anticipated conflict finally erupts, only to be immediately interrupted by the Tow-wouse explosion. Fielding's construction here is quite different from Cervantes' and Scarron's additions of new developments each time a commotion is apparently over. Having set the stage for a climactic scene, he introduces his new development before the showdown between the two parsons is really under way, amusingly *frustrating* the carefully built-up expectation and capping the sequence with a completely unexpected action, which, still more surpisingly, carries the reader back to the vein of comedy with which the novel began.

That opening comedy, so often regarded as a false start, on analysis proves to be a carefully thought-out sequence. In constructing the seduction episode, Fielding faced a complex of problems. He needed to sustain it sufficiently to avoid the impression of a fumbling incidental hit at *Pamela,* to satisfy the initial expectation of parodic comedy without making that the dominant expectation of the novel, and to establish the long-range anticipation of a return to this comic center. He had also to make his eventual romantic hero the vehicle for parodying his literary sister while not impressing the reader too strongly with his ridiculousness, and he had to poke fun at his innocence without inviting the reader to laugh at innocence itself. Fielding solved these problems with more success than has been generally acknowledged and also gave the episode an effective shape, by enlarging the basic germ of his comedy in two ways: adding a third agent in the person of Slipslop, and dividing the comedy of the seduction itself into two scenes. Adding Slipslop compounds the joke by placing Joseph under double attack, but beyond this it permits Fielding to create an amusing three-way interplay in which the innocent is humorously beset by both hypocrites, who are in turn both frustrated, and each fearful of being discovered by the other. It is as if Fielding, perhaps taking a cue from the successive matually embarrassing discoveries of Valville and de Climal, resolved to go Marivaux one better by compounding the hypocrite-seducing-innocent formula found in the beginning of both his novels. Fielding also uses Slipslop to focus the reader on Lady Booby's suffering as the primary comic object of the episode, reducing Joseph's actions to a secondary place.

Though the first bedside interview is an effective comic incident in itself, it is also a preliminary to the second interview. Parody of *Pamela* is implicit in the situation of the first scene, but it is not until the second scene that the comic interaction of mistress and servant is merged with explicit parody. Here the principal comic surprise is not the lady's violent reaction to an innocuous remark but the Pamelian declaration of virtue which triggers her fury. Joseph's diffidence in the first scene might be that of any prudent, slightly prudish servant lad, but here he is made to speak in the vein of the persecuted heroine, refers to the example of his sister, and at the close of the scene avers that "he had only spoke out of Tenderness for his Virtue." Thus the second scene pays off the promise of the parody, but it is also the climax of the episode in another way. In contrast to the first scene, the lady explodes early in the dialogue and continues to explode with each of Joseph's further Pamelian sentences; the greater part of the scene is given over to Lady Booby's rage. This, together with the fact that Joseph is here allowed to talk back resolutely (if somewhat priggishly) gives him a kind of comic triumph over the lady and leaves the reader with punitive satisfaction as the primary effect of the whole episode. To insure this effect and reduce Joseph's comic misfortunes to a secondary element, Fielding continues the episode beyond the footman's departure, following up this second scene with one in which "poor" Lady Booby must first suffer the impertinences of Slipslop and then pacify her out of fear of exposure.

At the close of this discussion of Fielding's incidents and episodes, it may be appropriate to summarize the distinctive qualities of his "Series of Actions," as they emerge against the background of its prototypes. When one compares the episode of the false promiser or the final night scene with their analogues in Cervantes, Lesage, and Scarron, one is struck by Fielding's capacity for maximizing comic effects by developing sustained or complex incidents from materials which his predecessors gave only cursory treatment. This development of incident is part of Fielding's remarkable concern, at every level of composition, to evolve from his materials effectively shaped or formed comic structures. The same interest in form evident in his conception of the novel as a whole is present in the little unmasking incidents, the clearly delineated movement of his comic fights, the dramatic interplay of his comic dialogues, the building of every incident to an effective comic climax, the topping of one climax by another, and the combining of incidents into sequences embodying their own structure of anticipation and comic resolution.

A second distinctive quality of Fielding's comic invention is the effervescence or dynamism of his unfolding narrative. Lesage may have invented a variety of comic figures and situations as extensive as Fielding's, and Cervantes is unmatched in his creation of an endless diversity of incidents from one complex comic source. But neither Cervantes, with his extraordinary invention of fantastic "adventures," nor Lesage, with his inevitable comic reversals, nor Marivaux, with his perfectly timed untimely arrivals, nor Scarron, with his unexpected explosions, achieved the kind of continuously surprising, rapidly flowing stream of comedy one finds in *Joseph Andrews*. This effect results in part from the character of the individual incidents which, in contrast to Marivaux's protracted scenes and prolonged analyses or Lesage's wandering episodes, are prevailingly taut and clearly structured and, in contrast to the brief adventures of Cervantes and Scarron, involve unexpected turns and avoid any predictable pattern. It results also from Fielding's delight in topping his own climaxes, and in connecting incidents in rapid sequence. And it results from his combination of diverse comic resources at close quarters: synthesizing comic mayhem with satirical comedy of character, or mistakes in the night with the relations between the principal figures; enriching a scene or an episode by the embellishment of a Mrs. Trulliber or a Mrs. Slipslop or a Lindamira; overlaying one joke upon another to squeeze all the comic variety of Cervantes or Lesage or the whole tradition into a work one-third the length of *Don Quixote*—so that the reader does not know from what quarter the next comic turn is coming. The unflagging zest of Fielding's comic invention, his delight in keeping the comic kettle boiling, even carried over into his revisions of the published novel, in which he added dozens of strokes to enrich the already exuberant narrative.[6]

Going beyond these generic characteristics, one may distinguish the specific emotional qualities of Fielding's mode of comedy. Of the three writers we are considering who developed their comedy out of the interactions of a sympathetic comic protagonist with various hypocrites or other antipathetic comic figures, Lesage is least interested in punitive comedy. In his episodes, the failure or disappointment of Gil Blas, rather than the exposure or embarrassment of the hypocrite, is the primary source of comic effect. The reader is untroubled by a succession of such episodes because the easygoing Gil Blas him-

[6] The most significant of these are listed and discussed in Martin C. Battestin, "Fielding's Revisions of *Joseph Andrews*," *Studies in Bibliography* 16 (1963): 81–117.

self reacts elastically to his misfortunes. In the comedy of Marivaux and Fielding, where the reader's moral sympathies and antipathies are more actively engaged, amusement is mixed with pains and satisfactions according to the fortunes of the hero or heroine and his or her antagonists. But whereas Marivaux's punitive effects are achieved by some sudden exposure, as in the confrontation between Valville and de Climal, or terminal event, as in Jacob's showdown with his master or his speech to the *directeur*, in his pivotal dialogues Fielding subjects his hypocrites to extended comic frustration and embarrassment, and there is nothing in the tradition like the sustained comic suffering of Lady Booby which arcs over the whole novel. This kind of comic satisfaction is a stronger element of our response to Fielding's novel because Adams and Joseph are less ambiguously sympathetic figures than Jacob or even Marianne, but also because the world of *Joseph Andrews* is a more savage one than that of Marivaux or even Lesage. Fraudulence and deceit are compounded by a prevalent meanness and gratuitous inhumanity, so that the reader more actively desires to see hypocrisy punished and is more intensely satisfied with this event.

The clear and consistent opposition between innocence and affectation, between good nature and ill nature, between victim and victimizer, generates a complementary effect which, though it may have been inspired by Fielding's recollection of the central sequence of Gil Blas's ironic disappointments, has no exact counterpart in the tradition. This is that peculiar sense of comic injustice generated by Leonora's denunciation of Horatio, Leonard's attack on Paul, the surly host's cursing of his well-meaning wife, Lady Booby's blaming of Joseph for misinterpreting her "innocent Freedom," and the corresponding postures of moral righteousness struck by the wounded hypocrites in their verbal duels with innocence. As each of his sympathetic principals makes, as it were, his or her formal entrance into the "world" of the novel—Joseph in the stagecoach episode, Adams as he enters the Dragon Inn, and Fanny when she arrives at the justice's—Fielding subjects him or her to the inhumane triumph of false wit or false learning. Although it has been suggested that this recurrent effect is a flaw in the novel,[7] it seems to me that this comic indignation is a major source of the reader's satisfaction with the final rewards of Joseph, Fanny, and Adams.

Perhaps most immediately palpable to the reader turning from the tradition to Fielding, and yet most difficult to define precisely, is the characteristic satiric realism of his comic vision. In one way or another, each of Fielding's predecessors regarded himself as a realist, bringing the fancies of romance down to earth. Though Marivaux and Lesage did not mock the romance tradition in the construction of their work as did Cervantes and Scarron, each explicitly distinguished his work from romance. As his remarks in book 3, chapter 1, indicate, Fielding was aware of this aspect of the tradition, and in constructing his own comic romance he seems to have set out to go his masters one better. Like Lesage, he creates a world in which chicanery and pretense are the order of the day, but he goes beyond Lesage in the extent to which he constantly surprises the reader with ironic glances at the realities of human nature. In the course of a story whose happy resolution is the conventional romantic marriage, Fielding depicts a half dozen quarreling couples. He turns Lesage's passing ridicule of a nervy fop into a "crack" at the world's false values and at the readiness of humanity to assist one to his destruction;[8] turns the "pure" comedy of Cervantes' and Scarron's battles and rows in the direction of satirical comment on marriage and the law; and invites the reader to compare his ironic "Unfortunate Jilt" with its conventional romantic counterparts, his bitter view of the

[7] See above, p. 111.
[8] See chap. 5, n. 2, above.

literary life with Cervantes' roseate picture, and his "true to life" version of the story of two friends with Cervantes' "Curious Impertinent."

The ironic or skeptical outlook implicit in these modifications might have produced a bitter or sneering kind of comedy; the moral seriousness underlying the comic indignation and punitive satisfaction, which prompts the satirist to crowd out the humorist in Wilson's tale, might have produced a more savage and angry kind of comedy. The genial blend of irony, compassion, and comic justice tempered with tolerance which does emerge from the novel, as well as its peculiar vivacity and pace, results not only from the nature of Fielding's comic actions but from the distinctive manner of their narration. But this is an aspect of Fielding's art deserving separate consideration.

III

The Manner of Fielding, Author of *Joseph Andrews*: The Art of the Narration

"Sundry Similes, Descriptions, and Other Kind of Poetical Embellishments": The Narrator as Comedian and Satirist

IN cautioning his readers against confusing "Performances . . . truly of the Comic Kind" with burlesques merely because of "a certain Drollery in Style," Fielding acknowledged the common association of facetious narrative manner with the Cervantean tradition. From the description of Senor Quesada poring over passages of chivalry whose meaning "Aristotle himself could never have found, though he should have been raised from the dead for that very purpose," to Marianne's running gabble with her supposed correspondent, sardonic commentary, playfully intrusive narrators, mock-heroic diction, and other burlesque gestures are staple ingredients of the comic romance. Much of Scarron's comic energy is channeled into his own clowning version of what Pope called Cervantes' "serious air," and Lesage and Marivaux each developed their own idiosyncratic modes of first-person narrative. Despite strong affinities to Scarron and especially Cervantes, Fielding's manner, too, is unmistakably his own. Indeed his performance in this respect is so inventive and exuberant, yet so skillfully controlled, as to make one wonder at his repeated insistence that "diction" or style is the least important literary element. To appreciate his achievement, it may be helpful to consider separately his use of the narration as a more or less independent source of comic pleasure, as a vehicle for satiric thought, and as a means of influencing the reader's response to individual incidents and the novel as a whole.

The most obtrusive elements of Fielding's narration, those "Parodies or Burlesque Imitations" in the "Descriptions of the Battles" mentioned in the Preface, have their direct antecedents in *Don Quixote* and *Le Roman comique.* A comparison of Fielding's most celebrated burlesque sequence, the description of the battle with the dogs (3:6), with the fullest examples of the mock-heroic manner in Cervantes (the battle with the Biscayan, pt. 1, 1:8–2:1) and Scarron (the fight between the players and the inn people, 2:7) reveals something of the characteristic bent of Fielding's comic narration. Each is a comic fight rendered in burlesque style, but Fielding's differs from his predecessors' in the extent to which the mock-heroic rendition itself is the source of the reader's amusement. In Scarron's account, such burlesque touches as the simile for the innkeeper—"furieuse comme une lionne à qui on a ravi ses petits (j'ai peur que la comparaison ne soit ici trop magnifique)"—and the description of Rancune—"seul contre plusieurs, et, par conséquent, plusieurs contre lui, ne s'étonna point du nombre de ses ennemis et, faisant de nécessité vertu, commenca à jouer des bras de toute la force que Dieu lui avait donnée, laissant le reste au hasard"—are truly embellishments. They add to our pleasure in the free-for-all, but the humor of that action, with its comically cumulative series of accidents, would remain if these narrative ornaments were removed. Similarly, in Cervantes' episode, though the mock-romantic hyperbole is more sustained, and it is not so easy to discriminate the action from the rendition, the narrator's hyperbolic manner enhances the parodic comedy of the action itself. It is a single combat between mounted opponents armed with "destructive steel," witnessed by ladies in distress—but one of the "knights" is a pidgin-tongued servant astride a mule with a cushion for his shield, and the other is the hack-mounted decrepit madman.

Recalling Fielding's description of burlesque, "appropriating the Manners of the highest to the lowest," one might conclude that the chief difference between Fielding's episode and those of his predecessors is one of degree. As Scarron widened the humorous disparity between subject and treatment by replacing Cervantes' armed and mounted combatants with the "lower" action of a roughhouse between tavern wenches and strollers, Fielding gave this burlesque mechanism a double turn of the screw, replacing human combatants with dogs, and substituting for generalized mock-heroic manner specific parody of Homer, the paradigm of the noble and exalted. But the difference is greater than this. Fielding's burlesque narration can hardly be called an embellishment. Except to the perverse eye of the "hunter of men," the sight of the sleeping Adams attacked by a pack of hounds is intrinsically a less comic action than Cervantes' and Scarron's battles. The narration here is the primary source of amusement, and not only for the "Classical Reader" who recognizes the invocation of the muse as the signal of that special "Entertainment" promised him in the Preface. To be sure, he is rewarded by a succession of humorously unexpected echoes or variations of the genealogy of Agamemnon's scepter, the description of Achilles' shield, characteristic Homeric epithet and simile, the intervention of a diety, the rapid-fire catalogue of the hero's decimation of an opposing host with vignettes or capsule biographies of perishing "warriors" incorporated in the account of their fall, and even, through the narrator's preoccupation with some of his epic conventions, the climactic effect of Achilles' delayed entrance into the fray. But the prolonged invocation and the description of the cudgel (each developed beyond any of the comparable mock-heroic gestures in the episodes of Cervantes and Scarron), the facetious extension of the latter by an account of the scenes *intended* to be inscribed thereon but omitted for lack of room, and the topical satiric humor in these scenes are obviously accessible to the reader unfamiliar with the *Iliad*. And from the narrator's request for supernatural assistance "in what I find myself unequal to," there unfolds the equally autonomous comedy of his difficulties with his task (see above, p. 145).

Subtler comic manipulations of the stylistic surface of the narrative are observable in Fielding's less spectacular burlesque passages. In the account of Adams' encounter with Fanny's assailant (2:9), the Homeric mannerisms of precise description and condition contrary to fact are assimilated to a humorous style which is not mock-heroic so much as pseudoscientific or pedantic, echoing the manner of a descriptive or philosophic treatise presented to the Royal Society.

He did not therefore want the Entreaties of the poor Wretch to assist her, but lifting up his Crabstick, he immediately levelled a Blow at that Part of the Ravisher's Head, where, according to the Opinion of the Ancients, the Brains of some Persons are deposited, and which he had undoubtedly let forth, had not Nature (who, as wise Men have observed, equips all Creatures with what is most expedient for them;) taken a provident Care, (as she always doth with those she intends for Encounters) to make this part of the Head three times as thick as those of ordinary Men, who are designed to exercise Talents which are vulgarly called rational, and for whom, as Brains are necessary, she is obliged to leave some room for them in the Cavity of the Skull: whereas, those Ingredients being entirely useless to Persons of the heroic Calling, she hath an Opportunity of thickening the Bone, so as to make it less subject to any Impression or liable to be cracked or broken; and indeed, in some who are predestined to the Command of Armies and Empires, she is supposed sometimes to make that Part perfectly solid.

As in the later account of the chamber-pot and slop-bucket battle preceding Fanny's abduction (3:9), this meticulous and overcircumstantial manner is amusingly inappropriate to the action being described, but in addition the very syntax is comic. As the discourse seemingly proliferates uncontrollably out of a modifier of a modifier of one of the two coordinate clauses supposedly containing the main thought of this narrative sentence, the reader is amused and then delighted to see the narrator thread his way through the obstacles created by his own compulsive parentheses to arrive at a coherent and grammatical destination.

The compositional comedy continues in the next paragraph, where the narrator, winded by his successful effort, eventually loses his precarious syntactical balance to a parenthetical renewal of the combined assault upon heroes and the argument from design, recovers himself by absurdly using pedantic reiteration to remind the reader of the violent action he has lost sight of, and makes his halting way to an appropriately huffing climax produced by compounding Scarron's juxtaposition of high-flown and plain descriptions.

Adams staggered at the Violence of the Blow, when throwing away his Staff, he likewise clenched that Fist which we have before commemorated, and would have discharged it full in the Breast of his Antagonist, had he not dexterously caught it with his left Hand, at the same time darting his Head, (which some modern Heroes, of the lower Class, use like the Battering-Ram of the Ancients, for a Weapon of Offence; another Reason to admire the Cunningness of Nature, in composing it of those impenetrable Materials) dashing his Head, I say, into the Stomach of *Adams*, he tumbled him on his Back, and not having any regard to the Laws of Heroism, which would have restrained him from any farther Attack on his Enemy, 'till he was again on his Legs, he threw himself upon him, and laying hold on the Ground with his left Hand, he with his right belaboured the Body of *Adams* 'till he was weary, and indeed, 'till he concluded (to use the Language of fighting) *that he had done his Business;* or, in the Language of Poetry, *that he had sent him to the Shades below;* in plain *English, that he was dead.*[1]

Of course, Fielding did not confine his stylistic humor to these mock-heroic battles. When he adapted Cervantes' description of Maritornes (pt. 1, 3:2) in his portrait of Slipslop (1:6), he was at least as much interested in the comic manner of the description as in its grotesque matter. Cervantes' "charming Original" is

a Broad-fac'd, Flat-headed, Saddle-nos'd Dowdy; blind of one Eye, and t'other almost out: However, the Activity of her Body supply'd all other Defects. She was not above three Feet high from her Heels to her Head; and her Shoulders, which somewhat loaded her, as having too much Flesh upon 'em, made her look downwards oftner than she could have wish'd.[2]

Fielding develops the stylistic hints of "not above three Feet high from her Heels to her Head," "somewhat loaded her," and "oftner than she could have wish'd" into a sustained amalgam of euphemism, qualification, and understatement, couched in a language of exaggerated elegance arranged in a formal pattern of syntactical parallelism and balance. His "fair Creature" is

a Maiden Gentlewoman of about Forty-five Years of Age, who having made a small Slip in her Youth had continued a good Maid

[1] Compare the opening of *Le Roman comique*, where the description of the sun charioteer's horses making good time downhill and frisking at the smell of sea air concludes: "Pour parler plus humainement et plus intelligiblement, il était entre cinq et six quand une charette entra dans les halles du Mans" (p. 3). Don Quixote himself employs a modest version of this device in the adventure of the enchanted bark: "Let us recommend our selves to Providence and weigh Anchor, or to speak plainly, embark and cut the Cable" (p. 633), and it reappears in an unlikely context when "amidst the Tears and Lamentations of his Friends, he gave up the Ghost, or to speak more plainly, died" (p. 934).

[2] It should be reiterated that throughout this discussion, as in the rest of the book, "Cervantes" refers to the Motteux-Ozell version.

ever since. She was not at this time remarkably handsome; being very short, and rather too corpulent in Body, and somewhat red, with the Addition of Pimples in the Face. Her Nose was likewise rather too large, and her Eyes too little; nor did she resemble a Cow so much in her Breath, as in two brown Globes which she carried before her; one of her Legs was also a little shorter than the other, which occasioned her to limp as she walked.

Whereas Cervantes' initial invective necessarily weakens the effect of his subsequent irony (the discovery that the wench's saving graces are deformities is expected after such an introduction), Fielding's passage is a progressively unfolding joke, as the accumulation of unattractive traits overpowers the narrator's effort to euphemize the grotesque.

If we compare this description with the picture of Mrs. Towwouse a few chapters later (1:14), we see that the grotesque matter is generally similar, but the manner is varied again.

Her Person was short, thin, and crooked. Her Forehead projected in the middle, and thence descended in a Declivity to the Top of her Nose, which was sharp and red, and would have hung over her Lips, had not Nature turned up the end of it. Her Lips were two Bits of Skin, which, whenever she spoke, she drew together in a Purse. Her Chin was peeked, and at the upper end of that Skin, which composed her Cheeks, stood two Bones, that almost hid a Pair of small red Eyes. Add to this, a Voice most wonderfully adapted to the Sentiments it was to convey, being both loud and hoarse.

Despite the ironic hyperbole of the last sentence, the style here is anything but euphemistic. The primary humorous device is plain directness. The bare Anglo-Saxon monosyllabic diction and blunt syntax, all the more striking when one reads the passage in its surrounding stylistic context, render vividly the "sweetness of temper" which the narrator tells us can be read in the lady's countenance. Apart from this dramatizing function, there is also something amusing about the writing of the passage itself, in which Fielding's "biographer" temporarily turns topographer, or naturalist, describing a person as if she were terrain ("descended in a Declivity to . . .") or a specimen of some sort ("at the upper end of that Skin, which composed her Cheeks, stood two Bones"), a procedure "wonderfully adapted" to his subject's hard-hearted "Insensibility of human Misery."

The variety of Fielding's stylistic humor is strikingly illustrated by his virtuoso use of the heroic simile, a device which Cervantes does not employ. Scarron's isolated mock-heroic comparisons are rather perfunctory: "Notre généreux comédien courrait donc après ces ravisseurs plus fort et avec plus d'animosité que les Lapithes ne coururent après les Centaures" (2:1). Fielding's energetic appreciation of the comic possibilities of the device is evident in his first use of it:

> As when a hungry Tygress, who long had traversed the Woods in fruitless search, sees within the Reach of her Claws a Lamb, she prepares to leap on her Prey; or as a voracious Pike, of immense Size, surveys through the liquid Element a Roach or Gudgeon which cannot escape her Jaws, opens them wide to swallow the little Fish: so did Mrs. *Slipslop* prepare to lay her violent amorous Hands on the poor *Joseph*, when luckily her Mistress's Bell rung, and delivered the intended Martyr from her Clutches. [1:6]

Perhaps with Homer's sequence of similes for the mustering Greek armies (*Iliad* 2: 455–83) in mind, he develops extended series of analogies to convey the astonishment of Lady Booby at Joseph's declaration of his virtue (1:8) and Trulliber's reaction of Adams' request for money (2:14), in each instance finding them all inadequate to express his subject. He starts another such series to describe the conflict within Lady Booby ("So I have seen, in the Hall of *Westminister;* where Serjeant *Bramble* . . . and Serjeant *Puzzle*. . . . Or, as it happens in the Conscience, where Honour and Honesty pull one way, and a Bribe and Necessity another . . ."), only to break off impatiently: "If it was only our present Business to make Similies, we could produce many more to this Purpose: but a Similie (as well as a Word) to the Wise" (1:9). He plays with the clichés of the device ("like a Cannon-Ball, or like Lightning, or any thing that is swifter, if any thing be" [4:7]; "As a Person who is struck through the Heart with a Thunderbolt, looks extremely surprised, nay, and perhaps is so too" [1 : 8]). He apparently completes an extended simile ("As a Game-Cock when engaged in amorous Toying with a Hen, if perchance he espies another Cock at hand, immediately quits his Female, and opposes himself to his Rival; so did the Ravisher"), then after a time returns to it unexpectedly, making fun of his own figure by treating it literally ("But *Adams*, who was no Chicken, and could bear a drubbing" [2:9]). As a climax to this running play, at the height of the battle with the dogs (3:6), he self-consciously eschews the simile for the sake of rapid narration, then *halts* the narration to discourse on the inadequacy of any simile for his hero: "Let those therefore that describe Lions and Tigers, and Heroes fiercer than both, raise their Poems or Plays with the Simile of *Joseph Andrews*, who is himself above the reach of any Simile." And with the descriptions of Slipslop's assault and Lady Booby's astonishment still fresh in the reader's memory, he declares with the solemnity of a neoclassical arbiter of "the rules" (2:1) "Similies . . . I think are now generally agreed to become any Book but the first."

As the preceding examples may suggest, the narrator's manner is really an amalgam of facetiously adopted manners. In addition to being the "sublime" poet of the mock-heroic and other passages of "very fine Writing," he is, following the lead of Cervantes and Scarron, the careful "true historian" or "biographer," delivering "all of Mr. *Joseph Andrews's* Speech which I could get him to recollect . . . as near as . . . possible in his own Words" (3:6); vouching for the "authentick Copy . . . *verbatim et literatim*" of the justice's "Depusition," "which we have with great difficulty procured" (4:5); and scrupulously discounting hearsay evidence: "I have heard it was remarked, that she [Lady Booby] fixed her Eyes on him much more than on the Parson; but this I believe to be only a malicious Rumour" (4:1).[3] He is a "learned" and "philosophical" writer, citing "Sayings of wise Men," but a trifle muddled as to his sources:

It is the Observation of some antient Sage, whose Name I have forgot, that Passions operate differently on the human Mind, as Diseases on the Body, in proportion to the Strength or Weakness, Soundness or Rottenness of the one and the other. [1:7]

Plato or *Aristotle*, or some body else hath said, That when the most exquisite Cunning fails, Chance often hits the Mark, and that by Means the least expected. *Virgil* expresses this very boldly:—

Turne, quod optanti Divum promittere nemo
Auderet, volvenda Dies en attulit ultro.

I would quote more great Men if I could: but my Memory not permitting me. . . .[4] [2:15]

[3] Except for the mock heroics derisive of chivalric romance, the most sustained component of Cervantes' manner is the posture of "true historian." In the first phase of the narrative he scans authorities and circumspectly sifts evidence: "Some Authors say, that his first Adventure was that of the Pass called *Puerto Lapice;* others, that of the Windmills; but all that I could discover of Certainty in this Matter, and that I meet with in the Annals of *La Mancha*, is, that he travelled all that Day" (p. 9). He laments Cid Hamet Benengeli's Arab bias, praises his exactness, and strives to supply his omissions: "He spy'd three Country-Wenches coming towards him from *Toboso*, upon three young Asses; whether Male or Female, the Author has left undetermined, tho' we may reasonably suppose they were She-Asses, such being most frequently us'd to ride on by Country-Lasses in those Parts" (p. 503). Like Fielding's narrator, he relies upon the first hand information of his hero—"Don *Quixote*, tho' he had a good Memory, remember'd only these here set down" (p. 574)—or other comically competent witnesses: "One of the Country-men that were by, happening to be a Notary-Publick, has it upon Record to this Day, that he threw it almost three quarters of a League; which Testimony has serv'd, and yet serves to let Posterity know that Strength is overcome by Art" (p. 567). In similar fashion, Scarron omits "cent belles choses" passing between the hero and heroine of his first *nouvelle* because he has not heard them and would not compose substitutes that might not do justice to the lovers "qui avaient bien plus d'esprit que je n'en ai, comme j'ai su depuis peu d'un honnête Napolitain qui les a connus l'un et l'autre (p. 27).

[4] In delivering the nuptial advice to Basil that Fielding adapted in *Don Quixote in England* (see above, p. 28), Quixote proffers "the Opinion of a

He is the mock-moralizing writer of a pseudo-exemplary story, presenting the comedy of Adams' "consolation" of Joseph (3:11) as "calculated for the Instruction and Improvement of the Reader," applauding Slipslop's relinquishment of Joseph (1:9) as "a Triumph over her Passion highly commendable" and expostulating in the manner of Pamela: "How ought Man to rejoice, that his Chastity is always in his own power, that if he hath sufficient Strength of Mind, he hath always a competent Strength of Body to defend himself: and cannot, like a poor weak Woman, be ravished against his Will" (1:18).[5]

Less specific in their eccentricity are two other narrative attitudes, one shading into the other. The narrator at times affects a naïve unawareness of the psychology of the characters: "having accidentally laid her hand on his" (1:5); "the Fellow who had taken poor *Fanny's* Purse, had unluckily forgot to return it" (2:13). The line between this deadpan narration and the ironic mode which is the most sustained element of Field-

Wise Man, whose Name I have forgot" (p. 582). Cervantes' narrator "philosophizes" much less than either the knight or his proverbose squire, and most of his handful of generalizing comments are "straight." Perhaps the closest he comes to the facetiousness of Fielding's manner is in this comment on the destruction of Quixote's books of chivalry: "several suffer'd in the general Calamity, that deserv'd to have been treasur'd up in everlasting Archives, had not their Fate and the Remissness of the Inquisitors order'd it otherwise. And thus they verify'd the Proverb, *That the Good often fare the worse for the Bad*" (p. 39). Scarron is more inclined to joking sententiousness, remarking "il est vrai qu'il n'y a rien de certain en ce monde" in recounting a mistake in the night (p. 11); cutting short his reflections on the pathos of an actor's life with the assurance "Il y a bien d'autres choses à dire sur ce sujet; mais il faut les ménager, et les placer en divers endroits de mon livre pour diversifier" (p. 25); and making light of Leandre's anxiety over his kidnapped beloved: "Quand on attend quelqu'un avec impatience, les plus sages sont assez sots pour regarder souvent du côté qu'il doit venir, et je finirai par là mon sixième chapitre" (p. 187). For a typical instance of Gil Blas' ironic reflections, see p. 56 above.

[5] The narrator's disinclination "to stain our Paper with" the "monosyllable, beginning with a B—" that so outrages Betty seems to be a mocking imitation of the kind of affected authorial delicacy Cervantes made fun of when he spoke of "a Swineherd getting together his Hogs (for, without begging Pardon, so they are call'd)" (p. 10; see the editor's note on the same page).

ing's composite manner is difficult to discern, but the narrator may be observed crossing it in a passage like this:

> But notwithstanding these and many other such Allegations, I am sufficiently convinced of his Innocence; having been positively assured of it, by those who received their Informations from his own Mouth; which, in the Opinion of some Moderns, is the best and indeed only Evidence. [1:16]

How effectively Fielding can combine these various facetious elements within a single humorous passage may be seen in the digression on ancestors at the beginning of the novel (1:2). The germ of this little sequence is found in the opening pages of *Don Quixote.* The first paragraph concludes: "Some say his Sirname was *Quixada*, or *Quesada* (for Authors differ in this Particular): However, we may reasonably conjecture he was call'd *Quixada* . . . tho' this concerns us but little, provided we keep strictly to the Truth in every Point of this History." This matter of little concern is still on the narrator's mind near the end of the chapter: "he determin'd to call himself Don *Quixote.* Whence the Author of this most authentick History draws this Inference, That his right Name was *Quixada*, and not *Quesada,* as others obstinately pretend." Four chapters later the point is reiterated: "Master *Quixada!* cry'd he (for so he was properly call'd when he had the right Use of his Senses . . .)."

Drawing from these hints the primary elements of his digression—the "biographer's" concern to sift truth out of uncertain and incomplete data, his argumentative manner, and his apparent inability to drop the subject which he says is unimportant—Fielding develops them into a little narrative comedy, mocking both rigorous historical method and the easy speculation of the antiquarian.[6] Lacking knowledge of Joseph's lineage beyond the third generation, his scrupulous historian

[6] For a possible particular object of Fielding's ridicule in this passage, see Arthur Johnstone, "Fielding, Hearne and Merry-Andrews," *Notes and Queries*, n.s., 7 (1960): 295–96.

will not affirm "whether he had any Ancestors before this."[7] But, having already implied its irrelevance, he "cannot omit inserting" a facetious epitaph, "almost out of the Stone with Antiquity," communicated by "an ingenious Friend" who "conjectures" it belongs to "the Founder of that Sect of laughing Philosophers, since called *Merry Andrews*." After this double digression, the narrator would drop the ancestry inquiry and "proceed to things of more consequence." Instead he resumes the digression. Dropping his inferential caution, he now maintains that Joseph "had as many Ancestors, as the best Man living," and that a look into the remote past might prove him related to "some Persons of very great Figure at present," concluding in the manner of a rhetorician:

> But suppose for Argument's sake we should admit that he had no Ancestors at all, but had sprung up, according to the modern Phrase, out of a Dunghill, as the *Athenians* pretended they themselves did from the Earth, would not this *Autokopros* have been justly entitled to all the Praise arising from his own Virtues? Would it not be hard, that a Man who hath no Ancestors should therefore be render'd incapable of acquiring Honour, when we see so many who have no Virtues, enjoying the Honour of their Forefathers?

What makes this a remarkable piece of humorous writing is not merely the variety of jokes combined within it, but the complex movement of the sequence as a comic argument. Proposing to tell us the story of Joseph Andrews, after one sentence the narrator finds himself stuck on the absurd question of whether or not his hero had any ancestors beyond his great-grandfather, decides to leave the question but can't, changes his stand on it, then ends up arguing its irrelevance, topping this serpentine sequence by unexpectedly dropping his clown's mask to make a satiric thrust at the decadence of modern aris-

[7] This may be an oblique play upon the fashionable reference to persons of "no family."

tocracy. Out of the narrator's apparent lack of control over his own discourse, Fielding fashions an effective comic structure.

The preceding examples may suggest something of the comic inventiveness of Fielding's narration; in the discursive surface of the narrative, as in the actions portrayed, something is always happening, and the same thing rarely happens twice. Through the diversity of his humorous rhetoric and the ingenuity of his variations, Fielding avoids the most obvious pitfall of burlesque narration, the tedium of the repeated joke. Some of Cervantes' mock-romantic devices, notably the hyperbolic accounts of Quixote's prowess, become increasingly predictable and unaffecting as the long narrative wears on. Through repetition, the epithets regularly applied to the Don go flat. The interweaving of a variety of comic manners and gestures makes Fielding's narration continually unexpected. The specifically mock-Homeric devices are kept fresh because they are embedded in a discourse containing other kinds of stylistic humor. Even the mock-Pamelian expostulation on male chastity is surprising because it occurs after the original parodic target has been lost sight of amid other comic embellishments. Nor are all of the jokes with *Pamela* so obvious as to become tedious. That tendency, noted in the contemporary *Essay on the New Species of Writing*, "to shew the Reader he would not permit the least Occasion to slip which offer'd an opportunity of amusing him"[8] is illustrated by what appears to be a routine narrative transition near the end of the novel (4:4). The paragon of feminine virtue has only just surprisingly appeared when her new husband is called from the room. The reader can envisage rich comic possibilities in the first interview between Lady Booby and her new niece, but Fielding derides

[8] *An Essay on the New Species of Writing Founded by Mr. Fielding, 1751*, ed. Alan D. McKillop (Los Angeles, 1962), p. 21. The anonymous critic is referring particularly to Fielding's chapter titles.

the unconscious vanity of Pamela's self-absorption as well as her "editor's" claims for the edifying effect of her actions by having his narrator conclude: "As their Discourse during his Absence would afford little Improvement or Entertainment to the Reader, we will leave them for a while to attend to Mr. *Booby*."

It is difficult to make a general comparison of Fielding's narrative humor with that of his predecessors without seeming to derogate that noble line of excellent foolers. Though it does in time wear thin, Cervantes' sustained sober mock-amplificatory style is one of the remarkable achievements of his remarkable book. The interruption of the combat with the Biscayan by the sudden end of the manuscript and the disclosure that the narrator of the first book is only a secondhand (or as it develops later, third hand) retailer of his story, followed by his search for the sequel, is certainly one of the most original narrative jokes ever fashioned. Scarron's narrator, with his pretense of making up his story as he goes along, his complaints about the fatigues of his work, and his running argument with imaginary critics, is a source of amusement in his own right. Jacob's long description of the conflict within him between *l'honneur* and *la cupidité*, in which each personified abstraction is endowed with its own characteristic speech, dwarfs the similar conflicts which Fielding portrays in Lady Booby(1:9 and 4:1).[9] Marianne's prattling memoirs are frequently interspersed with humorous digressions, and Marivaux builds a sustained comedy of her apologies to her imaginary correspondent for failing to stick to her story and keep her

[9] "Car, par exemple, la cupidité ne répondait à tout cela qu'un mot ou deux; mais son éloquence, quoique laconique, était vigoureuse.

"C'est bien à toi, paltoquet, me disait-elle, à t'arrêter à ce chimérique honneur! Ne te sied-il pas bien d'être délicat là-dessus, misérable rustre? Va, tu as raison; va te gîter à l'hôpital, ton honneur et toi, vous y aurez tous deux fort bonne grâce" (*Le Paysan parvenu*, p. 27). For the paragraph immediately preceding this excerpt, see p. 256 below.

authorial promises.[10] Though humorous narration is a much less conspicuous element in Lesage, Gil Blas's insouciant relation, punctuated by touches of euphemistic, ironic, and arch description, is a source of quiet amusement.

Still, when one turns from the work of any of these writers, even Cervantes, to *Joseph Andrews*, one is immediately aware of a greater comic energy or inventive vitality in the texture of the narrtion itself. In contrast to his predecessors, who frequently introduce a burlesque device perfunctorily or begin a humorous embellishment promisingly and then drop it, Fielding is almost never content with running out a stock facetious gesture; instead he shows a consistent concern with working out even the minor device or small unit of discourse to an effective comic conclusion, with as many unexpected and amusing turns along the way as possible. Although Scarron and Marivaux, in different fashions and degrees, each create more or less sustained comedies out of their respective narrators' relations to a suppositious reader, and Cervantes builds a similar running joke on the relation of his multipersoned narrator to his material, Fielding is unique in his development of a series of microcosmic humorous "dramas" (ranging in magnitude from his difficulties with the hounds battle and the ancestry digression down to the description of Slipslop) on or beneath the surface of the narrative, with his many-mannered narrator as their comic protagonist. A high point in this recurrent comedy of writing is reached in the apostrophe to Vanity (1:15), which, when compared to its prototype, Cervantes' apostrophe to Poverty (pt. 2, chap. 44), shows very clearly the distinguishing marks of Fielding's comic narration.

Each apostrophe begins in the classic manner of such exclamations ("O Poverty! Poverty! What could induce the great

[10] For a discussion of this aspect of Marianne's narration, and related tactics in other fiction, see Wayne C. Booth, "The Self-Conscious Narrator in Comic Fiction before *Tristram Shandy*" *PMLA* 67 (1952) : 163–85.

Cordova Poet to call thee a holy thankless Gift!"—"O Vanity! How little is thy Force acknowledged, or thy Operations discerned?"), but thereafter they take their separate ways. After questioning the Christian notion of poverty as a blessing, Cervantes' Moorish narrator presents a comicopathetic picture of genteel poverty: "Why dost thou intrude upon Gentlemen, and affect well-born Souls more than other People? Why dost thou reduce them to cobble their Shoes, and wear some Silk, some Hair, and some Glass Buttons on the same tatter'd Waistcoat, as if it were only to betray Variety of Wretchedness? Why must their Ruffs be of such a dismal Hue . . . ?" As the description continues the original apostrophized figure is supplanted by the Chaplinesque person of the poor gentleman: "Unhappy he, whose Honour is in continual Alarms, who thinks that at a Mile's Distance every one discovers the Patch in his Shoe, the Sweat of his Forehead soak'd through his old rusty Hat, the Bareness of his Clothes, and the very Hunger of his famish'd Stomach."

Fielding's narrator, on the other hand, sustains the personification of Vanity, the *femme fatale:* "How wantonly dost thou deceive Mankind under different Disguises? Sometimes thou dost wear the Face of Pity, sometimes of Generosity . . . . Is there a Wretch so abandoned as to own thee for an Acquaintance in publick? yet, how few will refuse to enjoy thee in private? . . . Thy Embraces are often the sole Aim and sole Reward of the private Robbery, and the plundered Province. It is, to pamper up thee, thou Harlot, that we attempt to withdraw from others what we do not want, or to with-hold from them what they do." Eventually other passions participate in the metaphorical drama—"Avarice itself is often no more than thy Hand-maid, and even Lust thy Pimp. The Bully Fear like a Coward, flies before thee, and Joy and Grief hide their Heads in thy Presence"—and the narrator becomes so caught up by his own device that he concludes by treating the abstraction as if it were a person. "I know thou wilt think, that whilst I abuse thee, I court thee; and that thy Love hath inspired me to write this sarcastical Panegyrick on thee: but thou art deceived, I value thee not of a farthing; nor will it give me any Pain, if thou should'st prevail on the Reader to censure this Digression as errant Nonsense." This crazily facetious turn is grounded in an ironically pointed logic: the narrator acknowledges that in developing his apostrophe he has indulged his own vanity in his "poetic" powers. Fielding then tops it with a still more surprising reversal, as the narrator delivers the *coup de grace* to the personage whose omnipotence he has just declaimed: "For know to thy Confusion, that I have introduced thee for no other Purpose than to lengthen out a short Chapter; and so I return to my History."

In comparison to Cervantes' haunting evocation of the life of the impoverished gentry, this elegantly turned apostrophe may seem merely clever, a brittle tour de force. But the very neatness with which the figure is worked out, the appositeness of its intersecting elements, adds force to the generalization Fielding would extend from the behavior of Barnabas and the surgeon to "that of many other Persons not mentioned in this History." While such satiric glances beyond the closed world of Don Quixote's adventures are infrequent, Fielding interlards his narrative with jibes at the manners and morals of his time and the more general failings of humanity. Such set pieces as this apostrophe, the "Dissertation concerning high People and low People" (2:13), and the "Philosophical Reflections" on female sexual hypocrisy (4:7) are only the most conspicuous elements of a satiric rhetoric which pervades the fabric of the narration, from the burlesque sequences to the ostensibly neutral mechanics of exposition.

The burlesque writing of Cervantes and Scarron is "pure" literary clowning. Its humor derives simply from the reduction of the devices and mannerisms of the chivalric and heroic romance writers to absurdity. Fielding, on the other hand, like Pope in "The Rape of the Lock," turns Homer's manner to satiric use, combining humorous play with glances at his society. Thus in the preabduction fight (3:9), Homer's formula for the description of a blow ("He threw, and caught Aineias in the hip, in the place where the hip-bone / turns inside the thigh, the place men call the cup-socket" [*Iliad* 5:305–6]) is given a satiric turn ("the Parson . . . having given him a Stroke over that part of the Face, where, in some Men of Pleasure, the natural and artificial Noses are conjoined"); and his measurement of heroic feats against the normal capacities of men ("But Tydeus' son in his hand caught / up a stone, a huge thing which no two men could carry / such as men are now, but by himself he lightly hefted it" [*Iliad* 5:302-4]) is subtly turned from magnifying the legendary past to derogating the decadent present ("Joseph . . . lifted up a certain huge Stone Pot of the Chamber with one Hand, which six Beaus could not have lifted with both" [3:9]). The convention of the personified dawn or sunset, ultimately derived from Homer, is similarly adapted. In Cervantes' most fully developed burlesque of this device, Don Quixote's own imagined "proper" beginning of his history, "the beautiful *Aurora*" is described as "having left her jealous Husband's Bed." Taking the hint, Fielding gives the idea a more worldly twist.

> That beautiful young Lady, the *Morning*, now rose from her Bed, and with a Countenance blooming with fresh Youth and Sprightliness, like Miss ———, with soft Dews hanging on her pouting Lips, began to take her early Walk over the eastern Hills; and presently after, that gallant Person the Sun stole softly from his Wife's Chamber to pay his Addresses to her. [3:4]

Earlier, he brings the poetic mythology down to a lower plane of the modern world.

> Now the Rake *Hesperus* had called for his Breeches, and having well rubbed his drowsy Eyes, prepared to dress himself for all Night; by whose Example his Brother Rakes on Earth likewise leave those Beds, in which they had slept away the Day. Now *Thetis* the good Housewife began to put on the Pot in order to regale the good Man *Phoebus*, after his daily Labours were over. In vulgar Language, it was in the Evening when *Joseph* attended his Lady's Orders. [1:8]

Individually, these little jests are as incidental in their satiric impact as the unexpected reference to the contemporary decadence of noble families at the close of the ancestry digression or the derision of the intellectuals of those men "predestined to the Command of Armies and Empires" concluding the description of Fanny's assailant. But they also figure in a more sustained ironic play upon a general aspect of Homer's narrative, through which Fielding draws a satiric contrast between his world and the literary universe of his "great Original."

As Richmond Lattimore has observed, the effect of Homer's similes and related devices in the *Iliad* goes beyond their figurative illumination of aspects of the story of the Trojan war.

> In simile, we are referred from the scene in the Iliad to a scene which is not part of the Iliad; sometimes to the supernatural, more often to the everyday world. Such passages represent in part an escape from the heroic narrative of remote events which is the poet's assignment and the only medium we know of through which he could communicate his craft. It is perhaps such a liberation that wittingly or not vitalizes the development within the simile (4. 452–56):
>
> As when rivers in winter spate running down from the mountains
> throw together at the meeting of streams the weight of their water
> out of the great springs behind in the hollow stream-bed,
> and far away in the mountains the shepherd hears their thunder;
> such, from the coming together of men, was the shock and the shouting.

Such similes are landscapes, direct from the experience of life, and this one is humanized by the tiny figure of the shepherd set against enormous nature.[11]

Lattimore's example indicates the characteristic content of Homer's similes. Drawn prevailingly from the phenomena of nature, the vicissitudes of the hunter, herdsman and shepherd, and simple domestic activities, these "scenes" and "landscapes" create an impression of a world the poet assumes as a familiar matrix of reference common to himself and his reader, (the world of men "such as men are now"), from which he may draw norms and analogies. Distinguishable as it is from the heroic world of Troy, this mosaic image of simpler rustic man encompassed by an awesome natural environment, enduring its pains and facing its terrors, is in its own way noble.

After employing Homeric animal imagery in his first similes for Slipslop, Fielding discovered that by drawing his comparisons from his own version of "nature" he could kill two birds with one stone, combining incidental satire with an implicit satiric characterization of the world assumed as a familiar point of reference between his reader and himself. Perhaps counting on even his "mere *English* Reader's" acquaintance with Pope's Homer, he seems deliberately to have replaced the primitive simplicity of ancient Hellas with the artifice and corruption of modern society, the ingenuous plain dignity of the husbandman with the petty meanness and duplicity of sophisticated "ladies" and "gentleman."[12] His awareness of this satiric strategy is implicit in the burlesque description of evening, where the two orders of imagery are juxtaposed. Except for the "lowering" of Thetis and Phoebus, the description of the

[11] *The Iliad,* translated by Richmond Lattimore (Chicago, 1951), p. 42. Passages cited earlier are from this translation.

[12] In Ian Watt's view, "Fielding's novel . . . reflects the ambiguous attitude of his age, an age whose characteristic literary emphasis on the mock-heroic reveals how far it was from the epic world it so much admired" (*The Rise of the Novel,* p. 254).

laborer returning home at nightfall and "the good Housewife" putting on the pot are reminiscent of similar homely vignettes in Homer; by bracketing this little scene with the picture of rakes arising, Fielding indicates that these gentlemen and their topsy-turvy routine are as normal a part of his assumed "every-day" world as the humble domestic scene might be in Homer's.

Thus, to describe the internal conflict of the love-tormented Lady Booby (1:9), the narrator draws upon analogies comically remote from the tender passion but also satirically emblematic of the state of his "normal" world: a litigation and a bribe. The first of these is presented in a parody of those extended similes in which Homer recounts a complex hypothesized action, but through the parody Fielding brings out the venality and perverse obfuscation of a process in which Justice is present only in the barely visible metaphor of her scales:

So have I seen, in the Hall of *Westminster;* where Serjeant *Bramble* hath been retained on the right Side, and Serjeant *Puzzle* on the left; the Balance of Opinion (so equal were their Fees) alternately inclined to either Scale. Now *Bramble* throws in an Argument, and *Puzzle's* Scale strikes the Beam; again, *Bramble* shares the like Fate, overpowered by the Weight of *Puzzle*. Here *Bramble* hits, there *Puzzle* strikes; here one has you, there t'other has you; 'till at last all becomes one Scene of Confusion in the tortured Minds of the Hearers; equal Wagers are laid on the Success, and neither Judge nor Jury can possibly make any thing of the Matter; all Things are so enveloped by the careful Serjeants in Doubt and Obscurity.

When Adams asks Trulliber for money (2:14), the narrator attempts to render his surprise by a series of hypothetical examples which constitute a kind of survey of the world and its ways.

Suppose a Stranger, who entered the Chambers of a Lawyer, being imagined a Client, when the Lawyer was preparing his Palm for the Fee, should pull out a Writ against him. Suppose an Apothecary, at the Door of a Chariot containing some great Doctor of eminent Skill, should, instead of Directions to a Patient, present him with a Potion for himself. Suppose a Minister should, instead of a good round Sum, treat my Lord ——— or Sir ——— or Esq; ——— with a good Broomstick. Suppose a civil Companion, or a lead Captain should, instead of Virtue and Honour, and Beauty, and Parts, and Admiration, thunder Vice and Infamy, and Ugliness, and Folly, and Contempt, in his Patron's Ears. Suppose when a Tradesman first carries in his Bill, the Man of Fashion should pay it; or suppose, if he did so, the Tradesman should abate what he had overcharged, on the Supposition of waiting. In short —suppose what you will, you never can nor will suppose any thing equal to the Astonishment which seiz'd on *Trulliber*, as soon as *Adams* had ended his Speech.

The figure approached in each of these "supposes," is, like Trulliber, a dishonest or venal follower of his calling. Thus the sequence presents a catalogue of corruption from trade to statecraft. But this is not all. In each of the hypothetical events, justice, retribution, candor, or decency unexpectedly rears its head: the villainous legal or medical practitioner receives a deserved dose of his own medicine, the briber turns honest Drawcansir, the sycophant becomes a moral censor, and customer and tradesman deal honorably and charitably with one another. By invoking these events as extreme sources of astonishment the narrator implies that they are so extraordinary as to verge on impossibility. In short, this is a world in which decency and justice are freaks.

The satiric vision of the world embodied in these burlesque passages is borne out in a sustained pattern of such thought conveyed through comments, amplifications, and asides interlineating the narrative. But for a writer commonly regarded as the very model of the "editorializing" novelist Fielding is surprisingly chary of allowing his narrator to express his satirical observations directly. Occasionally he reveals his awareness of human imperfection in a straightforward generalization ("So much delight do Men take in contemplating the Countenance of a Thief" [1:14]) or unequivocal narrative exposition ("The Master of the House . . . knew too much of the World to give a hasty Belief to Professions" [3:2]). But his more characteristic method is to express this vision through some form of irony or facetiousness. After sententiously observing (2:15), "And thus these poor People, who could not engage the Compassion of Riches and Piety, were at length delivered out of their Distress by the Charity of a poor Pedlar," he refers it to the reader "to make what Observations he pleases on this Incident." After Fanny has been rescued from rape by Adams (2:10), we are told "she suspected he had used her as some very honest Men have used their Country; and had rescued her out of the hands of one Rifler, in order to rifle her himself."[13] Lady Booby's civil reception of Pamela (4:9) is not to be wondered at, "for she was perfectly polite, nor had any Vice inconsistent with Good-breeding." The "warm Ingredients" of Betty's nature might have been controlled by "the Purity of Courts or Nunneries" (1:18). When the pudding-spattered Adams refers to his order (2:5), "the Gentlemen stared, (for he was too bloody to be of any modern Order of Knights)." Describing Joseph in his brother-in-law's suit (4:5), the narrator says none would suspect "as one might when my Lord———, or Sir———, or Mr.———appear in Lace or Embroidery, that the Taylor's Man wore those Clothes home on his Back, which he should have carried under his Arm." A few pages later (4:6) the mention of Joseph occasions this parenthesis: "whom for the Future we shall call Mr. *Joseph*, he having as good a Title to that Appellation as many others, I mean that incontested one of good Clothes." The "catastrophe" of "The Unfortunate Jilt" (2:4) is announced by a satiric

[13] For the relation of this passage, added in the second edition, to the fall of Walpole's ministry, see Martin C. Battestin, "Fielding's Changing Politics and *Joseph Andrews*," *Philological Quarterly* 39 (1960) : 39–55; and "Fielding's Revisions of *Joseph Andrews*," pp. 94–95.

observation delivered with the mock solemnity of a "philosophic" truth:

> But alas! as wise Men have observed, the Seat of Valour is not the Countenance, and many a grave and plain Man, will, on a just Provocation, betake himself to that mischievous Metal, cold Iron; while Men of a fiercer Brow, and sometimes with that Emblem of Courage, a Cockade, will more prudently decline it.

The pervasiveness of Fielding's satiric thought, the indirection with which it is frequently conveyed, and the variety of narrative devices through which it is introduced are further illustrated in his adaptation to this end of one of his most characteristic narrative procedures, the explanation of actions which the reader might find puzzling or "unnatural." It is in the guise of such "explanations" that his satiric essays on the "Ladder of Dependence" and the relations of "Miss" and "Master" are introduced. The narrator's very inference as to what sorts of actions are likely to seem incredible or "unnatural" to the reader carries its satiric implication. In the world of this novel, benevolent acts are so remarkable that they require some explanation; and the explanation usually reveals some less attractive motive than charity behind the action. When the hard-faced landlady cheerfully permits the travelers to leave without paying (2:15), the narrator, "lest *Fanny's* Skill in Physiognomy should be called in question," gallantly proffers the explanation: the woman acts out of a mistaken belief that Adams is related to the intimidating Trulliber. The rapid accommodation of Leonora's aunt with her niece (2:4), accomplished "with a more Christian Forgiveness than we generally meet with," is traced to her fears for her own reputation, established by "frequenting Church twice a day, and preserving the utmost Rigour and Strictness in her Countenance and Behaviour for many years."

On the other hand, after the reader has lived in the environment of the book for a while, he requires no explanations of ill-natured and selfish acts and may be ready to infer such motivations when they are not explicit. Fielding plays upon this disposition, inviting the reader to interpret Adams and Joseph's dispute over the horse (3:12) in the light of his knowledge of the world—"Perhaps, Reader, thou has seen a Contest between two Gentlemen, or two Ladies quickly decided, tho' they have both asserted they would not eat such a nice Morsel, and each insisted on the other's accepting it; but in reality both were very desirous to swallow it themselves"—then abruptly squelching the simile to emphasize his heroes' rare integrity: "Do not therefore conclude hence, that this Dispute would have come to a speedy Decision: for here both Parties were heartily in earnest, and it is very probable, they would have remained in the Inn-yard to this day, had not the good *Peter Pounce* put a stop to it." On other occasions he sharpens a jibe by offering an "explanation" where the reader requires none. Though the narrator offers to "help our Reader . . . as much as possible to account for" the zeal of Parson Barnabas and the surgeon in the prosecution of the highwayman (1:15), their action is not really puzzling. Though "neither of them were in the least interested in the Prosecution; neither of them had ever received any private Injury from the Fellow, nor had either of them ever been suspected of loving the Publick well enough, to give them a Sermon or a Dose of Physick for nothing," the reader, only recently reminded of the delight all men take in viewing the countenance of a thief, is ready to infer that the two doctors were motivated by a "natural" human eagerness to assist in the punishment of a fellow creature. Then the narrator reveals the unexpected absurdity of the two doctors' mutual aspiration to authority in the profession of neither.

Similarly, Slipslop's dramatic "cutting" of Fanny after her demonstrative reunion with Joseph (2:12) is not at all mysterious. The reader may easily attribute it to jealousy and frustration and, since the event occurs at the end of a chapter, assume he is to draw this inference for himself. The opening of the next chapter is thus surprising:

> It will doubtless seem extremely odd to many Readers, that Mrs. *Slipslop*, who had lived several Years in the same House with *Fanny*, should in a short Separation utterly forget her. And indeed the truth is, that she remembered her very well. As we would not willingly therefore, that anything should appear unnatural in this our History, we will endeavour to explain the Reasons of her Conduct; nor do we doubt being able to satisfy the most curious Reader, that Mrs. *Slipslop* did not in the least deviate from the common Road in this Behavior; and indeed, had she done otherwise, she must have descended below herself, and would have very justly been liable to Censure.

The real purpose of the first part of this paragraph is not narrative explication but comic amplification of Slipslop's affected behavior. The central irony of the latter part of the paragraph lies in the use of the word "unnatural." While ostensibly explaining mysterious conduct, the narrator in fact suggests that the actions of the novel, and the reader himself, exist in a topsy-turvy world in which such an action as Slipslop's is not only "natural" but right.

The subsequent "Dissertation concerning high People and low People," in which the narrator approaches this familiar world as a traveler or historian recording the bizarre institutions of a remote society, is as close to the manner of Swift as anything Fielding ever wrote.

> Now the World being thus divided into People of Fashion, and People of no Fashion, a fierce Contention arose between them. . . . In this Contention, it is difficult to say which Party succeeded: for whilst the People of Fashion seized several Places to their own use, such as Courts, Assemblies, Operas, Balls, &c. the People of no Fashion, besides one Royal Place called his Majesty's Bear-Garden, have been in constant Possession of all Hops, Fairs, Revels, &c. Two Places have been agreed to be divided between them, namely the Church and the Play-House; where they segregate themselves

from each other in a remarkable Manner: for as the People of Fashion exalt themselves at Church over the Heads of the People of no Fashion; so in the Play-House they abase themselves in the same degree under their Feet. This Distinction I have never met with any one able to account for; it is sufficient, that so far from looking on each other as Brethren in the Christian Language, they seem scarce to regard each other as of the same Species. This the Terms *strange Persons, People one does not know, the Creature, Wretches, Beasts, Brutes* and many other Appellations evidently demonstrate . . . .

Purporting to acquaint the reader with the norms of this world, Fielding presents its behavior as absurd and incomprehensible, "for those who are People of Fashion in one place, are often People of no Fashion in another." His exposure of its illusory values is in keeping with this donnish manner: "Nor is there perhaps, in this whole Ladder of Dependence, any one Step at a greater distance from the other, than the first from the second: so that to a Philosopher the Question might only seem whether you would chuse to be a great Man at six in the Morning, or at two in the Afternoon." And it is only in the paragraph following "this long Digression" that he emerges from behind the mask of detached curiosity: "If the Gods . . . made Men only to laugh at them, there is no part of our Behaviour which answers the End of our Creation better than this."

More characteristic of Fielding's own way is the early chapter (1:3) in which he formulates the character of the society less abstractly while ostensibly performing the routine expository task of introducing Adams and explaining his relation to Joseph. When the narrator, with deadpan humor, likens Adams' innocence to that professed by Cibber in his *Apology*, he appears to be distracted from his primary narrative purpose to topical invective; but he is also reminding the reader that the world he is to describe is one in which "such Passions as Malice and Envy" are to have considerable roles. In the course of the succeeding paragraphs the reader learns in passing that Adams' good qualities "so much endeared and well recommended him to a Bishop, that at the Age of Fifty, he was provided with a handsome Income of twenty-three Pounds a Year"; that Joseph's answers to questions about the New Testament were "better than Sir *Thomas*, or two other neighbouring Justices of the Peace could probably have done"; and that Joseph's father "had not Interest enough to get him into a Charity School, because a Cousin of his Father's Landlord did not vote on the right side for a Church-warden in a Borough Town." Adams' desire to further Joseph's education leads quite naturally to the information that he has "no nearer Access" to the Boobys than through Slipslop, "for Sir *Thomas* was too apt to estimate Men merely by their Dress, or Fortune; and my Lady was a Woman of Gaiety, who had been bless'd with a Town-Education, and never spoke of any of her Country Neighbours, by an other Appellation than that of *The Brutes*." Both regard Adams "as a kind of Domestic only, belonging to" the worldly parson whose parish he holds in cure. The apparently digressive history of that churchman's differences with Sir Thomas completes the casually assembled picture of the society, disclosing the passions of malice and greed, if not envy, at work in a Christian priest:

> . . . for the Parson had for many Years lived in a constant State of Civil War, or, which is perhaps as bad, of Civil Law, with Sir *Thomas* himself and the Tenants of his Manor. The Foundation of this Quarrel was a Modus, by setting which aside, an Advantage of several Shillings *per Annum* would have accrued to the Rector: but he had not yet been able to accomplish his Purpose; and had reaped hitherto nothing better from the Suits than the Pleasure (which he used indeed frequently to say was no small one) of reflecting that he had utterly undone many of the poor Tenants, tho' he had at the same time greatly impoverish'd himself.[14]

[14] Fielding sharpened this terminal point of his attack in the second edition. The original version makes no mention of the parson's satisfaction in the tenants' ruin (see *Joseph Andrews*, p. 347).

Although the burlesque passages in *Don Quixote* and *Le Roman comique* do not contain the satiric matter one finds embedded in Fielding's mock-heroics, there are anticipations of Fielding's satiric manner in the tradition. Near the beginning of her story, Marianne comments thus on the landlord and landlady who have stolen her protectress' money in the confusion attending her death:

Tout le monde de la maison paraissait s'intéresser beaucoup à moi, surtout l'hôte et sa femme, qui venaient tendrement me consoler d'un malheur dont ils avaient fait leur profit; et tout est plein de pareilles gens dans la vie: en général, personne ne marque tant de zèle pour adoucir vos peines, que les fourbes qui les ont causées et qui y gagnent.[15]

In the midst of his lengthy account of the conflict within him set up by his master's offer to finance his marriage to Genevieve, Jacob observes:

On trouvera peut-être les représentations que me faisait l'honneur un peu longues, mais c'est qu'il a besoin de parler longtemps, lui, pour faire impression, et qu'il a plus de peine à persuader que les passions.[16]

Something of Fielding's vision and manner is glimpsed in this account of the discovery of the stolen corpse in *Le Roman comique* (2:7):

La servante sauta au col de sa maîtresse, lui disant qu'elle avait trouvé son maître, avec un si grand transport de joie que la pauvre veuve eut peur que son mari ne fût ressuscité; car on remarqua qu'elle devint pâle comme un criminel qu'on juge.

And his explanation of apparently decent human behavior by the discovery of other motives is anticipated in Gil Blas's description (3:12) of the relationship between two leading actresses.

[15] *Marianne*, p. 24.
[16] *Le Paysan parvenu*, p. 27.

Florimonde que demeuroit dans une maison voisine, dînoit et soupoit tous les jours avec Arsenie. Elles paroissoient toutes deux dans une union qui surprenoit bien des gens. On étoit étonné que des Coquettes fussent en si bonne intelligence, et l'on s'imaginoit qu'elles se broüilleroient tôt ou tard pour quelque Cavalier: mais on connoissoit mal ces amies parfaites. Une solide amitié les unissoit. Au lieu d'être jalouses comme les autres femmes, elles vivoient en commun. Elles aimoient mieux partager les dépoüilles des hommes, que de s'en disputer sottement les soûpirs.

Even in Cervantes' predominantly benign narration there are glimpses of the outlook of Fielding's narrator, and of the world he describes, or rather constructs. When Quixote's battle with the lackey Tosilos is aborted (pt. 2, chap. 56), "the People went away, most of 'em very much out of Humour, because the Combatants had not cut one another to pieces to make 'em Sport; according to the Custom of the young Rabble, to be sorry, when, after they have staid, in hopes to see a Man hang'd he happens to be pardon'd."[17]

[17] An innkeeper's wife is "very different from the common sort of Hostesses, for she was of a charitable Nature, and very compassionate" (p. 95); the adventurers feast well on the spoils of the funeral procession, "the Priests, who had brought it for their own eating, being like the rest of their Coat, none of the worst Stewards for their Bellies" (p. 128); the judge is described as "sitting all the time more attentive" to the captive's story "than he ever did on the Bench" (p. 367); and the tears of his daughter's lovesick suitor are "enough to move a Heart of Cannibal, much more a Judge's, who (being a Man o' th' World) had presently the advantage of the Match and Preferment of his Daughter in the Wind" (p. 385). The extreme rarity of such satiric glances makes the sardonic picture of Quixote's mourners all the more disconcerting: "The whole Family was in Grief and Confusion; and yet, after all, the Niece continued to eat, the House-keeper drank, and wash'd down Sorrow; and Sancho Pança made much of himself: For there is a strange Charm in the Thoughts of a good Legacy, or the Hopes of an Estate, which wondrously removes or at least alleviates the Sorrow that Men would otherwise feel for the Death of Friends" (p. 934).

Despite its prevailing sweetness, "the Manner of Cervantes" seems to have exercised a more predominant influence over Fielding than that of any other precursor. His naïve deadpan irony is anticipated in the description of Maritornes as a "good-natur'd Thing," who, "whenever she had pass'd her Word in such Cases" as the assignation with the muleteer, "was sure to make it good, tho' she had made the Promise in the midst of a Wood, and without any

Although the proportion of such satiric reference and commentary in Fielding's narration is higher than in those of even Lesage or Marivaux, the difference between this aspect of Fielding's novel and the tradition is not merely quantitative. The satiric thought of Lesage and Marivaux, despite the recurrence of certain particular topics or themes, remains sporadic and incidental. Perhaps because he had Swift before him as a model, as well as the continental novelists, or perhaps as a consequence of his experience as a periodical essayist, Fielding forged his derisive comments on contemporary society into a cohesive pattern of thought. The ubiquitous satiric rhetoric which pervades the narrative, turning up unexpectedly in the midst of burlesque, casually inserted in a passing parenthesis, implicit in a seemingly routine narrative procedure, is brought to a head in a number of passages ranging in magnitude from the dissertation on high people and low people and the "philosophic Reflections" on feminine sexual hypocrisy down to the little collection of negative analogies for Adams' warm feelings toward the peddler, in which the narrator presents a more or less comprehensive characterization or summary of human behavior. The generalizations emergent from these several passages—that all men are slaves to the harlot Vanity; that the society is gov-

---

Witness at all" (p. 98); and with minor modifications this might be a piece of sustained narration from *Joseph Andrews*:

But Fortune, which, according to the Opinion of those that have not the Light of true Faith, guides, appoints, and contrives all things as it pleases, directed *Gines de Passamonte* (that Master-Rogue, who, Thanks be to Don *Quixote's* Force and Folly, had been put in a Condition to do him a Mischief) to this very Part of the Mountain, in order to hide himself till the Heat of the Pursuit, which he had just Cause to fear, were over. He discover'd our Adventurers much about the Time that they fell asleep; and as wicked Men are always ungrateful, and urgent Necessity prompts many to do Things, at the very Thoughts of which they perhaps would start at other Times, *Gines,* who was a Stranger both to Gratitude and Humanity, resolv'd to ride away with *Sancho's* Ass; for as for *Rozinante,* he look'd upon him as a thing that would neither sell nor pawn. . . . [p. 163].

erned by an absurdly artificial social snobbery; that "Miss" is so brought up to affect a revulsion from "Master" that she cannot acknowledge the sentiment of love without shame; that the various walks of life from the trade of tailoring to "that of prime-ministering" are strewn with venality and corruption; and that envy and cupidity are ruling attitudes to which there are few exceptions—together constitute a coherent and consistent view of the "world" as one dominated by affectation and ill nature.

The relation of this pervasive satiric rhetoric to Fielding's conception of his novel as a whole is obvious. It solidifies the impression of a world of vanity and hypocrisy which emerges from the actions themselves, emphasizing the exceptional character of the good nature and decency of Adams and his young charges and contributing to the reader's cumulative desire to see justice done and these virtuous protagonists rewarded; at the same time it continually points up the innocent parson's fundamental comic error, his radical misestimate of his fellow creatures and their ways. To the modern reader, this relationship may be all too obvious. Viewed in the light of Stephen Dedalus' ideal of "dramatic form" in which "the artist, like the God of the creation, remains within or behind or beyond or above his handiwork, invisible, refined out of existence,"[18] this incursion of satiric commentary may seem one of the more primitive aspects of Fielding's art. In the context of the novel as a whole, such rhetoric would appear to be redundant: its generalizations are precisely those which might be inferred from the actions of the novel themselves. If the story were related in a narrative devoid of such observations, the reader would still recognize that Fielding's fictional world is dominated by imposture and meanness. But the novel would be the poorer,

[18] James Joyce, *A Portrait of the Artist as a Young Man* (New York, 1956), p. 215.

and not only for the loss of the incidental pleasures of these satiric asides. Ian Watt has suggested that Fielding's departure from the "usual tenor" of his narrative to indulge in mock-epic writing diminishes "the reader's belief in the authenticity of the character or action . . . the conventions of formal realism composing an inseparable whole, of which the linguistic one is an inseparable part."[19] To the extent that these "poetical" passages and other conspicuous departures from straightforward narration are the vehicle of satire, their effect is precisely opposite. Through the pervasive imagery of a corrupt and decadent world extending beyond the confines of the actions he is relating, Fielding "convinces" the reader that his comic universe is not an artificial construct, that "Life" does indeed, as he argued in the Preface, "everywhere furnish an accurate observer with the Ridiculous."

He persuades us the more effectively precisely because his manner of conveying this body of satiric thought is not so blatant as it might have been in the hands of a less skillful writer. Because the incremental satire is often conveyed casually and by implication, the reader finds himself conditioned to accept a set of opinions about the state of the world without consciously being subjected to persuasion. When Hazlitt described *Joseph Andrews* as "a perfect piece of statistics" on "the general state of society, and of moral, political, and religious feeling in the reign of George II," he had the novel's incidents and characters in mind.[20] But how much is our sense of the "truth" of a Trulliber, or of a Lady Booby dictating to lawyer Scout, conditioned by the vision of "the general state of society" which the narration itself conveys? One wonders if Hazlitt's "recollection of Parson Adams sitting over his cup of ale in Sir Thomas Booby's kitchen" would have been so

[19] *The Rise of the Novel,* p. 255.

[20] *The Complete Works of William Hazlitt,* ed. P. P. Howe (London, 1931), 6:106. The subsequent quotation occurs on the following page.

disruptive of Burke's "ideal representation" of "the respect universally paid by wealth to piety and morals," if that image were not immediately followed by the expository chapter in which Adams' status "as a kind of Domestic only" is skillfully placed in the context of a world of meanness and injustice.

The Manner and the Form: The Narrator as Guide

At the close of his discussion "Of Divisions in Authors," Fielding speaks of "having indulged myself a little" at the expense of the "Curiosity of my Reader, who is no doubt impatient to know what he will find in the subsequent Chapters of this Book." The impression given here of an insouciant author who divagates whimsically from his proper narrative task is no more to be believed as an accurate representation of Fielding's composition than his comic stumbling over epic conventions in the midst of the dogs battle or the syntactical difficulties encountered in relating Adams' fight with the would-be ravisher. While "indulging" in peripheral burlesque and incidental satire, he never loses sight of his central constructive goals. The chapter on divisions is a case in point. Buried in the facetiae of Homer selling numbers of the *Iliad* by subscription and the use of chapters to prevent "spoiling the Beauty of a Book by turning down its Leaves" is the suggestion that his own narrative divisions are not merely arbitrary. They are related to the structure of his story ("It becomes an Author generally to divide a Book, as it doth a Butcher to joint his

Meat") and intended to assist the reader in comprehending it ("Those vacant Pages . . . placed between our Books . . . are to be regarded as those Stages, where, in long Journeys, the Traveller stays some time to repose himself, and consider of what he hath seen in the Parts he hath already past through"). Interposed at this point, the "digressive" chapter itself functions as such a "Stage," setting off the central sequence of Adams' adventures from the preliminary actions of book 1.

Analogously, those extended comparisons through which Fielding conveys his satiric vision of the world also serve dramatic functions. For all the unexpectedness of the comparison, the wrangle and confusion of the legal battle between Sergeant Bramble and Sergeant Puzzle is a vivid and accurate rendering of Lady Booby's tangled emotional conflict. The long series of "supposes" which interrupts Adams' interview with Trulliber is as effective and appropriate a device of amplification in its context as Homer's string of similes for the amassing Greek forces in the *Iliad*. This apparent distraction from the immediacy of the dialogue actually heightens its dramatic impact, comically emphasizing Trulliber's thunderstruck reaction to Adams' modest request, expanding the scale of the scene, and rendering, through the grand pause in the narrative and the mounting rhetoric of the series, the sense of the dumbfounded hog-seller's rising blood pressure.

Fielding's controlled use of his facetious paraphernalia is clearly demonstrated in the differing narrative treatment of the two bedside interviews between Joseph and Lady Booby in the opening episode. In initiating the conflict (1:5), he eschews all humorous narrative embellishment, concentrating on the comedy of the scene itself. In the second scene, having established the basic formula of the interaction between servant and mistress, he plays upon the reader's anticipations, bringing to bear his whole battery of ornaments. The "Panegyric or rather Satire on the Passion of Love" concluding the preceding chapter (1:7) focuses expectation on the scene, which is then introduced by the description of "the Rake *Hesperus*," but before relating the action the narrator must pause to vindicate the character of Lady Booby by offering a "luscious" description of Joseph. The dialogue itself is interrupted first by the mock simile for Joseph's surprise ("As a Person who is struck through the Heart with a Thunderbolt") and again, more protractedly by the narrator's half-dozen vain attempts to find an equivalent, ancient or modern, for the lady's reaction to Joseph's proclamation of his virtue. Like the unsuccessful effort to describe Trulliber's reaction to Adams' request, this apparent burlesque digression serves a dramatic function, vividly conveying the astonished hypocrite's "Silence of two Minutes" by freezing the action. Together these embellishments vary the comedy of the episode, but this is a minor function, since the seduction situation should be good for more than one scene. More significantly, Fielding employs these narrative devices to magnify the effect of the second scene, not only to top the first but to create an effective climax for the whole episode.

As these differences between the two seduction scenes reflect Fielding's concern with the effective form of the episode, so his diverse treatment of the two reunions between Joseph and Fanny reflects his consciousness of the form of the novel as a whole. At the second of these reunions (3:12), after the resolution of the kidnapping crisis and just before the final sequence, in keeping with the emergence of the lovers' fortunes as the center of expectation, the narrator exclaims:

> O Reader, conceive if thou canst, the Joy which fired the Breasts of these Lovers on this Meeting; and, if thy own Heart doth not sympathetically assist thee in this Conception, I pity thee sincerely from my own: for let the hard-hearted Villain know this, that there is a Pleasure in a tender Sensation beyond any which he is capable of tasting.

But after describing their earlier, more dramatic, reunion (2:12) he speculates "philosophically" whether Adams might not be the happiest of the trio and, while deciding the question in Joseph's favor, manages to refocus our attention on the Parson and his lamented *Aeschylus*. Then, to insure the subordination of the romantic story to the comic expectations centering on Adams and the world, he adds the "Dissertation on High People and Low People."

Obviously neither this little eassy nor its companion piece, the "Philosophical Reflections," is assimilated into the fabric of the narrative to the same extent as, say, the passing glances at Cibber and Rich. But Fielding seems to have exercised a judgment in the placement of these extended digressions comparable to that employed in the disposition of the histories of Wilson and Leonora. After the rapidly mounting sequence of surprising "adventures" which culminates in the meeting of Adams, Joseph, Fanny, and Slipslop, the "Dissertation" furnishes a needed pause in the action, permitting the reader to digest these unexpected developments and emphasizing the reunion as a significant event while leading us away from a sentimental preoccupation with it. Like the chapter on divisions, it is a "stage" in the development of the story, marking the convergence of the paths of Adams, Fanny, and Joseph and their denouement-prefiguring confrontation with Slipslop. Similarly the "Philosophical Reflections" (4:7) follow the most extended comic dialogue in the novel and mark a shift in Lady Booby's motives and objectives: from a simple object of her lust Joseph is elevated to the status of a potential husband.[1]

[1] The advertisement for this little essay, "the like not to be found in any light *French* Romance," as well as its substance, suggests that beneath its analysis of Lady Booby's psychology lies an indirect hit at *Pamela*. Certainly the account of how "Misses" of fourteen or fifteen begin "from almost daily falling in Master's way, to apprehend the great Difficulty of keeping out of it; and when they observe him look often at them, and sometimes very eagerly and earnestly too, (for the Monster seldom takes any notice of them till at this Age) . . . begin to think of their Danger" would call to the contemporary reader's mind the opening chapters of Richardson's novel. The subsequent account might pass for a synopsis of its central plot development:

The wiser Part bethink themselves of providing by other Means for their

These particular adaptations of narrative devices to immediate or long-range artistic ends are paralleled by a general accommodation of the several dimensions or aspects of the manner to each other and to the requirements of Fielding's "main end or scope." Although he made fun of the arbitrary neoclassical rules concerning the deployment of epic machinery, he seems to have worked into his specifically mock-epic strain with some care. Apparently concerned to avoid that impression of mere burlesque which "vulgar Opinion" derives from "the Dress of Poetry," he develops this vein gradually—if not avoiding similes in the first book, confining himself to these and short burlesque descriptions. In his first comic battle (2:5) there is no play on Homer's description of warfare. This specific parody is introduced in Adams' tussle with the ravisher and subsequently developed in the climactic battle with the dogs and the preabduction fight. Then in the closing stage of the narrative, in the account of Joseph's fight with Didapper's servant (4:7), the mock-heroic manner is modified in keeping with the emer-

---

Security. They endeavour by all the Methods they can invent to render themselves so amiable in his Eyes, that he may have no Inclination to hurt them; in which they generally succeed so well, that his Eyes, by frequent languishing, soon lessen their Idea of his Fierceness, and so far abate their Fears, that they venture to parley with him; and when they perceive him so different from what he hath been described, all Gentleness, Softness, Kindness, Tenderness, Fondness, their dreadful Apprehensions vanish in a moment; and now (it being usual with the human Mind to skip from one Extreme to its Opposite, as easily, and almost as suddenly, as a Bird from one Bough to another;) Love instantly succeeds to Fear.

The parenthesis hits at one of the most vulnerable points in Richardson's conception, the instant ease with which the heroine accepts her persecutor as suitor, while the rest of the account suggests that his conversion is the result of her conscious manipulation, a subtler version of the basic premise of *Shamela*. In this context, the culminating point of Fielding's little case history—that young ladies schooled from infancy in prudery "still pretend the same Aversion to the Monster: And the more they love him, the more ardently they counterfeit the Antipathy," by the "constant Practice of which Deceit on others, they at length impose on themselves, and really believe they hate what they love"—may be intended to apply to Pamela as well as to Lady Booby.

gence of Joseph as romantic hero.[2] Within the hunting episode itself, there is a comparable gradual transition from "our ordinary Style" to the full epic manner. In the preliminary part of the incident, before the invocation of divine assistance to describe Joseph's entrance into the fray, the narrative begins to wax facetious and a shade overprecise and elegant, describing Adams' flight almost as that favorer of "the *Pedestrian* . . . to the *Vehicular* Expedition" himself might:

> He with most admirable Dexterity recovered his Legs, which now seemed the only Members he could entrust his Safety to. Having therefore escaped likewise from at least a third Part of his Cassock, which he willingly left as his *Exuviae* or Spoils to the Enemy, he fled with the utmost speed he could summon to his Assistance.[3] [3:6]

The synthesis of the diverse aspects of the narration involves something more fundamental than this kind of stylistic blending or the adaptation of individual narrative flourishes to artistic functions. The incorporation of satiric matter in mock-heroic passages is not in itself enough to solve the basic problem of integrating the roles of the comedian and the satirist in a single authorial figure. Implicit in the satirist's role is a worldly shrewdness, an awareness of human foibles and vices, which exceeds that of any of his characters. Potential in the tradition of the humorous narrator is a kind of clowning which might undercut the effectiveness of the satirist. That this potentiality never becomes actual in *Joseph Andrews* can be attributed to

[2] There is less emphasis on burlesque and facetious turns and more on the vivid recording of the actions themselves; and the Homeric anatomic precision is used to deliver unusually strong direct disapproval: "that part of his Neck which a Rope would have become with the utmost Propriety."

[3] Another kind of blending can be observed in the handling of the "Unfortunate Jilt," which begins in a formal and slightly solemn narrative style characteristic of the conventional exemplary novel and gradually merges into the manner of the main narrative, complete with mock-Pamelian expostulation and facetious sayings of wise men—at the cost of the lady narrator's dramatic identity.

Fielding's careful subordination and control of the "Merry Andrew" in the complex image he creates of himself.

In this connection it is instructive to compare the opening of *Joseph Andrews* with that of *Le Roman comique.* Scarron begins his brief opening chapter with an extended burlesque description of the horses of the sun's chariot racing for their watery home, concluding "Pour parler plus humainement et plus intelligiblement, il était entre cinq et six quand . . . ." After relating the entrance of his motley strollers into Mans, he pauses to defend himself against an imagined critic's objection to his comparison of Rancune carrying a bass viol to a tortoise on its hind legs ("mais j'entends parler des grandes tortues qui se trouvent dans les Indes et, de plus, je m'en sers de ma seule autorité"). And after some further account of the troop and their reception, he concludes "cependant ques ses bêtes mangèrent, l'auteur se reposa quelque temps et se mit à songer à ce qu'il dirait dans le second chapitre." Thus from the outset we are made conscious of a facetious and whimsical narrator whose preoccupation with his task we expect to be almost as important a comic object as the story he will relate. The narrative proper of *Joseph Andrews* begins with similar fooling in the pursuit of Joseph's ancestry (1:2), but before playing the role of fumbling "biographer" Fielding is careful to establish himself as a wit in the introductory discussion (1:1) "of writing Lives in general, and particularly of *Pamela;* with a Word by the bye of *Colley Cibber* and others."

Although this opening chapter has been read as a continuation of Fielding's theorizing in the Preface, it seems to me that one function of this second literary discussion is to project his character as the "implied author" of this story, a character or dramatized personality to be distinguished from the reflective artist who writes the Preface. In the Preface, the historical Henry Fielding stands apart from the work he has constructed, expounding for his "mere *English* Reader" his specific conception of that work, which includes as one dimension of its art the expression by the author of an image of himself within the novel which will serve his artistic ends. This "second self" is no simple ironic *persona* like Swift's conscientious projector in "A Modest Proposal," nor is he, like Parson Oliver in *Shamela*, the author turning his collar in plain view of the reader before delivering his explicit judgments. There is no overt pretense of creating a fictional narrator, like Cervantes' "Arab Historian"; rather the effectiveness of Fielding's narration derives from his skill in fostering the illusion that his constructed self *is* the author, an author whose complex but coherent personality exercises a correspondingly intricate and subtle influence upon the reader.[4]

In contrast to Scarron's burlesque beginning, the opening paragraphs of Fielding's first chapter might be the beginning of a moral essay in *The Champion:*

[4] The manner of the Preface is entirely serious, without irony or facetiousness; the "immense Romances" mockingly hyperbolized in book 3, chapter 1, are drily described as containing, "I apprehend, very little Instruction or Entertainment." After the Preface's careful and systematic distinction of comic romance from other species of writing, in the opening chapter "the authentic History with which I now present the public" is casually lumped together in the category of "Lives" with *Pamela*, Cibber's *Apology*, and fabulous chapbooks. The convention between implied author and reader of referring to this work of fiction as a "biography" or "history" is maintained in all three of the internal prefatory chapters.

The concept of "implied author" or "second self" described here is generally that developed by Wayne C. Booth, *The Rhetoric of Fiction* (Chicago, 1961), although he might not agree with my conclusion that the narrator or 'I' of the work, in his view "seldom if ever identical with the implied image of the author" (p. 73), is precisely that in *Joseph Andrews*. Where I use the terms *narrator* and *author* interchangeably, I refer to this composite figure. For a thorough discussion of the problems of recovering the views of the historical Henry Fielding from this constructed image, see Sheldon Sacks, *Fiction and the Shape of Belief* (Berkeley, 1961). The second chapter presents a detailed examination of the influence of the narrator's judgments, and those of the characters, upon the reader's responses in book 1 of *Joseph Andrews*.

> It is a trite but true Observation, that Examples work more forcibly on the Mind than Precepts: And if this be just in what is odious and blameable, it is more strongly so in what is amiable and praiseworthy. Here Emulation most effectually operates upon us, and inspires our Imitation in an irresistible manner. A good Man therefore is a standing Lesson to all his Acquaintance, and of far greater use in that narrow Circle than a good Book.
>
> But as it often happens that the best Men are but little known, and consequently cannot extend the Usefulness of their Examples a great way; the Writer may be called in aid to spread their History farther, and to present the amiable Pictures to those who have not the Happiness of knowing the Originals; and so, by communicating such valuable Patterns to the World, he may perhaps do a more extensive Service to Mankind than the Person whose Life originally afforded the Pattern.

Though the initial observation is trite, the writer's stylishly ordered logical development of it is not, and the first impression is that of an articulate, judicious, somewhat pious moral observer. But as the gentleman goes on to cite, without deviating from his initial sobriety, a series of wonder books and nursery tales in which "Delight is mixed with Instruction, and the Reader is almost as much improved as entertained," that impression must be revised. When the same moralizing rhetoric is turned to biting ridicule of Cibber, and the ensuing "authentic History" is offered as an example of the exemplary power of another, the reader may want to reconsider those opening paragraphs. In the light of what follows, the attribution of "irrestible" power to emulation can be seen as hyperbolic, and such phrases as "amiable Pictures" and "valuable Patterns" have a hollow ring. The elegant expository development is, on second thought, oddly disproportionate to the obvious point being made. We sense that we may have been successfully hoodwinked by an author skillful enough to persuade us to take seriously a passage written tongue in cheek.[5] Yet our initial im-

[5] In the *Champion* for June 10, 1740, Fielding expounded the opposite view of the comparative effect of positive and negative example, explaining

pression is only modified, not canceled. Though he ridicules the moral pretensions of some books, and the simple-minded notion of exemplary literature espoused by the author of *Pamela*, the tenor of his attack on Cibber's truckling vanity indicates that he is not cynically indifferent to moral questions. Since the "solidity" of the opening sweetly naïve posture only heightens our estimate of the capacity of its artful forger and of the worldly-wise view that transcends it, we anticipate a correspondingly sophisticated view of the moral implications of human actions in the story to follow.

The impression of a knowing yet morally sensible "implied author" created in this carefully turned opening chapter is not weakened by the apparent stumbling of the ancestry digression or any of the other narrative jokes which follow. Though this author may get himself into compositional predicaments, or strike a burlesque pose, or feign dimmer perception than the reader's, the reader realizes these are the contrivances of a superior wit agreeably indulging his playfulness for their mutual amusement or to make a point, but refusing to be truly distracted from his central narrative aims merely for the sake of a laugh. He does not, like Scarron or Marianne, make himself the butt of a running joke based on the casualness of his composition or his inability to cope with his authorial task; instead, his feigning of inadequacy is more likely to be an ironic

---

it with a view of human nature that contrasts forcibly with the sanguine piety of these paragraphs: "I shall venture to carry this speculation a little farther, and to assert that we are much better and easier taught by the examples of what we are to shun, than by those which would instruct us what to pursue; which opinion, if not new, I do not remember to have seen accounted for, though the reason is perhaps obvious enough, and may be, that we are more inclined to detest and loathe what is odious in others, than to admire what is laudable" (Works 15 : 330–31). Battestin, *The Moral Basis of Fielding's Art*, pp. 33–34, reads these opening paragraphs as Fielding's announcement of his intention to "present the examples of two such good men named Joseph and Abraham," and traces their sentiments to a sermon of Isaac Barrow. For a reading of the chapter closer to the one I have given, but still regarding the opening paragraphs as essentially serious, see Sacks, pp. 70–71.

means of ridiculing his subject, as when he protests his inability to relate the conversation between Squire Booby and the justice (4:5) "which rolled, as I have been informed, entirely on the subject of Horse-racing." Nor does he, like Marianne, prattle along the side avenues of thought which arrest her charmingly scatterbrained relation at every half step or, like Scarron's narrator, advertise his tendency to digress. Instead, his digressions are disguised or given narrative pretexts, and, unlike any of his predecessors, he repeatedly brings his divagations to a well-turned conclusion, even when, as in the ancestry discussion, his discourse seems to have gotten out of hand. The very qualities of his humor and satire—the virtuosity of his burlesque and facetious writing, the invention of his wit, the trenchant perceptions embodied in his satiric digressions, and the coherent point of view which emerges from the whole body of satiric thought—contribute to the reader's confidence in him. The cumulative effect of his comic and satiric brilliance is virtually to intimidate the reader, an effect enhanced by the realization, from the revelation of Fanny's existence, if not before, that he is in the hands of a storyteller knowing more than he chooses to reveal and deliberately manipulating his story, and his reader, for his own purposes.[6]

One effect of this cumulative impression of the author's brilliance, probity, and, especially, command, is to head off potential serious responses to the trials and difficulties of his amiable protagonists. If, at the most threatening moment of the homeward journey, the author can refer to Fanny's abduction as "this Tragedy" and in the same breath turn to satiric commentary on the contemporary fashion of theatrical interludes before relaying an incidental comic dialogue "of no other Use in this History, but to divert the Reader," that reader is not likely to

[6] Booth, "The Self-Conscious Narrator in Comic Fiction before *Tristram Shandy*," remarks on the functional control of Fielding's digressions.

entertain any serious apprehension over the innocent maiden's fate. This maintenance of comic confidence, which has been noted by several recent critics,[7] is only one element of a more complex function which the "implied author" serves throughout the novel. In addition to being a "humorist" and a "satirical dog," the commenting or reacting author serves as the reader's trusted norm or guide for his own responses to the actions of the novel.

In devising this aspect of the narration, Fielding might well have taken his own response to *Pamela* as a warning. Richardson's decision to let the heroine tell her own story created problems of which the author himself seems to have been scarcely aware. The vulnerability of Pamela as a literary creation lies in that very moral perfection which is designed to make her exemplary. When a character is put forth as supernally good, and especially through her own account, those very strokes which in another portrait might be regarded as humanizing touches appear to the skeptical reader (and we are all skeptical when continually reminded that we are in the presence of a paragon) as signs of fraud. Many readers, including Fielding, have found it difficult to believe in the pious humility of the heroine or in the seriousness of her situation because of her obsessive narrative preoccupation with the most trivial details relating to herself, her situation, and her precious "papers." If the sufferings of an innocent virgin in the absolute power of a dissolute master bent on her undoing, related in a way which would seem to guarantee the most pathetic effect—through the maiden's own account recorded while the action is still in progress—could produce this unintended reaction, might not a reader lose his way among the mutually qualifying and potentially confusing

[7] See R. S. Crane, "The Concept of Plot and the Plot of *Tom Jones*," *Critics and Criticism* (Chicago, 1952), pp. 641–42; McKillop, *The Early Masters of English Fiction*, pp. 109–11; Booth, "The Self-Conscious Narrator in Comic Fiction before *Tristram Shandy*," pp. 178–79; and Ehrenpreis, p. 36.

evaluations and responses involved in Fielding's unfamiliar combination of amiable and antipathetic comedy? For he would have the reader amused by Joseph's embarrassed priggishness and Adams' persistent mistakes and misplaced vanity while still distinguishing these sympathetic comic figures from the antipathetic ridiculous persons surrounding them. He would have him view Adams' naïveté from the superior perspective of his own sophistication while still preserving his affection and admiration for that good man's innocence. He would have him sufficiently involved in the fortunes of his young hero and heroine so that he will feel some mild concern when they are threatened and rejoice when they attain their happiness, yet sufficiently detached to view their crises with equanimity and even amusement. The narrator helps the reader to strike the proper balance among these attitudes and responses, leading him between the Scylla of cynicism lurking in the satiric content of the narration and the Charybdis of sentimentality yawning within a story of innocent young lovers in a hostile or indifferent world.

The moral limits of the narrator's amusement are clearly drawn. Though capable of facetiously describing the comically misdirected "Exhortations of Parson *Adams* to his Friend in Affliction" (3:11) as "some of the best and gravest Matters in the whole Book," he does not, like the roasting squire, delight in turning "even Virtue and Wisdom themselves into Ridicule." Though he reveals himself a person of much greater sophistication than any of the "people of fashion" in his story, his acquaintance with the "polite" world has not corrupted his basic sympathies with the good-natured and the innocent, wherever they may be found. Implicit in his ironically euphemized description of Adams' inadequate pay is a moral indictment of society antithetical to the outlook of a Lady Booby, who would divert her guests (4:9) "with one of the most ridiculous Sights they had ever seen, which was an old foolish Parson, who, she said laughing, kept a Wife and six Brats on a Salary of about twenty Pounds a Year." Within the same chapter (1:12) containing the sardonic "so perfectly modest was this young Man; such mighty Effects had the spotless Example of the amiable *Pamela*" occur such phrases as "poor *Joseph*," "his miserable Being," and "the poor Wretch." Similar expressions of compassion, especially for the defenseless Fanny, are found throughout the narrative.

The author echoes Mr. Wilson's preference of the honest pleasures of the simple life over the vanities of "high life" ("They made a Repast with a Cheerfulness which might have attracted the Envy of more splendid Tables" [3:5]; "for Hunger is better than a *French* Cook" [3:8]; "retired to a very homely Bed . . . however, Health and Fatigue gave them a sweeter Repose than is often in the power of Velvet and Down to bestow" [3:8]).[8] A related theme contrasts the true satisfactions of good nature, fellow-feeling, and love with the inevitable dissatisfactions of the self-seeking, vanity-driven, and envy-eaten ("For let the hard-hearted Villain know this, that there is a Pleasure in a tender Sensation beyond any which he is capable of tasting" [3:12]). After describing the joy of the country people (4:1) at the return of their patroness "with the Offalls of whose Table the infirm, aged, and infant Poor are abundantly fed, with a Generosity which hath scarce a visible Effect on their Benefactor's Pockets," the author compares their reception of Adams:

But if their Interest inspired so publick a Joy into every Countenance, how much more forcibly did the Affection which they bore Parson *Adams* operate upon all who beheld his Return. . . . The

[8] Although Joseph first sounds this note on his "deathbed" ("The poorest, humblest State would have been a Paradise; I could have lived with thee in the lowest Cottage, without envying the Palaces, the Dainties, or the Riches of any Man"), the narrator's voicing of it is concentrated in the aftermath of the Wilson episode, where it is plainly intended to reinforce the point of the good man's retirement from the world's vanities.

Parson on his side shook every one by the Hand . . . and exprest a Satisfaction in his Face, which nothing but Benevolence made happy by its Objects could infuse.

An important part of the narrator's guiding strategy is his characterization of the reader to whom he frequently addresses his remarks. He assumes the same "good-natured Reader" whom Fielding addresses in the closing paragraphs of the Preface, one who will respond sympathetically to "the Goodness of [Adams'] Heart," who will find the lovers' reunion (2:12) "a very delightful Adventure," and who "will see something which will give him no great Pleasure" (4:12) in the peddler's disclosures concerning Fanny's infancy. But in keeping with his vision of the world, the author also postulates other kinds of readers, invoking them to cajole or shame us ("If thy own Heart doth not sympathetically assist thee in this Conception, I pity thee sincerely from my own" [3:12]) into the proper attitude. The reader may either sympathize, as the narrator hopes he will, with Adams' joy at the rescue of his son (4:8) or be classified among "some few Readers" who will regard Adams' behavior as "very low, absurd, and unnatural." He (or rather she) may share in the joy of the lovers' embraces (2:12) or be aligned with those "Prudes . . . offended at the Lusciousness of this Picture." He may number himself among the "true Lovers" who "will represent to their own Minds without the least Assistance from us" the happiness of Joseph and Fanny (2:13) or be numbered among those "who have never been in love" and so are not "capable of the least Conception" of their state. To prevent this rhetoric of feeling from producing a more sentimental response than would be consistent with his overall comic aim, the author balances it with some humorous play on these "tender Sensations." About to describe Fanny (2:12), he indulges in mock hyperbole, "Reader, if thou art of an amorous Hue, I advise thee to skip over the next Paragraph," hoping that he himself "may escape the Fate of *Pygmalion*." His inference near the close of the seduction episode (1:9) that "the Reader is doubtless in some pain" for Joseph is clearly ironic. And at the climax of the kidnapping sequence (3:12) he is similarly playful, using the language of melodrama to insure a comic response:

> Neither the facetious Dialogue which pass'd between the Poet and the Player, nor the grave and truly solemn Discourse of Mr. *Adams*, will, we conceive, make the Reader sufficient Amends for the Anxiety which he must have felt on the account of poor *Fanny*, whom we left in so deplorable a Condition. We shall therefore now proceed to the Relation of what happened to that beautiful and innocent Virgin, after she fell into the wicked Hands of the Captain.

Despite the rarity of good sense and good nature in the "world" as he describes it, Fielding in fact counts on a reader whose moral sensibility is reasonably acute and whose heart is in the right place. Although the "values" and sympathies of the "implied author" emergent from the whole fabric of the narrative help to guide, or perhaps more accurately to confirm, this reader's general attitudes and expectations, within his major comic scenes the narrator's reference to his own or the reader's judgments or feelings is remarkably infrequent. He expects the reader to distinguish between a Joseph and a Lady Booby, or an Adams and a Trulliber, and he so constructs his incidents and characters as to facilitate such moral differentiations without explicit narrative interpretation. His intrusive judgments are reserved for more ambiguous situations.

Thus when Parson Barnabas eavesdrops on the injured Joseph's soliloquy (1:13) we are to find the footman's apostrophe to Pamela and the melodramatic rhetoric of his "death-bed" speech amusing, but not to agree with Barnabas' judgment of the speech as "nothing but a Rhapsody of Nonsense." In relating the incident, Fielding makes no comment on the behavior of either character. Yet his subsequent parenthetical remark that "notwithstanding Mr. *Barnabas's* Opinion, he [Joseph] had not been once out of his Senses since his arrival at the Inn" is not a surprising disclosure but a humorously unnecessary explanation of what should already be clear to the reader. Before Joseph begins to speak, the character of the complacent parson is succinctly drawn by the simple chronicle of his activities on reaching the inn:

> Mr. *Barnabas* . . . came as soon as sent for, and having first drank a Dish of Tea with the Landlady, and afterwards a Bowl of Punch with the Landlord, he walked up to the Room where *Joseph* lay: but, finding him asleep, returned to take the other Sneaker.

Obviously such a person might find Joseph's preference of love in a cottage to "Palaces . . . Dainties, or . . . Riches" incomprehensible. But the reader is expected to sympathize with the romantic and Christian sentiments distinguishable beneath the burlesque excesses of Joseph's declamation. Fielding makes the moral opposition unequivocal by having Barnabas conclude "he had heard enough" just after Joseph exclaims "I must think of another World," thereby neatly exposing the hollowness of the earthbound parson's vocation.[9]

On the other hand, when he came to depict his true parson's insensibility to Joseph's feelings as a lover, the problem of the reader's response was sufficiently nice to warrant some guidance. In the scene in which Adams' lecture against the passions is disrupted by his grief for his supposedly drowned son (4:8), Fielding would have us laugh at the Parson's unfeeling and imperceptive advocacy, in the face of his own contradictory example, of a philosophy condemning the natural feelings which are the very wellspring of his goodness, but he would not have us laugh at those feelings themselves. Therefore he hopes "the Reader will sympathize" with Adams' joy at the lad's recovery

[9] Of course, the reader's interpretation of the scene is also influenced by his recent memory of the scenes between Joseph and Lady Booby, and the more immediate context of his mistreatment by the highwaymen and coach passengers.

and invites him to savor his gratitude toward his rescuer: "Reader, he felt the Ebullition, the Overflowings of a full, honest, open Heart towards the Person who had conferred a real Obligation, and of which if thou can'st not conceive an Idea within, I will not vainly endeavour to assist thee." At the same time, he would give the exasperated lover the comic "satisfaction" which at this point in their relationship we feel is his due without reducing Adams to a punitive butt. So when the recovered parson resumes his lecture, we are told "the Patience of *Joseph*, nor perhaps of *Job*, could bear no longer." The similitude humorously expresses the reader's own feeling and harmlessly discharges the comic anger generated by Adams' obtuseness. Yet he would not have the reader's siding with Joseph lead him to confuse this sharpest opposition between the two protagonists with the numerous earlier conflicts of amiable and antipathetic figures; so he introduces into this closed situation reminders of the prevalently ill-natured world which has been so inimical to both. The person reporting the drowning "had been a little too eager, as People sometimes are, from I believe no very good Principle, to relate ill News." More emphatically, Adams' feelings are magnified by a preceding set of negations:

> What were his Sensations? not those which two Courtiers feel in one another's Embraces; not those with which a great Man receives the vile, treacherous Engines of his wicked Purposes; not those with which a worthless younger Brother wishes his elder Joy of a Son, or a Man congratulates his Rival on his obtaining a Mistress, a Place, or an Honour.

The subtlest of the narrator's helps, the conjecture that when Joseph offers him the consolation of a heavenly reunion "the Parson did not hear these Words, for he paid little regard to them, but went on lamenting," epitomizes the complexity of response elicited in this scene. Read one way, it is part of the rhetoric designed to preserve our sympathetic view of Adams: the "historian's" explanation prevents the reader from concluding that the idea of a future life is as meaningless to Adams as it was to Barnabas. But read less benignly it is the "naïve" deadpan ironist's reminder of the ineffectuality of argument, *any* argument, against the force of immediate deep human feeling, and thus, by extension, of the essential error of Adams' stoical doctrine.

As this incident suggests, even when the author intrudes his guidance, he relies on implication and inference. By so doing he prevents his conduct as interpreter and judge from becoming oppressive. Perhaps the most striking aspect of this restraint is the fact that, despite his implicit disapproval of the values and conduct of the "world" he delineates, he rarely expresses a direct negative opinion or feeling concerning the characters and actions he describes. Nor does the prevailing irony of his narration have the biting edge of his manner in *Jonathan Wild.* Even in the longer satiric digressions one finds nothing like this:

> . . . for he was none of those half-bred fellows who are ashamed to see their friends when they have plundered and betrayed them; from which base and pitiful temper many monstrous cruelties have been transacted by men, who have sometimes carried their modesty so far as to the murder or utter ruin of those against whom their consciences have suggested to them that they have committed some small trespass, either by the debauching of a friend's wife or daughter, belying or betraying the friend himself, or some other such trifling instance. [Works 2:34–35][10]

Fielding's irony in *Joseph Andrews* is closer in spirit to the intention he attributed to those writers who "endeavour to de-

[10] Another gauge of the mildness and indirection of the narrator's satiric expression is the scathing rhetoric which Fielding put into the mouth of Don Quixote. A good example is the speech near the opening of Act II of *Don Quixote in England,* in which he proclaims hypocrisy the deity men worship, sees each man rising "to admiration by treading on mankind," and bitterly spells out the world's definition of the good-natured man as "one who, seeing the want of his friend, cries, he pities him," concluding "let them call me mad; I'm not mad enough to court their approbation" (*Works* 11:32).

ceive the reader by false glosses and colours, and by the help of irony at least to represent the aim and design of their heroes in a favourable and agreeable light." The extenuation of Adams' failure to heed Joseph's words is not an isolated phenomenon. Far from sharing the roasting squire's "strange Delight" in "every thing which is ridiculous, odious, and absurd in his own Species," he seems to acknowledge the defects of his characters with great reluctance and at times in spite of himself. Slipslop emerges as a grotesque despite his efforts to describe her "nicely," and Lady Booby's staring at Joseph in church (4:1) is disclosed despite the narrator's belief that it is "only a malicious Rumour." He refuses to be particular about the travelers' itinerary (3:2) when they approach "the Seat of the *Boobies* . . . as that is a ticklish Name, which malicious Persons may apply according to their evil Inclinations to several worthy Country 'Squires, a Race of Men whom we look upon as entirely inoffensive, and for whom we have an adequate Regard, [and] we shall lend no assistance to any such malicious Purposes." Concerned to "preserve the Character" of Lady Booby, "who is the Heroine of our Tale," he describes the "vast Temptation" of Joseph's person "which overcame all the Efforts of a modest and virtuous Mind," hoping that the reader's "Good-nature will rather pity than condemn the Imperfection of human Virtue" (1:8).

These ironic expressions of an indulgent view of human frailty and a disinclination to slander are manifestations of a consistent posture which the author maintains throughout the novel. While ridiculing and satirizing through irony, facetiousness, and other forms of indirection, he puts himself forward as remarkably kind, generous and amenable, an uncritical and incorrigible apologist. What he says in mitigation of Joseph's slow comprehension of Lady Booby's intention both exemplifies and summarizes this aspect of Fielding's self-characterization: "That he did not discern it sooner, the Reader will be pleased to apply to an Unwillingness in him to discover what he must condemn in her as a Fault" (1:10).

The diverse elements of the narrator's humorous manner and the peculiar indirection of his satiric rhetoric contribute to this unified impression. More often than not, his narrative explanations of events are in apology for some character's conduct. Even the dissertation on high people and low people is offered to "vindicate the great Character of Mrs. *Slipslop*." The author's feigning of naïve unawareness of his characters' motives; the "historian's" concern with accuracy and fairness, and his discountenancing of rumor and gossip; the "moralist's" hopeful emphasis on the value of positive examples and his tendency to confine his expostulations to praise of virtue rather than condemnation of vice; the recurrent euphemism, understatement, overprecision, and elegance which add up to a kind of humorously extreme politeness of style ("a little too eager, as People sometimes are, from I believe no very good Principle, to relate ill News"); and even the "epical" burlesque through which the writer's subjects, be they ever so low, are "ennobled" and "elevated"—all these aspects of the narration can be subsumed under this characterization. From the naïve assumption in the opening paragraph of the "irresistible" force of moral emulation and the author's subsequent defense of his ancestorless hero to the mildly deploring conclusion of the penultimate chapter ("Lady *Booby* . . . left . . . in an Agony, which was but too much perceived, and not very charitably accounted for by some of the Company"), the author's overt manner is almost a caricature of that benevolent disposition valued in the novel and so lacking in the world he describes.

The effects of this characterization are complex. In a sense, the implied author transcends in his own person the psychological limits he imposes on his characters, retaining Adams' incorrigible inclination to think well of his fellows despite an undeceived knowledge of the world more penetrating and subtle than that of the mature Wilson. From this standpoint, his charitable attitude encourages the reader to adopt a similar view of the actions and persons he depicts, mellowing the potentially stronger punitive effect of the comedy. But in the context of the novel we are also likely to regard the narrator's gift for polite extenuation as a benign comic weakness, compounded of innocence and timidity. As a consequence of this view, his satire and ridicule carry all the greater force. The "truth" comes out, as it were, in spite of his charitable efforts to gloss it over; and the reader, comforted by the thought that even this superior author has his human failing, and conscious for the moment of his own greater sophistication, is eager to seek out the foible the "naïve" narrator has missed. Paradoxically, though the mildness of the author's manner makes the impact of the comedy less sharp and biting than it might be if he had the character of a "hater," this manner also contributes to that funding or accumulation of comic indignation which we have noted as an essential part of the emotional structure of the novel. For he does not discharge the reader's feelings through direct invective until the closing chapters of the novel, when his outright denunciation of the pettifogging Scout and his fellow "Pests of Society" (4:3), and his scornful description of Didapper, "the little Person or rather Thing that hopped after Lady *Booby*" (4:9), contribute to the punitive satisfaction of the conclusion.

The prevailing restraint and indirection of Fielding's guidance and, more pointedly, the quasidramatic form of his major comic interviews, support William Empson's claim that in writing his first novel "he discovered how much work he could leave the public to do for him."[11] But he also seems to have

[11] "*Tom Jones*," reprinted from *Kenyon Review*, vol. 20 (1958), in *Fielding: A Collection of Critical Essays*, ed. Ronald Paulson (Englewood Cliffs, N.J., 1962), p. 138.

understood better than any contemporary novelist the work he might do to provide a controlling framework of judgments, attitudes, and expectations within which the reader's inferences might operate. If he drew hints from the continental comic romance tradition for some of the strategies and devices he employed to influence the reader, he went beyond any of them in his sustained concern with the impact of his story as an essential dimension of its form, and his awareness that all the elements of his work—from the ordering and shaping of its episodes to the narrator's little jokes—might be disposed to this end.

Fielding's claim to have written a kind of book "hitherto unattempted in our Language" is validated in a sense he may not have intended when one compares this aspect of his achievement with the cruder rhetoric of *Pamela*. Whereas Defoe and Smollett seem to have been either indifferent to the problems of influencing the reader's response or naïvely confident that they might be solved simply by telling him what to think and feel—regardless of any conflicting implications of the actions and characters themselves, Richardson, like Fielding, was aware of the need to manipulate his reader's sympathies and antipathies in the service of his distinctive literary aim. But his first "little book" did not confront Fielding with anything approaching the subtle planning and management of effects he was later to discern in *Clarissa*. The heavy and ubiquitous editorializing of the heroine's narrative—designed to insure her our admiration and sympathy while making vivid the "reality" of her situation—succeeded by its very intensity in arousing the skeptical resistance of at least one "good-natured reader." Beneath this discursive rhetoric, Richardson could be observed patching up the form of his exemplary romantic melodrama by a transparent process of serial revision and persuasion after the fact. The central problem of his plot conception was how to wring the requisite pathos, terror, and admiration from Pamela's persecution in the complication while still preserving her persecutor as a suitably meritorious reward for her virtue in the denouement. Instead of building up the duality of Mr. B's character through fallible signs in the first part of the narrative, as Fielding, or even Scarron, might have done, Richardson first maximized his villainy to heighten the effects of the heroine's plight, then, after his radically unprepared conversion to a solicitous spouse, supplanted him in the villain's role with his haughty sister, Lady Davers, against whose violent abuse the failed rapist could now assume the role of benevolent protector. This process of retroactively reshaping the reader's view of the action is continued more directly and thoroughly in the sequel, which Richardson seems to have undertaken partly to answer the criticisms of the novel. When the domesticated Mr. B is called upon to give his account of the events formerly described by Pamela, the device of multiple viewpoints which was to become an effective source of dramatic irony and suspense in *Clarissa* is plainly a kind of literary cheating. After revealing an unsuspected struggle to conquer his "guilty passion," the hero reconstructs his early invasion of the maiden's bed (in which, hand in her bosom, he had coolly requested Mrs. Jervis to "just step up stairs, and keep the maids from coming down") as a flustered chapter of mischances in which he "had no such intention as they feared," and he conveniently omits any reference to the direr Lincolnshire phase of his persecution culminating in an undisguisable rape attempt.

If, as it has recently been plausibly argued, Richardson designed this account and the less disguised defences of the probability and ethical and social validity of his story in *Pamela II* as a rebuttal to *Shamela*,[12] Fielding's counterreply in *Joseph Andrews* was not confined to the opening parody or the occasional hits at Mrs. B's snobbery and intellectual pretension.

[12] Owen Jenkins, "Richardson's *Pamela* and Fielding's 'Vile Forgeries'," *Philological Quarterly* 44 (1965) : 200–210.

In contrast to Richardson's jerry-built rhetorical structure, he offered another kind of evolving narrative, whose seemingly casual shifts and changes were part of a planned system of actions with its own internal probabilities and ethical and emotional coherence. Viewed in this context Fielding's skillful synthesis of ethical matter into a carefully controlled dynamic narrative form is all the more impressive. If *Joseph Andrews* does not approach the complexity and magnitude of his achievement in *Tom Jones*, it anticipates the art of that masterpiece more significantly than has been generally acknowledged.

Index